PROFIT FROM THE PEAK

PROFIT FROM THE PEAK

The End of Oil and the Greatest Investment Event of the Century

BRIAN HICKS
CHRIS NELDER

WILEY

John Wiley & Sons, Inc.

Published by John Wiley & Sons, Inc., Hoboken, New Jersey.
Published simultaneously in Canada.

For general information on our other products and services or for technical support, please contact our Customer Care Department within the United States at (800) 762-2974, outside the United States at (317) 572-3993 or fax (317) 572-4002.

Wiley also publishes its books in a variety of electronic formats. Some content that appears in print may not be available in electronic formats. For more information about Wiley products, visit our Web site at www.wiley.com.

Library of Congress Cataloging-in-Publication Data:
Hicks, Brian, 1968–
    Profit from the peak: the end of oil and the greatest investment event of the century / by Brian Hicks and Chris Nelder.
        p.   cm.
    Includes index.
    ISBN 978-0-470-12736-0 (cloth)
        1. Petroleum industry and trade.   2. Energy industries.   3. Commodity futures.
I. Nelder, Chris, 1964–   II. Title.
    HD9560.5.H47   2008
    333.8'23—dc22
                                                                        2007047638

Printed in the United States of America.
10 9 8 7 6 5 4 3 2 1

CONTENTS

PART I. THE CRISIS IN A BARREL

PART II. MAKING MONEY FROM THE FOSSIL FUELS THAT ARE LEFT

LIST OF FIGURES

LIST OF TABLES

ACKNOWLEDGMENTS

First and foremost, the authors would like to thank the Association for the Study of Peak Oil (ASPO), without whose work this book would not have been possible. It is an admirable organization whose members' selfless efforts are often difficult and costly, yet freely given for the benefit of all, and they deserve our thanks. We would specifically like to thank Colin Campbell, Matthew Simmons, Kjell Aleklett, Rembrandt Koppelaar, Frederick Robelius, Jean Laherrère, Tom Whipple, Steve Andrews, and Randy Udall for their work. We have also benefited greatly from the work of David Hughes.

Likewise, the many contributors and editors of the online forum The Oil Drum have been the source of excellent charts and countless important insights in this book. For their work—particularly that of Samuel Foucher, Jeffrey Brown, Dave Cohen, Robert Rapier, Euan Mearns, Stuart Staniford, Tony Ericksen, and Roel Mayer—we are particularly grateful.

For general inspiration and big picture guidance, we owe a deep intellectual debt to Richard Heinberg, Julian Darley, Paul Hawken, Charles Hall, Tad Patzek, Albert Bartlett, Kenneth Deffeyes, Michael Ruppert, and the team at From the Wilderness. All of them have written many excellent papers and books that we highly recommend to your attention.

We would also like to acknowledge the willing assistance of Pat Lasswell, David Ryba, Aaron Task, and Jamie Lee for teaching, answering random technical questions, checking our numbers, and being part of the general intellectual milieu that produced this book.

And most of all, we must thank M. King Hubbert, whose original insight on peak oil is a gift to humanity—if we have the courage to apply it. As he famously remarked, "Our ignorance is not so vast as our failure to use what we know."

INTRODUCTION

Peaking [oil production] will result in dramatically higher oil prices, which will cause protracted economic hardship in the United States and the world.

—THE HIRSCH REPORT

If Iraqi production does not rise exponentially by 2015, we have a very big problem, even if Saudi Arabia fulfills all its promises. The numbers are very simple; there's no need to be an expert. . . . Unfortunately, there's a lot of talk, but very little action. I really hope that consuming nations will understand the gravity of the situation and put in place radical and extremely tough policies to curb oil demand growth.

—FATIH BIROL, CHIEF ECONOMIST OF THE INTERNATIONAL ENERGY AGENCY (IEA)

The world has never faced a problem like this. Without massive mitigation more than a decade before the fact, the problem will be pervasive and will not be temporary. Previous energy transitions (wood to coal and coal to oil) were gradual and evolutionary; oil peaking will be abrupt and revolutionary.

—THE HIRSCH REPORT

There is no doubt that world oil and gas production will peak. The only questions are: exactly when, the extent of the decline, and what we will do about it.

Oil accounts for 40 percent of our overall energy consumption, and over 90 percent of the energy we use for transportation.

Essentially everything in our modern lives is made with some contribution from oil. For example, oil and gas are embedded into every aspect of making a common shirt: from the feedstock to make nylon, to running the looms, to transporting the shirt to a store, to the transportation used to take the shopper to and from the store.

Oil and natural gas are also embedded into every aspect of the food we eat, from the field to the table. On average in America, every calorie of food we consume requires 10 calories of fossil fuel energy to create and bring it to our tables.

Consider this short random list of everyday items made from oil:

Air conditioners, ammonia, antihistamines, antiseptics, artificial turf, asphalt, aspirin, balloons, bandages, boats, bottles, bras, bubble gum, butane, cameras, candles, car batteries, car bodies, carpets, cassette tapes, caulking, CDs, chewing gum, cold remedies, combs/brushes, computers, contact lenses, cortisone, crayons, creams, denture adhesives, deodorant, detergents, dice, dishwashing liquid, dresses, dryers, electric blankets, electrician's tape, fertilizers, fishing lures, fishing nets, fishing rods, floor wax, footballs, glues, glycerin, golf balls, guitar strings, hair (synthetic), hair coloring, hair curlers, hearing aids, heart valves (artificial), heating oil, house paint, ice chests, ink, insect repellent, insulation, jet fuel, life jackets, linoleum, lip balm, lipstick, loudspeakers, medicines, mops, motor oil, motorcycle helmets, movie film, nail polish, nylons, oil filters, paddles, paint brushes, paints, parachutes, paraffin, pens, perfumes, petroleum jelly, plastic chairs, plastic cups, plastic cutlery, plastic wrap, plywood adhesives, refrigerators, roller-skate wheels, roofing paper, rubber bands, rubber boots, rubber cement, rubbish bags, running shoes, saccharine, seals, shirts (synthetic fabrics), shoe polish, shoes, shower curtains, solvents, spectacles, stereos, sweaters, table tennis balls, tape recorders, telephones, tennis rackets, thermoses, tights, toilet seats, toners, toothpaste, transparencies, transparent tape, TV cabinets, typewriter/computer ribbons, tires, umbrellas, upholstery, vaporizers, vitamin capsules, volleyballs, water pipes, water skis, wax, wax paper.[1]

We are not just "addicted to oil," as President George W. Bush has famously admitted. We're deeply, completely, utterly dependent on it, in every way. And there are no easy alternatives.

For the past 50 years, we have explored the entire earth intensively looking for more oil. But despite the latest technology and the most elaborate efforts, global oil discovery peaked in 1962 and has declined relentlessly ever since. Generally, we are finding less and less oil each year, and for the past 25 years, we have consumed more oil than we have found. In 2006 we found about 6 billion barrels of oil, but we consumed 28 billion, and the trends continue in the direction of increasing demand and decreasing supply.[2]

In this book, we take a hard look at the future of oil and gas, and how to invest in what's left. Then we explore the potential (and the limitations) of each of the major energy alternatives, and the carefully considered investing angles on each one.

Although this is a study in how to profit from the peak, we hope it is also more than that: a sober look at the future of humanity as a whole. On current trends, humanity could reach the peak of food, water, and all forms of energy by 2020. What are we doing about it? Are we doing anything about it? Is anybody driving this bus, or are we all passengers?

Ultimately, one simply wants to know: Where are we? Where are we going, and what are our options for the future? How can we find a way forward to prosperity amid the coming changes?

This book attempts to answer these questions.

PART

THE CRISIS IN
A BARREL

CHAPTER

1

DECEMBER 2005: THE MONTH THE DEVIL WEPT HIS TRILLIONTH TEAR

This could become the biggest energy issue the world has ever faced.

—Matthew Simmons

In December 2005, the Oil Age came to a quiet end. In that month, the world consumed its one-trillionth barrel of oil. In the blink of an eye, half of the world's known oil reserves were gone.

With roughly a trillion barrels remaining, and considering the fact we are consuming over 85 million barrels every single day, the world has only about 30 to 40 years' worth of oil left at present rates of consumption. But as we shall see in the following pages, the reality of declining oil production will have much more immediate effects. Shortages and persistently higher prices are the first indicators, which are already here. Higher prices will undoubtedly lead to reduced demand, and the oil that remains will last a little longer.

But it appears certain that within the next decade, and possibly *within the next three years*, we will be forced to start living with progressively less energy each year, every year, for the next century—with profound effects on the economy and just about everything in life as we know it.

This is the most serious challenge the world has ever faced.

From our current vantage point, in the optimistic first years of a new millennium, most people believe that cheap and abundant oil and natural gas will continue to provide us with low gasoline and grid electricity prices for at least several decades more, just as they have in the past. This is especially true for the pundits and analysts who regularly appear on television to talk about how improved technology will continue to lower energy costs and bring as much energy to market as we demand.

But, according to Matthew Simmons, the top oil investment banker in the world and an energy adviser to President George W. Bush, the idea that cheap oil would last forever is a twenty-first century myth: "The religion was faith-based, not fact-based! It was an illusion!"[1] At the first Association for the Study of Peak Oil and Gas (ASPO) conference in 2005, Simmons observed that the peak oil problem had started to look like a "theological debate," and quoted Dr. Herman Franssen, saying, "It is time to leave 'I believe' inside a church."[2]

Here are the facts: The largest oil reservoirs are mature, and their production is falling. Approximately three-quarters of the world's current oil production is from fields that are two or three decades old, past their peaks and beginning their declines. Much of the remaining quarter comes from fields that are 10 to 15 years old. New fields are diminishing in number and size every year, and this trend has held for over a decade.[3]

And enhanced oil recovery technology, rather than making ever-greater amounts of oil available, has had the perverse effect of simply allowing us to deplete the existing oil basins more quickly. Instead of creating future supplies of cheaper energy, enhanced oil recovery has caused us to sell the supply of those high-quality, nonrenewable resources as quickly and as cheaply as possible—leaving little for the future, and that at a much higher price.

To put oil depletion in context, consider these facts:

- For every calorie of food that we consume in the United States, 10 calories of fossil fuel input were needed in the form of fertilizers (made from natural gas); pesticides and herbicides (made from oil); fuel to run the machines that plant, tend, harvest, transport, and process the goods; and fuel to deliver them to your grocery store and keep them cold there. And that doesn't even count the energy needed to transport you to the store, and you and your groceries back home, nor the energy used to cook the meal.

■   The massive inputs of fossil fuels into food production are what have permitted the world population to increase from around 1.5 billion people at the turn of the twentieth century to its current level of around 6.7 billion people. (See Figure 3.1 in Chapter 3.)

In a very straightforward way, food *is* oil and gas. According to noted peak oil author Richard Heinberg, food travels an average of 1,300 miles from the farm to the plate in North America, leading critics such as James Howard Kunstler to decry the "3,000-mile Caesar salad" that travels from California's breadbasket, the San Joaquin Valley, to his table in Scranton, Pennsylvania.

But peak oil challenges more than our ability to feed ourselves.

The security costs alone of having the U.S. military protect the oil supplies of the Persian Gulf are around $44 billion per year.[4]

In fact, an in-depth analysis of the true total economic cost of the nation's growing dependence on imported oil is estimated at $825.1 billion—almost twice the President's $419.3 billion defense budget request. And much of that goes into the pockets of people who hate us.

Our dependence on oil—of which nearly two-thirds is imported—is a constant drain on the nation's treasury, not to mention the blood of its soldiers.

To the local population of oil-rich Central Asian states—Uzbekistan, Turkmenistan, Tajikistan, Kyrgyzstan, Kazakhstan and Azerbaijan—oil was once seen as a blessing from nature and a wealth lubricant to their economies.

Today they have a new name for oil: "Devil's tears." The Devil's tears in these regions—as well as many other parts of the globe—have led to corruption, kidnappings, murder, political instability and oppression, economic decline, environmental degradation, coups d'état, and often bloody civil wars.

Unfortunately, we see the Devil crying for years to come.

We need oil for nearly everything we do, and our entire infrastructure is built on the assumption that there will always be more when we want it, with very little storage or slack along the way. We have a serious challenge ahead of us.

CHAPTER

2

WHAT IS PEAK OIL?

It's quite a simple theory and one that any beer drinker understands. The glass starts full and ends empty, and the faster you drink it the quicker it's gone.

—COLIN CAMPBELL

Before we can begin to understand the concept of peak oil, we need to understand what oil is, how it is produced and measured, and the factors that influence its production.

WHAT IS OIL?

While it is often said that oil is made of "dead dinosaurs," dinosaurs comprise a tiny fraction of the organic matter from which oil is formed. So, while dinosaurs did flourish during the Jurassic and Cretaceous periods (208 million to 65 million years ago), a great deal of the fossil fuels were formed from plants and animals that preceded them.

According to standard geological theory, oil is formed over a period of millions of years by the decomposition of organic matter through the following process. (See Figure 2.1.)

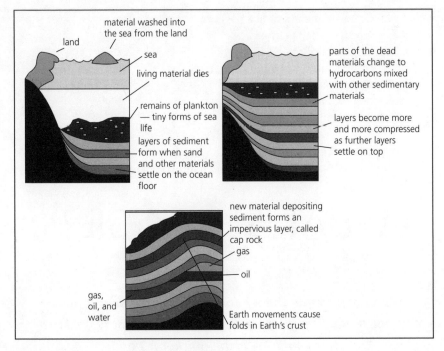

material washed into
the sea from the land

land

sea

living material dies

remains of plankton
— tiny forms of sea
life

layers of sediment
form when sand
and other materials
settle on the ocean
floor

parts of the dead
materials change to
hydrocarbons mixed
with other sedimentary
materials

layers become more
and more compressed
as further layers
settle on top

new material depositing
sediment forms an
impervious layer, called
cap rock

gas

oil

gas,
oil, and
water

Earth movements cause
folds in Earth's crust

FIGURE 2.1 *Oil Formation Process*

Source: The Energy Institute and www.schoolscience.co.uk.

At the edges of the world's primeval oceans, algae, plankton, marine plants and animals, and fecal matter migrated to basins and clefts in the ocean's floor via the cyclical exchange of seawater with nutrient-rich freshwater from the land. The deposited organic matter settled into the basins and oxidized as it decomposed, eventually depriving the ocean depths of oxygen. In this anaerobic environment, bacteria converted the lipids (fats, oils, and waxes) into a waxy substance called kerogen.[1]

These cyclical deposits alternately silted over, creating layers of sediment that sank upon previous layers, compressing them into sedimentary rock. To create oil, the source rocks in an oil basin must contain at least 2 percent organic matter. Source rocks with 5 percent or better are considered to be extremely rich sources,[2] but they comprise less than 1 percent of all sedimentary rocks.[3]

The source rocks are then buried, through various kinds of geological movement, to a depth of at least 7,500 feet, but not more than 15,000 feet—what is called the "oil window." At those depths and pressures, the rock encounters the right amount of heat—about 100 to 150°C—to cook the organic matter in a process called thermal depolymerization and to break down its long organic molecules into smaller chains of hydrocarbons that can make oil.

A hydrocarbon is simply one or more carbon atoms linked together and bound to some number of hydrogen atoms. For example, the simplest hydrocarbon is one carbon atom and four hydrogen atoms, given a chemical formula of CH_4, which is methane, a natural gas.

If the hydrocarbons have five to 20 carbon atoms in the chain, they produce liquid crude oil. Fewer than five atoms will create a natural gas. Oil may also be mixed with sulfur, natural gas and natural gas liquids, water, and other minerals.

Kerogen that is buried deeper than the oil window then enters the "gas window," of 150°C to 175°C, at which temperatures it will be broken down into smaller molecules to make natural gas.[4] (At higher temperatures than that, the gas would be destroyed.)

Once broken into smaller hydrocarbons, the oil must migrate back toward the surface through porous reservoir rocks that have sufficient permeability, or the ability for a liquid to flow between the pores, so that the oil can rise (floating on top of subterranean water). Oil that bubbles up all the way to the surface is biodegraded by bacteria.

Ninety percent or more of the oil ever formed did escape, and made its way to the surface in a "seep," where it biodegraded away. The remaining 10 percent, still trapped in reservoirs underground, is what we have been producing.

In order for the oil to be trapped in a reservoir, there must be a dome, a cap rock typically made of a fine-grained mudstone or salt, which forms a tight seal and keeps the oil from escaping further upward. Remember, we're talking about geological time frames. Even a drop-sized leak in the cap would drain a billion-barrel oil field in 100 million years.

Coal has a similar formation process, only instead of starting with oceanic organisms, it begins with primeval steaming swamps. The compression and decomposition of the plant matter forms peat, which, after being buried by layers of rock and heated over geological time frames, becomes coal. Coal formed at the same temperatures as oil is bituminous coal; at higher temperatures it becomes anthracite, and at lower temperatures, lignite. Most of the coal we harvest today was formed 300 million or even as long as 400 million years ago.

The large majority all of the oil, shale, and tar sand deposits in the world were formed during the Carboniferous period, about 354 to 290 million years ago, but deposits have been found dating back to the late Cretaceous period

(144 to 65 million years ago).[5] Those periods were especially warm periods in the earth's history, and produced lush blooms of plants and animals both on land and in the sea. Deposits of oil and coal earlier than that tend to be gas-prone, having been buried more deeply and hence cooked at higher temperatures.

As Colin Campbell put it, "The great bulk of the world's oil was formed at just two very brief moments of extreme global warming 90 and 150 million years ago."[6]

Abiotic Oil

For the sake of completeness, we should mention that there is an alternate theory of oil formation, which holds that oil can also be formed by nonorganic processes occurring in carbon deposits deep within the mantle of the earth. Originally proposed by a Russian geologist in 1951, the theory has attracted a small following of adherents, and has been promoted vigorously by astrophysicist Thomas Gold. By this theory, oil would not be a *fossil* fuel at all, nor would it be a finite resource, since it could be still forming today. Opponents of peak oil theory are fond of trotting out the meager data on this theory as supposed proof that peak oil is a hoax.

The vast majority of geologists discount the theory, however, and we give it no further consideration here.

HUBBERT'S PEAK

Peak oil is a theory that explains how, for a given oil-producing region, oil production tends to increase for some time, reach a peak right around the halfway point, and then taper off, in a modified bell curve shape.

What the bell curve describes is the *rate* of production, not the volume of oil produced. This is an important concept because peak oil theory is often mischaracterized as a "running out of oil" problem, when it's really about the *flow rate* of the oil. Perhaps the most succinct phrasing of this point was made by Dr. Jean-Marie Bourdaire, a sometime director of the International Energy Agency (IEA) and the World Energy Council: "It's not the size of the tank which matters, but the size of the tap."

This is because all economies depend on constant growth, which in turn depends on constantly increasing the rate of energy production. After we pass the peak rate of production, we have to live with less and less oil each year, rather than more and more. This is a difficult realization, for we have generally managed to increase oil production continuously since the birth of the oil industry, long before any of us living today were born. The assumption of endless growth upon which we have built our economies are about to be shaken to the core. This is a fundamental shift in the basis of our reality, and it will change the world as we know it.

The peak oil theory was originally proposed by a geologist named M. King Hubbert (1903–1989). Dr. Hubbert worked for Shell Oil for over 20 years, then as a senior research physicist for United States Geological Survey (USGS) for 12 years, plus holding professorial positions in geology at the University of California at Berkeley and Stanford University. His bell curve model came to be known as Hubbert's Peak (also sometimes referred to as the Hubbert Curve).

Hubbert's insight was simple: The production curve of a given oil province is very similar to its discovery curve, just delayed some years later.

He used the model to predict in 1956 that the United States would reach its oil production peak in 1970—a prediction that was scoffed at by his peers and that inspired ridicule right up through 1970, when critics pointed out—quite rightly—that the country had never produced more oil than it did that year.

And in 1971, the United States began its relentless descent into the second half of its age of oil, just as Hubbert had predicted. (See Figure 2.2.)

In 1975, Hubbert's theory was vindicated, as the National Academy of Sciences accepted his calculations on oil and natural gas depletion and admitted that its earlier, more optimistic estimates had been incorrect.[7]

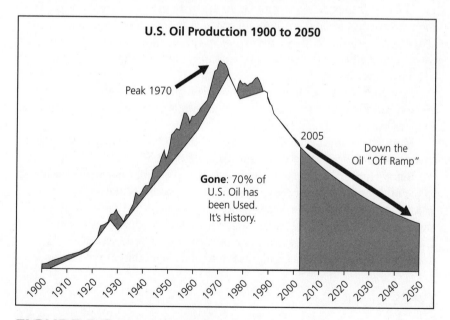

FIGURE 2.2 *U.S. Oil Production Profile*

Source: ASPO Newsletter No. 77, May 2007.

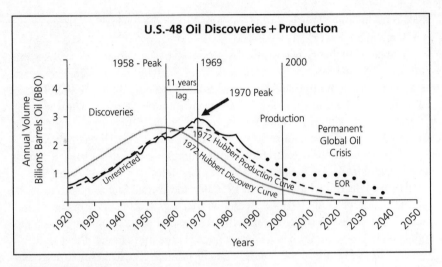

FIGURE 2.3 *US-48 Hubbert Curves*

Source: Hubbert Center Newsletter 97/1.

Hubbert is thus credited with being the first man to use geology, physics, and mathematics to predict future oil production from a reserve base.

This relationship between discovery and production has since been proved conclusively all over the world. For example, consider the United States' oil history, as shown in Figure 2.3.

Applying the same analysis to global oil production, we find a similar relationship between the two curves, but with a different time lag between them, as shown in Figure 2.4.

Shifting the time scale of the graph highlights the similarity of the oil discovery and production curves, as shown in Figure 2.5.

Since Hubbert developed his theory, many authors have studied it and applied it to individual oil provinces and to the world. While various modifications to the theory have been made, such as modified curve-fitting techniques and mathematical linearization, which have produced results that are a few years plus or minus from a straight Hubbert Curve analysis, his core insight remains true and is highly useful to understanding oil production.

TYPES OF OIL

Not all crude oil is the same. It comes in different grades, and some types of oil are better suited to making certain products than others.

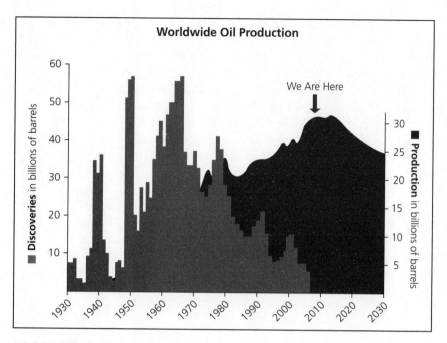

FIGURE 2.4 *World Hubbert Curves*

Source: ASPO Newsletter No. 77, May 2007.

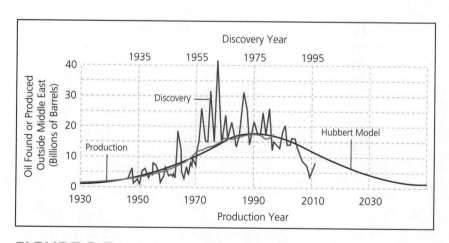

FIGURE 2.5 *Time-Shifted Hubbert Curves*

Source: Colin Campbell and Jean Laherrère, *The End of Cheap Oil.*

The first difference is the viscosity—how heavy (or gooey) the oil is—which is measured by its gravity on the American Petroleum Institute (API) Scale. Depending on the API gravity, crude oil may be classified as light, medium, or heavy. Light crude oil is defined as having an API gravity higher than 31.1°, medium oil as having an API gravity between 22.3° and 31.1°, and heavy oil as having an API gravity below 22.3°. (Note: The higher the number, the lighter the crude.) Oil that is too thick to flow naturally, such as the oil found in tar sands, is called bitumen and has an API below 10°.[8]

The second difference is the sulfur content. In order to refine oil into most products, the sulfur must be removed. "Sweet" oil contains less than 0.5 percent sulfur, and "sour" oil contains more.

Light sweet oil is most easily refined into the products we use. The heavier and sourer it is, the harder it is to produce light products like gasoline.

Since we have used the world's best oil first, the remaining oil is progressively heavier and sourer. Figure 2.6 from the Energy Information Administration (EIA) illustrates the point for non-Organization of Petroleum Exporting Countries (OPEC) oil producers.

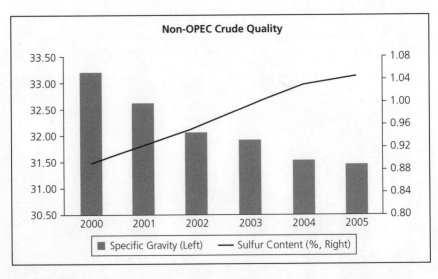

FIGURE 2.6 *Non-OPEC Crude Quality*

Source: Energy Information Administration, www.eia.doe.gov/oiaf/aeo/conf/pdf/saunders.pdf.

REFINING

Light sweet oil is refined in a simple refinery, whereas heavy sour oil must be refined in a complex refinery that includes specialized components to remove sulfur and other compounds.

Refining is essentially distillation. The crude oil is heated under carefully controlled conditions, in a process known as fractional distillation, or "cracking." Because crude contains a mix of short and long hydrocarbons, they will boil off at different temperatures. The lightest (shortest) hydrocarbons, like the components of natural gas and gasoline, will rise easily to the top under moderate temperatures, and the heaviest hydrocarbons, best suited for wax and asphalt, will need to be heated to much higher temperatures. As the various components of the oil boil off, they are separately collected. (See Figure 2.7.)

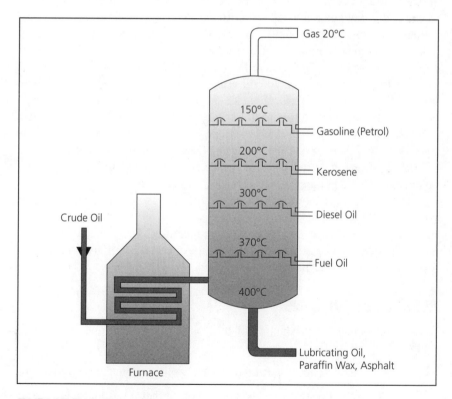

FIGURE 2.7   *Oil Refining*

Source: Mrs. T.C. Knott.

It's easy to see why light sweet crude is the most desirable grade of crude oil. Its very desirability is also the reason why global production of it peaked first, in 2005.[9] The majority of the world's known remaining oil is heavy sour crude, and most of the untapped resources are even heavier and sourer than the heavy sour crude produced today. Most of the remaining oil in Saudi Arabia and Venezuela, for instance, is heavy crude, and much of it is sour.

This is a major factor in today's high oil prices. Refining capacity for heavy sour crude is limited, and the available supply of oil to those refineries is ample—just as the Saudis say it is.

OIL PRICES

Light sweet crude is the grade most often quoted in the financial press as the "price of oil." But in actuality, there are dozens of different grades of crude traded every day and delivered to various collection points before being distributed to refiners. Those deliveries, in turn, were purchased on the futures market a month or more in advance; in the United States these trades are executed on the New York Mercantile Exchange (NYMEX).

The most commonly quoted oil price in the United States is West Texas Intermediate (WTI), which is a light sweet crude (about 0.24 percent sulfur)[10] delivered to the collection point in Cushing, Oklahoma. Another often-cited crude benchmark is North Sea Brent Crude, which is a different grade of light sweet oil (0.37 percent sulfur) produced from the North Sea and typically refined in Europe; it is traded on the London ICE exchange operated by Inter-continentalExchange, Inc.[11]

Although the price of oil is set on the futures market, where it may vary widely over time, the actual production cost of the oil is quite stable, as it is based on the fixed costs of the oil rigs and pipelines. The production cost of Saudi Arabian oil, which is among the cheapest to produce in the world, is as low as $1.50 to $2.00 a barrel.[12]

RESERVES REVISIONS

In order to predict the production of oil from a given field, one needs three numbers:

1. How much oil has been extracted to date, known as cumulative production.

2. An estimate of reserves, or the amount of oil that is left to produce from the field.

3. The amount of oil that remains to be discovered and exploited.

Together, these numbers add up to the estimated ultimately recoverable (EUR), also known as the ultimate recoverable resource (URR), which is the total number of barrels that will have been extracted when production ceases.

Obviously, knowing the EUR is key to predicting the production profile of a field, given the cumulative production and the knowledge that the peak usually occurs around the halfway point.

To establish what the EUR of an oil field might be, a host of methods will be employed, such as analyzing the geography of the area, drilling test wells, measuring the depth and characteristics of the reservoir using sensors, trying to identify the perimeter, and taking seismic readings. All the collected data is then fed into advanced computer modeling tools, which produce models that geologists can analyze. So estimating the EUR is part art and part science, but the estimates have become increasingly accurate and are rarely far off today.

Over time, it is normal for the EUR to grow somewhat under honest reporting as new information about the field comes to light and the application of new methods improves the recoverability factor.

The same principles apply to the EUR of an entire oil-producing nation. At first, the EUR is usually stated conservatively; then as time goes on and estimates give way to proven production, it will grow a little. As oil is actually produced and the total known production grows, we can backdate that oil to the original date of discovery and come up with a fairly accurate production profile.

Political Reserves

But the statement of oil reserves has always been fraught with dishonest reporting, driven by political and economic factors. Only in a few parts of the world—such as Norway, the United Kingdom, and the United States—are the current reserves numbers considered to be fairly accurate and transparent. In the rest of the world, particularly the Middle East, reserves numbers are highly suspect.

Each producing region has had its own motivations for misstating or being deliberately vague about its oil reserves numbers. Western companies can increase their valuations in the stock market, which is to say their perceived value, by exaggerating estimates. Rather than stating the worst-case, 90 percent probability estimate, they might cite their best-case, 10 percent probability estimate. (Experience has shown that the P50, or 50 percent probable, estimate is usually close to the right number.)[13]

The Soviet Union had a long history of stating wildly improbable reserve estimates, because doing so increased its perceived strength on the world stage. As an example of how much these numbers can differ, in 1996 *World Oil* estimated Former Soviet Union (FSU) reserves at 190 billion barrels, but the *Oil and Gas Journal* gave it only 57 billion.[14]

For OPEC producers, the motivation has in part been due to the quota production scheme of the organization. Each producer's permissible production quota is based on a percentage of its EUR. So in order to increase production—and thus increase revenues, which in the case of Middle East producers constitutes the vast majority of the state's income—an OPEC member must increase the EUR of its total reserves, so that its quota can be increased.

During the so-called quota wars of the 1980s, all major OPEC producers radically increased their stated reserves, in some cases doubling or tripling them virtually overnight, *without discovering any additional oil!*

Even the International Energy Agency (IEA), not an entity known for sticking its neck out, has said, "The hike in OPEC countries' estimates of their reserves was driven by negotiations at that time over production quotas, and had little to do with the actual discovery of new reserves."[15]

The reserves restatement game began in 1985, when Kuwait reported an increase of 41 percent, from 64 billion barrels (Gb) to 90 Gb.

Then, in January 1988, Abu Dhabi and Dubai each reported a tripling of their reserves, and Iran, Iraq, and Venezuela all doubled theirs, presumably to maintain parity of production among OPEC members. And in January 1990, Saudi Arabia reported a 50 percent increase. (See Figure 2.8.)[16]

Taking a closer look at this phenomenon, let's consider the reserve statements of Kuwait, a country with no undeveloped fields and quite mature existing fields, whose output is well known. (See Figure 2.9.)

The declining line indicates the backdated estimate, showing that the originally claimed reserves were 64 billion barrels in 1984 and were gradually trending toward 50 billion—the latter being consistent with IEA and BP models, which are well-respected in the industry.

Yet, Kuwait's publicly stated reserves (the top line in the chart) leaped from around 64 billion barrels to around 92 billion barrels in 1985, without any new discoveries, and that number has actually increased to 100 billion in the 20 years since. Despite having produced a great deal of its oil over that time, Kuwait hasn't reduced its remaining reserves a whit!

But now the truth is coming out.

For the purposes of an example, let's trace Kuwait's reporting over time:[17]

1984: Kuwait reports a EUR of 86 Gb, with 22 Gb produced and 64 Gb of reserves.

1985: Kuwait increases its reserves number to 90 Gb without discovering any new oil, effectively claiming that its remaining reserves are equivalent to the initial report of the total discovery.

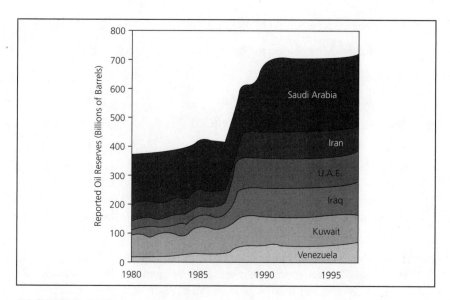

FIGURE 2.8 *Political Reserve Additions*

Source: Colin Campbell and Jean Laherrère, *The End of Cheap Oil.*

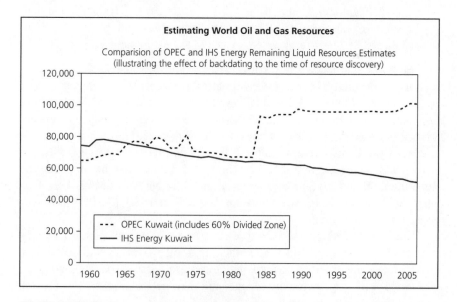

FIGURE 2.9 *Kuwait Oil Reserves History*

Source: Euan Mearns. Data: 2007 BP Statistical Review of World Energy.

1987: Reserves increased to 92 Gb.

1991: Reserves increased to 95 Gb, then reduced to 94 Gb in 1992.

2003: Reserves increased to 97 Gb.

2004: Reserves increased to 99 Gb.

2005: Reserves increased to 102 Gb.

January 2006: Industry newsletter *Petroleum Intelligence Weekly* (*PIW*) says it has seen internal Kuwaiti records showing reserves are actually about 48 billion barrels, noting that the public figures do not distinguish between proven, probable, and possible reserves. Kuwait's former oil minister, Sheikh Ahmad al-Fahd al-Sabah, dismisses the report as a partial picture, and other oil officials say the report is inaccurate.[18]

Early June 2007: Kuwait's current oil minister, Sheik Ali Jarrah al-Sabah, says that Kuwait's proven reserves (presumably P95 reserves) are actually 48 Gb, but that its probable reserves (presumably P50 or less) are 150 Gb.[19]

Late June 2007: Oil company engineers working in Kuwait informally confirm the 48 Gb estimate, and suggest that it might even be a bit optimistic. The main source of the oil, Kuwait's Greater Burgan Field, has been in operation since 1938 and so should be well into the decline of its maturity, and new reserves are expected to be comparatively small.[20]

We know that since 1984, Kuwait has produced some 12 Gb of its oil. Now, if the original 64 Gb reserve estimate was correct (implying an EUR of 86 Gb) and we subtract 12 Gb, that would leave Kuwait with 52 Gb left, barring additional discoveries. And 52 is very close (given the degree of uncertainty associated with such estimates) to the 48 now claimed.

What does this example tell us? It tells us that the reserves revisions were indeed spurious, and that the original estimates, less the oil produced since then, should give us a fairly accurate estimate. And this is precisely what the Association for the Study of Peak Oil and Gas (ASPO) has been doing for world estimates.

The sort of disingenuous reserve reporting we have chronicled here is characteristic of most of OPEC and other major oil producers, with the honest numbers kept under wraps. Indeed, the figures are considered state secrets, as oil remains their top source of revenue, and their geopolitical power rests on their oil production capacity.

We may also be certain that the nonbackdated data available from oft-cited sources such as the United States Geological Society (USGS) is highly unreliable, which is unfortunate considering how vitally important it is for the world to know how much oil there is left. Government and corporate planning in response to peak oil might be radically different if the peak is now than if it will be 50 years from now, but as long as the press keeps reporting the inflated USGS numbers, and everybody keeps believing them, the truth about peak oil will remain obfuscated.

Until a way is found to increase the transparency of reserves reporting, perhaps through an international agreement to allow independent auditing of national reserves, the only prudent course of action is to use all the production data we have to backdate the reserves numbers, which should be adjusted to P50 numbers.

As we have seen, the results of such analysis paint quite a different picture than the official reserves. For example, OPEC's own EUR claim is 2,138 billion barrels. But using a backdated geological model, Phil Hart and Chris Skrebowski[21] calculate that the OPEC estimate is overstated by 250 billion barrels,[22] putting the EUR at around 1,888 billion barrels. Using a similar model, Dr. Colin Campbell and Jean Laherrère calculate that it is no more than 1,800 billion barrels.[23] If the backdated models are correct, then OPEC's total reserves have been overstated by about 14 percent.

There is still much debate over the world's EUR. For one issue, some analysts define EUR as conventional oil, while others define it as "all liquids," including every kind of fossil fuel oil. There are differences over potential new discoveries. There is disagreement about the potential contribution of new technology to improve recovery techniques. There is even some debate about the amount of oil that has been produced, due to, again, opaque reporting. But the consensus is clear enough from a big-picture standpoint, and the variance is small enough to provide some guidance to public policy makers.

David Woodward, general manager of the Abu Dhabi Company for Onshore Oil Operations, compared 40 estimates of the world's EUR published between 1975 and 1993. According to Woodward, "There is a fair degree of consistency among the estimates, with the average value being 2,000 billion bbl [barrels] and most [70 percent] falling in the range of 2,000 to 2,400 billion bbl."[24]

Unfortunately, not all estimates and methodologies are equally valid. Many estimates—particularly the ones quoted in the press—are based on chart analysis, treating oil as if it were not a finite resource, or on the application of economic theory to past production profiles, as if the past were a guaranteed indicator of the future.

Having studied many such papers, we have come to regard the work of Colin Campbell and the ASPO as the most reliable analysis, as it has been done by highly experienced geologists who have done the tedious and difficult

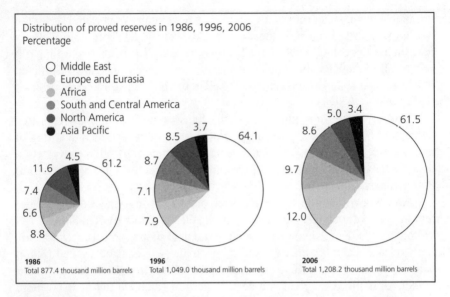

FIGURE 2.10   *Distribution of Proven Reserves in 1986, 1996, and 2006*

Source: BP Statistical Review of World Energy 2007.

work of examining the data on all of the world's significant oil fields—more than 18,000 of them—field by field, adjusting the numbers as needed to reflect true probability, and backdating the reserves.

We may still have an overestimation problem, principally owing to poor data from the Middle East, where more than half of the world's remaining oil lies.[25] If the world has 906 billion barrels to go, and the overestimate—what Colin Campbell has called "political reserves"—is indeed 300 billion barrels worldwide, then the overestimate accounts for about a third of world's remaining "proven reserves"![26] (See Figure 2.10.)

Note that the U.S. share of the total declined from 11.6 percent in 1986 to 5.0 percent in 2006, while the Middle East share remained just over 61 percent.

IMPORTANCE OF GIANT OIL FIELDS

Oil fields vary greatly in size from very large to very small, but the largest fields contribute far more oil to the global supply than most of the small ones put together. This concept is well understood in geological circles. Half of all oil produced comes from just 0.03 percent of all oil fields.

This is significant because the largest fields are few in number, and when they're past their peaks, then so is the world. No quantity of smaller fields could possibly make up for the depletion of the largest ones.

Recent insights on the importance of giant oil fields principally owes to the work of Matthew Simmons, CEO of Simmons & Co. International, the world's top oil investment banking firm. He undertook a comprehensive study of the world's largest fields, one by one, in order to understand the world's production curve.

Simmons divided the world's fields into 120 giants—defined as producing at least 100,000 barrels per day (bpd)—and thousands of lesser fields. He then compiled data on each giant field's production and published his results in a groundbreaking 2002 white paper entitled "The World's Giant Oil Fields."

He found a number of surprises in his analysis:

My biggest surprises of this study were first, how difficult it was to even obtain data on current production rates. Second, how critically important this relatively small population of oilfields still is to the world's total oil supply. Third, how old many of these fields are, particularly the largest of these fields. Fourth, the total lack of good data on the decline rates for almost all of these giant fields. My last surprise was the consistently smaller size of each new generation of giant fields.

Table 2.1 shows Simmons' 2002 aggregation of the giant fields and their production.

In 2002, the 32,350,000 bpd from these giant oil fields comprised 47 percent of the annual total. But in 2005, an updated analysis on the world's giant oil fields by Fredrik Robelius estimated that the contribution from 333 fields with production over 100,000 bpd was 61 percent of the world total.[27]

Simmons' graphical representation of the world's oil fields illustrates the enormous importance of the giants. (See Figure 2.11.)

But the world's giant oil fields are aging. In Simmons' 2002 analysis, the average age of the world's 14 largest fields was 43.5 years—which is definitely mature. (Typically, a large oil field goes into decline after 50 years.) And the average age of the world's 19 largest—fields that produced over 500,000 bpd—was 70 years!

As in all things, with age comes reduced production. Simmons demonstrated it in Table 2.2.

Simultaneously, the number of giant fields discovered is declining, and the discoveries are progressively smaller, as shown in Figure 2.12.

Clearly, we are not on course to repeat the oil bonanza of the past.

TABLE 2.1 **Summary of Giant Oil Fields**

Giant Fields Production (000s bpd)	No. of Fields	Total Production (000s bpd)	Pre-1950s	1950s	1960s	1970s	1980s	1990s
					Era Discovered			
1,000+	4	8,000	2	1		1		
500–999	10	5,900	2	3	3	1	1	
300–499	12	4,100	3	1	6	1	1	
200–299	29	6,450	8	4	6	9	1	1
100–199	61	7,900	5	8	13	13	11	11
Total	116	32,350	20	17	28	25	14	12

Source: Matthew Simmons, "The World's Giant Oil Fields," working paper, 2002. www.nps.edu/cebrowski/Docs/energy/giantoilfields.pdf.

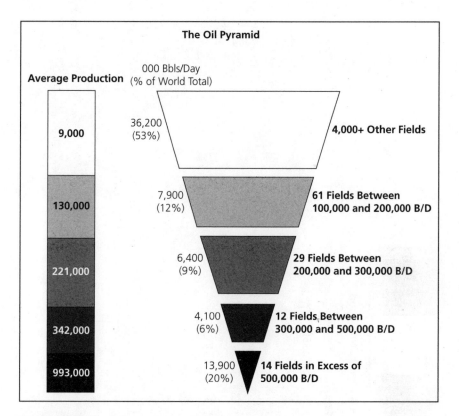

FIGURE 2.11 *Simmons' Oil Pyramid*

Source: Matthew Simmons, "The World's Giant Oil Fields," working paper, 2002.
www.nps.edu/cebrowski/Docs/energy/giantoilfields.pdf.

WHEN IS THE PEAK?

Many analysts have attempted models of world oil production, using various methodologies and various definitions of the oil that is counted (which may include condensates, natural gas liquids, natural gas plant liquids, and heavy oils including oil from tar sands, etc.) in order to predict the peak. While the estimates vary, there is a fairly good locus of consensus around the 2009–2012 time frame among geologists and oil industry analysts (economists and government data keepers tend to have much more optimistic predictions).

A recent study by Dr. Samuel Foucher (aka "Khebab") on the peak oil forum The Oil Drum compared 19 projections by well-known analysts, which demonstrates the approximate consensus of opinion. (See Figure 2.13.)

TABLE 2.2 Giant Oil Fields' Production (000s Barrels per Day)

000 B/D	Giant Oil Fields' Production						Percent	Total Production
	Pre-1950s	1950s	1960s	1970s	1980s	1990s		
1,000+	5,700	1,100	0	1,200	0	0	25%	8,000
500–999	1,500	1,700	1,600	600	500	0	18	5,900
300–499	900	300	2,300	300	300	0	13	4,100
200–399	1,700	900	1,400	2,000	200	200	20	6,400
100–299	550	1,100	1,700	1,700	1,500	1,400	25	7,950
	10,350	5,100	7,000	5,800	2,500	1,600	100%	32,350
Percentage of Total	32%	16%	22%	18%	8%	5%		100%

Source: Matthew Simmons, "The World's Giant Oil Fields," working paper, 2002. www.nps.edu/cebrowski/Docs/energy/giantoilfields.pdf.

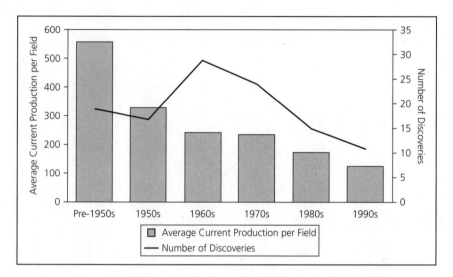

FIGURE 2.12 *Giant Field Discoveries, Pre-1950s to 1990s*

Source: Matthew Simmons, "The World's Giant Oil Fields," working paper, 2002. www.nps.edu/cebrowski/Docs/energy/giantoilfields.pdf.

ASPO's most recent model for regular conventional oil, last updated in September 2007, puts the global EUR at 1,900 billion barrels, with a peak date of 2005, where 1,001 billion barrels have already been produced and there are 899 billion barrels to go.

For all liquids, ASPO estimates the EUR is 2,500 billion barrels, including heavy oil (which includes tar sands and oil shales) and deepwater and polar oil, and natural gas liquids, with a peak date of 2010, 1,102 billion barrels produced to date and 1,398 billion barrels to go.[28]

ASPO's estimate in chart form is shown in Figure 2.14.

PIRA Energy Group, one of the world's leading energy analyst companies, largely agrees with ASPO's assessment. PIRA believes that non-OPEC conventional crude and condensate production peaked in 2006, which was precipitated by Angola joining OPEC. Non-OPEC production coming from producers in decline is 47 percent, and PIRA does not believe that the rest can even make up for the loss of Angola's production, let alone global depletion. Therefore, PIRA believes that future growth will have to come from OPEC and unconventional sources.[29]

Now, as we have seen, different definitions of what is measured make it difficult to identify a consensus on oil production numbers. ASPO's database

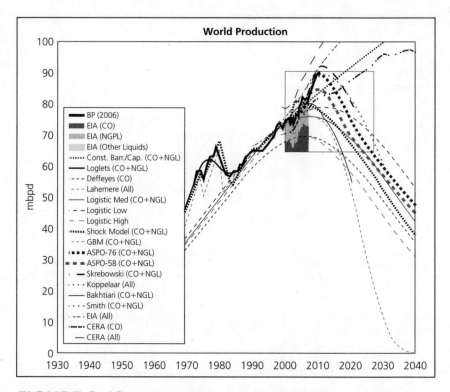

FIGURE 2.13 *World Oil Production (Crude Oil Plus Natural Gas Liquids) and Various Forecasts (1940–2050)*

Source: Samuel Foucher, Post to TheOilDrum.com, www.theoildrum.com/node/2620.

shows a peak of "conventional oil" in 2006 at 65.7 million barrels per day, and "all liquids" in 2011 at 89.39 mbpd, but the *Oil and Gas Journal* reports 2006 production of 72.49 mbpd.

Data published by the Energy Information Administration (EIA) also supports the apparent peak of conventional oil, showing that it reached a high of 74.151 million barrels per day in May 2005, but has tapered off since then, standing at 73.1 million barrels per day in January 2007.[30]

The trend is clearly evident in Figure 2.15, an aggregate chart by Tony Eriksen ("ace" at The Oil Drum), which includes both conventional crude and lease condensates.[31] He describes it as follows:

World C&C production continues to retain its May 2005 peak and is forecast to decline by 1%/yr until 2009. The decline rate steepens to 4%/yr until 2012.

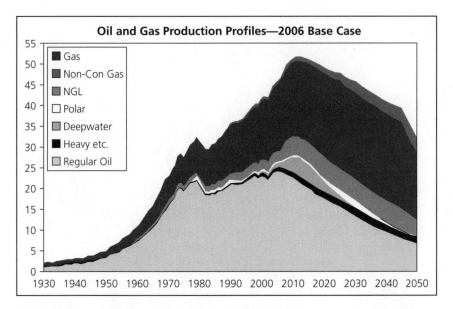

FIGURE 2.14 *World Oil Production (All Liquids)—ASPO 2006 Base Case*

Source: ASPO Newsletter, No. 78, June 2007.

The main reason for the end of the total liquids plateau in 2009 is that the C&C production decline rate changes from 1%/yr to 4%/yr in 2009.[32]

Another well-respected oil commentator who believes we have already peaked is Ali Samsam Bakhtiari, a retired director (now deceased) of the National Iranian Oil Co. (NIOC). For more than 30 years he has studied the oil industry, and has an enviable collection of databases on the world's oil production. He sees the definitive peak of conventional oil in 2006 (he excludes natural gas liquids from his numbers, which account for about 3 million barrels per day of the world's total petroleum use of 85 mbpd):

After some 147 years of almost uninterrupted supply growth to a record output of some 81–82 million barrels per day in the summer of 2006, crude oil production has since entered its irreversible decline. This exceptional reversal alters the energy supply equation upon which life on our planet is based. It will come to place pressure upon the use of all other sources of

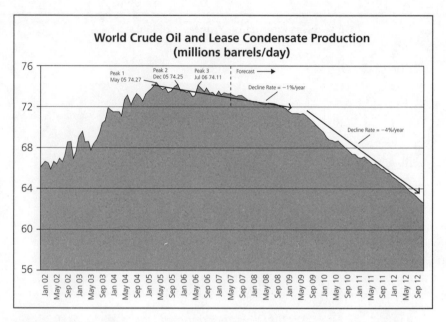

FIGURE 2.15 *World Crude Oil Plus Lease Condensate Production*

Source: Tony Eriksen. Data from the EIA, Chris Skrebowski, and others. www.theoildrum
.com/node/2716.

energy—be it natural gas, coal, nuclear power and all types of sundry renewables, especially biofuels. It will eventually come to affect everything else under the sun.[33]

Dr. Foucher simplified his chart of various predictions (Figure 2.13) by calculating mean and median estimates, as shown in Figure 2.16.

As the chart shows, the variance between estimates is negligible enough that we can call the date of the peak "soon enough." Peak oil is such an enormous turning point for the world that it doesn't matter if the peak is plus or minus five years from a given date—our call to action will be the same, albeit perhaps slightly more or less urgent.

As ASPO puts it: "Arguing endlessly over the precise date of peak also rather misses the point, when what matters is the vision of the long slope that comes into sight on the other side of it."[34]

Indeed, as Matthew Simmons has often pointed out, we won't know the global peak until it is well in the rearview mirror. Political matters and

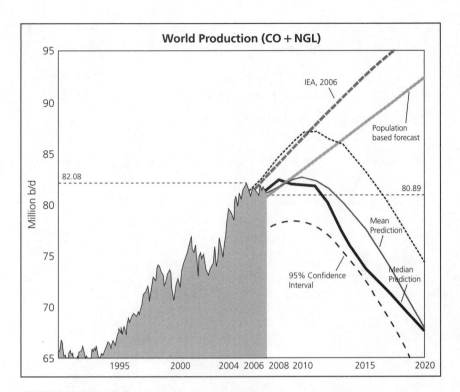

FIGURE 2.16   *World Oil Production (Crude Oil Plus Natural Gas Liquids) Consolidated Forecasts*

Source: Samuel Foucher, Post to TheOilDrum.com, www.theoildrum.com/node/2620.

"above-ground events" cause fluctuations in oil production that would not occur if it were simply a matter of geology and supply and demand.

EXPORTS

Another way of looking at the production picture is exports, because what we in the United States really care about is not overall production, but the availability of the two-thirds of our lifeblood that is imported.

Exports are currently running at 47 million barrels per day,[35] a little more than half the total production of 85 mbpd. But for net importers, dependence on exports is particularly pronounced: Just the top 15 exporters account for

84 percent of the total oil exported worldwide, and production in half of them is either flat or in decline.[36] (See Table B.1, "Top Oil Producers and Peak Production.")

A June 2007 study by Rembrandt Koppelaar of ASPO-Netherlands looked at just the global oil exports from 2002 to 2007. He concluded:

1) Total world exports of all fuel liquids have been on a plateau since the end of 2004, and declined slightly in the last year, despite production increases.

2) Liquids exports from non-OPEC countries as a whole have declined since the beginning of 2004.

3) OPEC liquids exports have increased until the end of 2005, followed by a short plateau after which a slow decline set in, mainly due to declining production in Saudi Arabia.[37]

Figure 2.17 shows his chart of global exports.

So, while global liquids production increased by 1 mbpd from 2005 to 2006, the amount exported was flat. Koppelaar explains: "This plateau implies

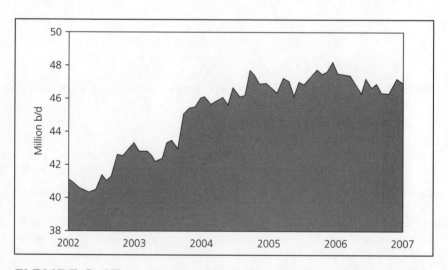

FIGURE 2.17   *World Liquids Exports, January 2002–February 2007*

Source: Rembrandt Koppelaar, Oilwatch Monthly, June 2007, www.peakoil.nl/
wp-content/uploads/2007/06/oilwatch_monthly_june_2007.pdf.

that all liquids production growth in producer countries has been absorbed by internal markets in recent years."

Indeed, as independent oil analyst Jeffrey Brown has observed, the increase in domestic consumption by the top 10 net oil exporters from 2000 to 2006 is equal to all of Nigeria's net exports in 2006.[38]

In other words, as producer countries grow up and continue to industrialize, they consume more of their own production and are unable to increase exports. This further confirms that any additional oil for export will have to come from OPEC, particularly Saudi Arabia.

Consequently, the data gatherers have issued some rather shrill calls recently for them to increase production:

The EIA warned that "OPEC must increase oil production by more than a million barrels per day if a rise in prices is to be avoided in the coming months."[39]

And the IEA head said, "OPEC needs to raise its crude oil output in the coming months to ensure an adequate supply."[40]

But OPEC has declined: "OPEC notes oil markets remain well supplied and market fundamentals do not require any additional supply from the Organization at this time. . . . A combination of current high inventory levels and increasing OPEC spare capacity, which is expected to reach around 15 percent in the second half of this year, means there are adequate supplies available to cope with any upward revisions to oil demand forecasts."[41]

There are just a few problems with OPEC's perspective.

First, nobody believes there is much actual spare production capacity outside of Saudi Arabia. The rest of the OPEC producers pretty much have their taps wide open. (Kuwait might have a little spare capacity, but probably nothing significant in the big picture.)

Second, not many believe that Saudi Arabia actually has 15 percent spare capacity.

Third, of the 11 OPEC nations (prior to Angola's joining, just recently), only one has increased its production since September 2005, and that was a tiny 30,000 barrels per day bump for Libya. All the others have declined, for a total decline of 2 million barrels per day.[42] That may be due to voluntary production cuts in accordance with OPEC's agreements, or it may be involuntary.

A chart of OPEC exports in aggregate (Figure 2.18) tells the story plainly.

As we can see, there is clearly a yawning gap opening between production and demand in 2007 for those of us who depend on imports, possibly as much as a 2 percent gap. And if the reduction in exports is in fact due to declining production, then we are clearly past the peak.

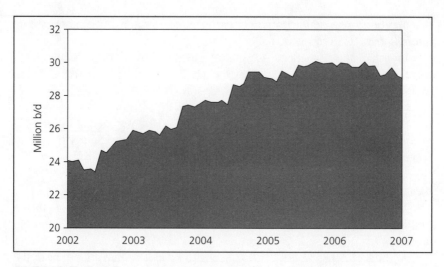

FIGURE 2.18 *OPEC Liquids Exports, January 2002–February 2007*

Source: Rembrandt Koppelaar, Oilwatch Monthly, June 2007, www.peakoil.nl/wp-content/uploads/2007/06/oilwatch_monthly_june_2007.pdf.

Whether OPEC doesn't increase its exports because it can't—due to factors such as geological limits, security problems, lack of capacity, and increased domestic demand—or because it won't—because it is better for its long-term profitability—or all of the above, we cannot know. And OPEC is certainly not telling.

But there is another possibility, elegantly argued by oil analyst Dave Cohen in a June 2007 article, "A Paradigm Shift."[43] He suggests that what is really going on is that OPEC producers (particularly Saudi Arabia) have realized that they are back in control of the world market, since non-OPEC producers are pumping flat out, and that they really don't need to try to keep oil prices any lower than they are now.

They have also realized that they'll make far more profit by selling refined products than by selling crude, and their investment in future projects reflects that. Cohen explains:

Based on the outlook of growing demand for their oil and gas, by 2011 the countries of the Middle East will invest some $94 billion in their oil and gas upstream sectors, more than half of which will go to expand oil production capacity. This is in addition to more than $240 billion of investment in the mid and downstream oil and gas chains and petrochemicals. . . . Of the

$70 billion Saudi Arabia is investing by 2012, only $18 billion is for upstream expansions.[44]

The rest is for finished products like gasoline, chemicals, and plastics. And that really makes perfect sense for them: Why let foreign companies reap the refining profit, and why ship crude around the world when shipping refined products costs less?

That approximately $350 billion that Middle East producers are preparing to invest in oil production and processing would seem to suggest that they have high confidence in its future.

However, these additional investments, upstream or downstream, won't be coming online before next year, and some may take four years or more.

In the meantime, it looks like we're going to have to finally learn to live within our energy budgets, rather than assuming that there will always be more when we need it.

RESERVE REPLACEMENT AND DEEPWATER DRILLING

For large, integrated oil companies like ChevronTexaco and ExxonMobil, their stock valuation depends on maintaining their reserves as well as the revenue they derive from depleting their producing fields, because reserves are the company's future. So historically they have tended to prospect for new oil—or, because promising drilling targets are fewer and fewer in recent years, to prospect on Wall Street and buy up smaller companies—such that they could maintain a relatively steady reserve/production ratio.

But a healthy stock depends on constant growth as well, so they also need to continually increase production rates.

However, at the current rates of depletion, large, integrated oil companies need to replace 137 percent of their reserves in order to compensate for depletion and increase production at 3 percent, while maintaining a constant reserve/production ratio.

Over the past three years, they haven't been able to keep up. From 2004 to 2006, the world's major oil companies managed to replace only 91 to 92 percent of their reserves, according to a June 2007 report by Bear Stearns & Co.[45]

Meanwhile, the cost of finding and developing new oil rose by 28 percent since 2005—an ominous indication.[46]

Where will the oil majors find those additional reserves? There are only two significant regions of the world where oil development is relatively young and reasonably sized new fields can be produced: the area around the Caspian Sea in eastern Asia, and Africa. However, both areas are rife with conflict between the locals and the oil companies, and both are caught up in geopolitical tensions that foster terrorism. The Caspian region is also a geographically challenging place to do anything, and an even harder place to defend. In short, it is now, and it will continue to be, very difficult to produce oil from these regions and bring it safely to market.

That leaves primarily deepwater drilling in friendly areas as the next frontier for oil. Although the first deepwater wells—wells drilled in more than 1,000 feet of water—were drilled in the 1970s, up until the 1990s, deepwater drilling was too difficult and expensive to make economic sense.[47] But between the world's existing onshore and shallow-water offshore fields having largely been exploited, and the developing areas like the Caspian Basin and Africa being risky and difficult places to invest hundreds of millions of dollars in drilling rigs, combined with a historically high price for oil, deepwater drilling is the next near-term frontier.

Deepwater drilling rigs are marvels of technology and achieve drilling depths that were unheard-of a decade ago. But there is a limited supply of these high-specification floating rigs, and they're very expensive to build and to rent. So those that have them, like Transocean Inc. (NYSE: RIG) have a book of business extending more than a year in advance, at ever-increasing day rates—as much as $600,000 per day![48]

As an indication of how much effort the large oil companies now have to expend in order to increase their reserves, in April 2007, ExxonMobil set a new world record depth for an oil well, drilling over seven miles into the ocean floor off the coast of Russia.[49]

DIFFERING PROJECTIONS

Given the enormous amount of data available about oil production, one might expect there to be more agreement than there is about the future of oil. A word about this schism among observers is in order.

We have seen the emergence of two general camps: the "late peak" or "no peak" camp, who believe that oil production can be increased over at least the next 30 to 50 years to meet demand, and the "early peak" camp, who believe that the peak is imminent, either in the recent past or within roughly the next five years.

The latter camp mainly comprises geologists, many of them retirees who spent their careers working for Big Oil; data hounds and mathematical wizards; professors and scientists from academia; and environmentalists and activists of all stripes who recognize that peak oil is the flip side of global warming and a host of other issues that concern them.

In the other camp are primarily economists, governmental data-gathering organizations such as the EIA and IEA, and current representatives of oil companies. These agents all have a vested interest in maintaining business as usual, and are under intense pressure from both government and industry to come up with optimistic forecasts showing that oil supply will meet demand. Stories are legion of scientists within these organizations who have come up with a set of numbers based on good analysis, only to have those numbers adjusted by political powers-that-be to project a more optimistic scenario.

One such organization known for its rosy production forecasts is Cambridge Energy Research Associates (CERA), which is often consulted by the media when the question of oil supply comes up. Usually CERA is represented by one man, Daniel Yergin, an oil analyst whose book *The Prize: The Epic Quest for Oil, Money & Power* (Free Press, 1993) is well respected, but whose forecasts are less so. CERA's clients are energy companies, and its production forecasts in recent years have been well off the mark. These forecasts have not been reproducible by credible independent scientists in the field, and the estimates have been consistently high.

For example, in March 2006 CERA presented a model for UK 2006 oil production capacity showing around 2,350,000 barrels per day, but the actual production turned out to be 700,000 barrels per day lower—an error of 42 percent for a very recent forecast of a country whose oil production history is well known and whose data is very transparent![50] And in 2002, CERA forecast that gas production in the United States would increase by 15 percent by 2010, where in reality it has declined by 4 percent. Now most gas wells in the United States are depleted in three years or less.[51]

For another example, in February 2007, the IEA, OPEC, and the U.S. Department of Energy/EIA were all still projecting that non-OPEC supply would grow by almost 1.1 to 1.3 million barrels per day in 2007,[52] even though everyone knows that non-OPEC supply has been flat for the past four years straight! Such projections are so devoid of reality that it really begs the question how trustworthy their other estimates are.

While the EIA, IEA, *Oil & Gas Journal*, and other energy data keepers are all reasonably well respected for their gathering and analysis of historical data, that respect evaporates when it comes to predictions. The optimism of their predictions seems specifically designed to please their masters and to avoid panic within the populace, not to accurately predict future production.

One former high-ranking U.S. energy official was blunt about it: "It would be a huge mistake to base U.S. energy policy on what the USGS thinks about future oil supplies, and the Energy Information Administration has put out such overblown numbers, and done it with such arrogance, that it should be statutorily barred from answering questions about oil."[53]

Apparently it would also be a mistake to even trust the published data on past production from some sources. According to a July 2007 study by Dow Jones Newswire, which looked at ConocoPhillips data on United Arab Emirates (UAE) member Dubai's oil production before the Dubai government took over operation of its fields from ConocoPhillips in April 2007, the data being issued by the Dubai government is wrong by as much as two-thirds. Dow Jones' calculations put the sheikdom's output at somewhere between 65,000 and 80,000 barrels per day, versus the UAE government web site's claim that the output is 240,000 barrels per day.[54]

If we can't even trust historical production data, then what sort of foundation do we really have for projecting future output?

IEA's Confession

The reality gap in official estimates closed a little bit in July 2007, when the IEA issued its "Medium Term Oil Market Report" on the five-year outlook for oil. For the very first time, the agency admitted that they had doubts that oil supply could keep up with global demand. The report was blunt: "Despite four years of high oil prices, this report sees increasing market tightness beyond 2010. . . . It is possible that the supply crunch could be deferred—but not by much."

This was a major departure for the agency, which for over 30 years has predicted that supply would meet whatever the demand is projected to be. See Figure 2.19.

Essentially, the report's conclusions boil down to this:

- Demand is rising at about the rate of 2.2 percent a year through 2012, primarily driven by the developing world's consumption, which is rising three times as fast as in the OECD countries. Transportation fuels will be the largest source of demand, by far.

- Non-OPEC production is expected to increase from 50 million barrels per day today to 52.5 mbpd by 2012, but the growth rate will diminish by 2009, and most of the additional production will be from unconventional sources such as natural gas liquids, tar sands production, extra heavy oil, coal to liquids, and biofuels.

- OPEC spare capacity will increase slightly from 2.5 mbpd in 2007 to a high of 3.4 mbpd in 2009, then decline to just 1.5 mbpd (1.6 percent of demand) by 2012. Some 70 percent of the increase will have to come from Saudi Arabia.

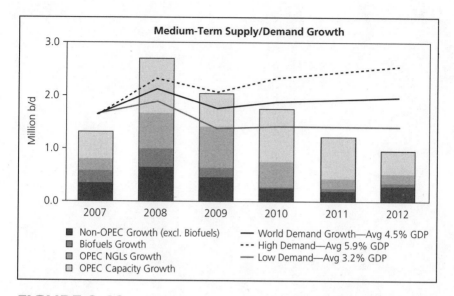

FIGURE 2.19 *International Energy Agency Medium-Term Supply/ Demand Growth*

Source: IEA, "Medium Term Oil Market Report," July 2007. http://omrpublic.iea.org/ mtomr.htm.

- Depletion rates are worrisome: "Net oilfield decline rates average 4.6% annually for non-OPEC and 3.2% per year for OPEC crude. Aggregate levels mask much sharper declines in a 15–20% per annum range for mature producing areas and for many recent deepwater developments. All told, the forecast suggests the industry needs to generate 3.0 mb/d of new supply each year just to offset decline. Notwithstanding, above-ground supply risks are seen exceeding below-ground risks in the medium term."

- Rising project costs, shortages of labor and materials, and geopolitical problems will continue to plague world oil production and conspire to create uncertainty and delay projects, so supply could fall short of demand by 2010. And shortages of natural gas are even more imminent.

In order to meet demand by 2012, the IEA projects the need for the increases by OPEC states, as shown in Table 2.3.

TABLE 2.3   IEA Forecast of OPEC Production by 2012

Producer	Increase by 2012 (mbpd)	Production in 2012 (mbpd)
Saudi Arabia	1.77	12.57
United Arab Emirates	0.50	3.38
Angola	0.50	2.17
Kuwait	0.42	3.06
Nigeria	0.37	2.84
Qatar	0.21	1.16
Algeria	0.19	1.56
Libya	0.17	1.92

Source: IEA, "Medium Term Oil Market Report," July 2007. http://omrpublic.iea.org/mtomr.htm.

But how likely are these increases? In June 2007, small increases from Angola, Iran, Nigeria, and the UAE were almost completely offset by declines totaling 70,000 bpd from Iraq, Indonesia, and Venezuela, and Saudi Arabia informed its Japanese customers that it would continue to export less than the established contract volumes.[55] Is this a recipe for continuously increasing production?

The IEA even acknowledged the peak of non-OPEC conventional oil, although they couldn't quite bring themselves to say it:

The concept of peak oil production and its timing are emotive subjects which raise intense debate. Much rests on the definition of which segment of global oil production is deemed to be at or approaching peak. Certainly our forecast suggests that the non-OPEC, conventional crude component of global production appears, for now, to have reached an effective plateau, rather than a peak.[56]

Redefining conventional crude oil by including sources like tar sands and coal to liquids is really bending over backward in order to call the top a "plateau" instead of a "peak," but at least they admitted that non-OPEC conventional crude capacity is maxed out.

In summary, we are in a situation where demand is increasing exponentially and supply is decreasing exponentially, which points to near-certain shortages by 2010.

Said Lawrence Eagles, head of the IEA's oil industry and markets division: "The results of our analysis are quite strong. Either we need to have more supplies coming on stream or we need to have lower demand growth."

Since we know that supply is limited, and we have no reason to think that supply will increase substantially in the next five years, prices will have to rise to force demand back into balance with supply.

Pickens' Slim Pickin's

One of the most respected observers on peak oil is legendary oilman T. Boone Pickens, a man with over four decades of experience in the oil business who has earned his reputation by making prescient bets on the oil market. His Dallas-based hedge fund, BP Capital, has had returns exceeding 800 percent since 2001.

In April 2007 he spoke frankly to the Petroleum Professional Development Center at Midland College in Texas. "Yes, I believe in peak oil," he said. "Matt Simmons and I talked today and we're on the same team. If, as Daniel Yergin believes, there's so much more oil left, why doesn't oil production move up instead of staying flat? Global demand is 85 million barrels [per day], or 31 billion barrels a year. The world hasn't replaced the oil it's been producing since 1985. So if there's so much oil left, I don't understand why production hasn't gone up. All the big fields are declining and all the current drilling does no more than hold off the decline. So the next step is decline. We can't hold on to 85 million barrel a day production."[57]

Looking out through the end of 2007, he saw oil demand rising to 86 or 87 million barrels a day but production staying flat, sending prices back into record high territory.

In a March 2007 interview at the *Forbes* magazine CEO conference, Pickens summed up the situation like this: "The world has been looked at. There's still oil to be found, but not in the quantities we've seen in the past. The big fields have been found and the smaller fields, well, there's not enough of them to replenish the base. . . . If I'm right, we're already at the peak. The price will have to go up."[58]

As indeed it has!

DRILLING LIKE NEVER BEFORE

The United States is a good example of discovery and production profiles, having been thoroughly surveyed and being the beneficiary of the world's very best oil expertise and production technologies.

The U.S. has now burned through 70 percent of its oil. Since its all-time production peak in 1970, the postpeak decline in production has been relentless—despite the most aggressive drilling and production techniques ever used.

In the first quarter of 2007, oil drilling in the United States reached a 21-year high, drilling an estimated 11,771 oil wells, natural gas wells, and dry holes.[59] And yet, overall production continues to decline.

As we have seen, the first part of an oil field's production is easy and cheap; then it becomes progressively more expensive and difficult to produce, requiring more advanced technology and more investment of energy to retrieve declining amounts of oil.

Oil fields are typically produced in three stages: Primary recovery is the first stage, wherein oil comes out of the reservoir due to its own pressure. When the natural pressure begins to falter, then secondary recovery techniques are used, such as injecting water or natural gas into the reservoir, additional "infill" drilling, or advanced horizontal drilling. These two stages yield a worldwide average of about 33 to 35 percent recovery of the original oil in place (OOIP). The remaining oil is typically "stranded" and unrecoverable, because it's too hard or too expensive to pump out.[60]

New enhanced oil recovery (EOR) techniques can squeeze just a bit more of this oil out of the reservoir, by injecting something that will cause some of the remaining oil to be dissolved into a fluid that can be pumped out. Such techniques include injection of various substances such as CO_2, hydrogen sulfide (sour gas), other hydrocarbons, or nitrogen; thermal methods, such as injecting hot water or steam; and chemical methods, such as injecting polymers and surfactants (foam).

Enhanced oil recovery techniques have been deployed in the United States for three decades, and have been applied to many mature oil basins elsewhere in the world, so the effect of EOR is well known. Experience has shown that EOR does not much affect the date of an oil field's peak production, nor its peak rate. What it does do is extend the tail of the production chart, making it thicker and longer. (Likewise, increasing the drilling rate does not increase the rate at which oil is found or produced, at least in the United States.[61])

Of course, that's still a good thing, because it buys us time to make the adjustments we need to prepare for a world of declining fossil fuel inputs.

There are hopes that in the coming decades, EOR can be further improved, such that it might even achieve a 50 percent rate of ultimate recovery. This will require intensive research and development (R&D) and government support to streamline regulatory approval, fund the R&D work, and expedite the permitting of projects. It remains to be seen whether EOR will live up to these expectations.

Depletion Rates

Of the top 20 oil-producing countries in the world, accounting for 85 percent of all oil produced, half are in decline. (See Appendix B.)

There is no question that three of the four supergiant oil fields are past their peaks: Daqing in China, Cantarell in Mexico, and Burgan in Kuwait.

The fourth and the largest of them all, 50-year-old Ghawar in Saudi Arabia, may be past its peak as well. However, the opacity of Saudi reporting makes it difficult to know. A comprehensive, well-by-well study[62] of Ghawar by geochemist and energy analyst Euan Mearns on The Oil Drum estimates that it is somewhere between 69 percent and 72 percent depleted, and if so, then it is well past its peak, and probably going into steep decline. (See Figure 2.20.)

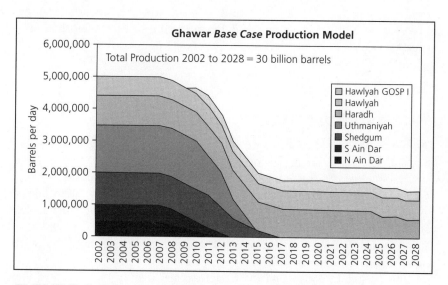

FIGURE 2.20 *Euan Mearns' Ghawar Production Model*

Source: Euan Mearns, Post to TheOilDrum.com, http://europe.theoildrum.com/node/2507.

Other studies have estimated that the depletion rate of Ghawar could be as high as 8 percent per year,[63] which would be a catastrophic decline, possibly brought about by the excessive injection of water to maintain production flows. However, that would be more or less in line with Matthew Simmons' estimate that the average rate of decline from Saudi fields is a relatively high 7 percent per year.[64]

According to Matthew Simmons, if Ghawar has passed its peak, then by definition the world has passed its peak, so great is the contribution to the world supply that Ghawar provides. It would mark the beginning of the end of the Oil Age, because there is nothing else that will suffice to maintain energy supplies: "There isn't any case you could make, by any stretch of the imagination, based on anything we know, that you could go elsewhere to make up the difference. This could become the biggest energy issue the world has ever faced."[65]

Indeed, Saudi Arabia's production has declined slightly since 2005, despite a radically increased program of drilling. Figure 2.21, prepared by oil analyst Stuart Staniford, vividly demonstrates the relationship.

We should note that this is a fine example of how neoclassical economics doesn't work very well with nonrenewable and nonsubstitutable resources. God will not put more oil in the ground just because we are willing to pay more for it.

Unfortunately, despite the immense risk that depletion poses to the world's economies, no one is responsible for tracking depletion or warning anyone about it. It has been remarked that peak oil is like a planeload of passengers having a huge party, descending quickly on a crash trajectory, with nobody in the cockpit.[66]

INFRASTRUCTURE ISSUES

The biggest contributors to world oil production are the largest and most mature fields, which are in decline. Therefore, there is little incentive to keep investing in the infrastructure that pumps, refines, and distributes oil.

According to Matthew Simmons, 80 percent of the world's energy delivery system is corroded—literally rusting through—and desperately in need of refurbishing.[67] We saw the effects of this problem in March 2007, when a section of British Petroleum (BP)'s pipeline in Prudhoe Bay sprung a leak and spilled a small amount of oil.

But the public outcry and the Congressional inquiry that followed the spill almost universally failed to identify the real issue. Senators called BP's management to task for having failed to "pig" its pipelines according to

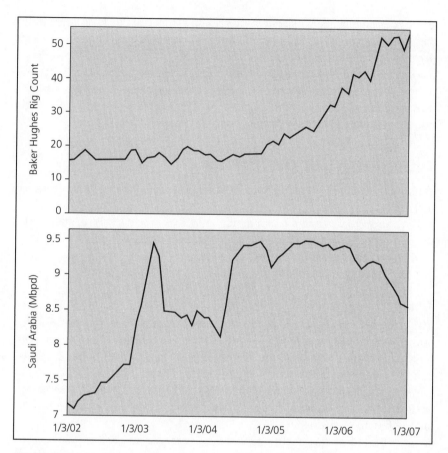

FIGURE 2.21 *Baker Hughes Oil Rig Count in Saudi Arabia, Jan 2002–Jan 2007 (top) vs. Saudi Arabian Oil Production, Jan 2006–Jan 2007 (bottom)*

Graph is not zero-scaled to better show changes.

Source: Stuart Saniford, Article on TheOilDrum.com, "Depletion Levels in Ghawar (Updated)," www.theoildrum.com/files/saudi_2_07.png original, updated and revised in www.theoildrum.com/node/2563.

Data sources: U.S. EIA, *International Petroleum Monthly* (http://www.eia.doe.gov/ipm/supply.html), Table 1.1; IEA, "Oil Market Report," Table 3; and Joint Oil Data Initiative for oil supply. Baker Hughes for rig counts.

standard maintenance procedures. BP acknowledged its lack of attention to the pipelines, but never admitted that it wasn't even trying to maintain them because the output from the fields has fallen toward the marginal low end of production. BP is just running down the clock on the capital investment and hoping that it can continue to use the pipelines just long enough to produce the last bit of oil. The company certainly would not see any financial justification for reinvesting in that infrastructure.

THE BOTTOM LINE ON PEAK OIL

Taking into account all of the preceding information, what's the bottom line on peak oil?

We know that demand is continuing to increase mercilessly. In June 2007, the IEA reported that world demand would increase by 1.7 mbpd over 2006, maintaining the growth rate of recent years.

So what may we expect from supply?

Timing

The date of the global oil peak cannot be known until it's in the past. But we do know that it will be affected by both belowground factors, such as geologic limits, and aboveground factors. The latter group includes geopolitical events, like the continuing kidnappings and infrastructure attacks on oil facilities in Nigeria; weather events, such as hurricanes in the Gulf of Mexico; the timing of investments; and the availability of everything from basic building materials and fuel to skilled labor.

About half of the world's largest producers are in decline. The United States, United Kingdom, Norway, and Indonesia are all past their geological peaks, and China will soon be past hers. Mexico, Kuwait, and Russia are past their peaks due to a host of political and geological factors, ranging from a lack of sustained investment to resource mismanagement. And major OPEC producers, including Iran, Iraq, and Venezuela, have passed their peaks as well, albeit more due to political factors than anything else.

Russia, Iran, Venezuela, and Mexico may soon cease to be net exporters, as the growth of their economies increases their domestic needs. This drying up of exports will be felt most keenly by heavily dependent importers such as the United States, even before the actual geological peak of global production.

Supply from all non-OPEC producers has been stagnant for about six years now, and current projections say that it will likely reach its absolute peak some time between now (2007) and 2010, although it may continue on a plateau until 2012–2015.[68]

Flat non-OPEC production will put the burden of increased production squarely on OPEC.

The ASPO projects that supply from OPEC producers will increase through 2010, but other observers say it will peak much later, perhaps as late as 2025 or even 2050. However, the available data is opaque, so it is very difficult to project. The supply outlook for the OPEC states not located in the Persian Gulf, especially Nigeria, Venezuela, and Indonesia, is uncertain, but it is clear that they won't be able to make up for depletion of non-OPEC producers.

That leaves the Persian Gulf OPEC producers as the last remaining hopes against an imminent peak—or more accurately, that leaves Saudi Arabia, because the other OPEC producers have little spare production capacity and are not on a trajectory to have significantly more anytime soon.

Figure 2.22 shows the EIA's projection, from its 2007 World Energy Outlook.

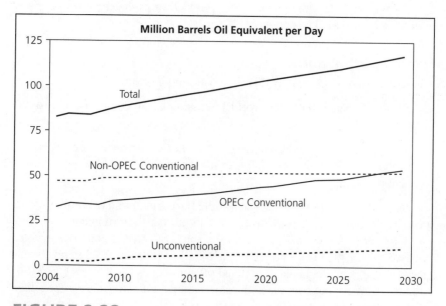

FIGURE 2.22 *Energy Information Administration World Liquids Production, 2004–2030*

Source: Energy Information Administration, International Energy Outlook 2007, www.eia.doe.gov/oiaf/ieo/pdf/0484(2007).pdf.

OPEC has held firmly to its contention that the market is well supplied with crude, and that there is no need to increase production right now. In OPEC's view, the bottleneck is in complex refining capacity. There is plenty of heavy sour crude to go around, but there is limited capacity to process it.

If that is true, then the shortages that have been anticipated by peak oil analysts since light sweet crude peaked in 2005 should soon materialize. At least until the world can build more complex refining capacity—and there are investments in that under way in the Middle East, in particular—we may expect gasoline prices to continue to rise along with the tightness of light sweet crude supply.

And naturally, those who understand the market's complexities—such as you, dear reader—may expect to reap stunning profits by investing in the large independent American heavy sour crude refiners, Valero and Tesoro.

By 2010–2012, then, the world will be looking to Saudi Arabia for any increases in global production. If demand remains strong and the Saudis are unable or unwilling to significantly increase production, then it seems likely that we will see the global peak in oil production in that time frame, right around 2010 as ASPO has predicted.[69]

Uneven Distribution

The remaining oil is unevenly distributed around the world:

■ Some 85 percent of the world's remaining oil comes from just 20 countries.

■ The 14 largest oil fields, located in six countries, produce over 20 percent of the world's oil supply. The four largest of those produce over 12 percent of the total.

Most of the world's oil is in the Middle East, a cauldron of conflict where it can be very difficult to provide a secure investment environment.

Two-thirds of the world's oil is in the hands of Muslim countries that are opposed to U.S. policies. And according to oil consultancy PFCEnergy, three-quarters of it is in the hands of national oil companies (NOCs) such as Saudi Arabia's Aramco,[70] and all the major international oil companies put together have less than one-quarter of it under their control.

The situation could be even worse. The *Economist* puts the NOCs' share of the world's proven oil reserves at 90 percent,[71] and oil analyst Tom Petrie estimates that it's actually closer to 93 percent. Both note that the world's 13 largest oil companies are NOCs, and the biggest of the international oil majors, ExxonMobil, is only the 14th largest.[72]

Either way, NOCs are clearly in a position to dictate the terms of future development deals. Unless the international oil majors—overwhelmingly companies from countries in the West that are past their own production peaks and anxious to replace falling reserves—want to go out of the oil business entirely, they have to play ball with the NOCs. Because that's where the oil is.

Unfortunately, the NOCs are notorious for political entanglements, cost overruns, and project delays, and the world is truly at their mercy.

The *Economist* explains:

> Few of the princes, politicians, and strongmen who wield ultimate authority over these firms can resist the urge to meddle. At best, that leads to the sort of inefficiencies found at most state-owned firms: overstaffing, underinvestment, and so on. At worst, business of pumping and selling oil is totally subsumed by politics, as in the case of Petroleos de Venezuela, one of the biggest NOCs. In either case, NOCs produce less oil, more expensively, than they should.[73]

This state of affairs doesn't seem likely to change, barring a major geopolitical shake-up. NOCs have learned a thing or two from their long partnerships with the big Western majors, and are now capable of taking on complex projects on their own. They don't need the majors as badly anymore, and tend to use them for their exploration and production (E&P) expertise and then toss them out just when the going gets sweet.

These days, says ConocoPhillips chief executive James Mulva, "Big Oil is not so big."

It's as though the adults of the oil industry have been forced to sit and watch as the children take control.

On the other hand, slowing oil production today will no doubt be a boon for the future, when we will value the remaining oil much more and use it more judiciously.

Depletion

Global oil depletion is the biggest threat to future production, and it is remorselessly relentless. The accepted average world depletion rate is about 2.5 percent annually, but in Saudi Arabia, the largest producer, it may be closer to 8 percent, and Mexico's Cantarell oil field is being depleted at a catastrophic rate, possibly as high as 15 percent.

Discovery

The world passed the peak of discovery between 1962 and 1964 (depending on whose numbers you use).[74] We now find only one barrel of oil for every three we produce,[75] and the ratio is only getting worse. The fields we're discovering now are progressively smaller, in more remote and geographically challenging locations.

Seventy percent of our daily oil supply comes from oil fields that were discovered prior to 1970.[76]

Enhanced Recovery Technology

Peak oil skeptics and large oil company executives frequently claim that enhanced oil recovery technology will put fears of shortages to rest. A high-enough oil price, they say—and $60 is usually the number cited—will spur investment in enhanced recovery technology and breathe new life into old wells.

In a June 2007 speech, BP group chief executive Tony Hayward pinned supply shortages primarily on a chronic lack of investment, noting the industry's lackluster returns and low oil prices in the past two decades.

"For instance," he explained, "we produce on average only one-third of the oil in known fields. And we know equally well that it is conceivable to push average recovery rates to 65 percent or even 80 percent with the right technology. Indeed, it has already risen by about 10 percent in the last 30 years."

What he didn't explain is that the enhanced recovery doesn't increase the peak *rate* of production; it only increases the EUR.

But he also let on that perhaps our estimates of future production should be taken with a grain of salt:

> For many years, we have, as an industry, over promised and under delivered in terms of production. . . . Many of these problems are political, caused by bureaucracy and corruption, civil strife and war, or changing fiscal and regulatory regimes creating uncertainty.[77]

Indeed they are. But whether the proximate reasons are aboveground or belowground, peak is peak, and it's very close at hand. We're going to need all the time we can get to prepare for the reality of declining oil.

No Magic Bullets

As Roger Bezdek puts it, "There are no magic bullets, only poison pills."

Unconventional oil resources, such as oil shales and tar sands, cannot substantially affect the peak. Technologies such as recovery of oil from oil shales have yet to be proven at a commercial scale, their economics are still unknown and there are major environmental issues that are still unresolved. And the technologies that are functional at a commercial scale, such as Alberta's tar sands, are expensive and slow to build, as well as environmentally damaging (or at least questionable), and the net energy returned is low.[78]

The net effect of unconventional oil, including that from the tar sands, and advanced oil recovery technology will be to dampen the slope of the post-peak decline and extend the tail to produce more of the original oil over a longer period of time. It won't substantially change the date of the peak or the peak rate of production.

All in all, far from being a panacea, unconventional oil is a story of getting less for more effort and expense every year.

ASPO anticipates that overall world oil production will likely peak and plateau between now and 2015.[79] It seems that Colin Campbell's estimate could prove correct: "My numbers give 2005 for let's say the cheap, easy stuff and 2011 for all categories, but that it's coming is beyond any serious debate whatever."

Matthew Simmons concurs:

> As I look, every month, at the best data we have, which is fuzzy data, it is getting harder and harder to imagine that we could actually grow crude oil supply another three or four or five million barrels a day. You've got every OPEC producer basically now flat out. They all claim they have spare capacity, but when oil prices got to be almost $80 a barrel, not a single one of them were increasing their production. Saudi Arabia said they have two million barrels a day, or two and a half million barrels a day of shut-in supply, [but] their imports to the member countries of the IEA have been flat to declining the last five years. If they had spare capacity they would have sold into a rising market! Venezuela's oil is in decline, Nigeria's oil is in decline, Indonesia is now becoming an oil importer, [and] Iran's oil industry is in shambles, so from a prudent planning standpoint, I think we should assume we have peaked. And if I'm wrong, I bet I'm wrong by two or three years, but why quibble over two or three years?[80]

THE HARD TRUTH

To recap what we know about oil peaking, the trends are clear: The biggest and most productive oil fields are all in decline or soon will be, and the rate of decline increases each year past the peak.

New finds are smaller and smaller and are just barely able to compensate for the decline from larger fields; they will not allow us to increase overall production any further. Finding new oil is becoming increasingly difficult and expensive, and the oil is of progressively lower quality, because we have used the best and easiest to produce oil first. New discoveries are harder to produce due to their suboptimal locations and geological characteristics, and producing oil from the mature fields requires increasing energy inputs, more advanced technology, and more expense.

With supply and demand in ever-tighter balance, prices will continue to rise, and unconventional oil cannot resolve the tension: In 1997, the net wellhead cost of Saudi oil was only 95 cents a barrel, but at $60 a barrel, oil produced from Canada's tar sands may yield only a 10 percent profit.[81]

Considering that the world is completely dependent on this resource, and considering that the peak of conventional oil is probably two years in the past, and the peak of exotic, unconventional, and hard-to-produce "all liquids" is at most only two to four years in the future, it is quite clear that the world has precious little time to begin preparing itself for the second half of the age of oil.

CHAPTER

3

WANTED: FIVE NEW SAUDI ARABIAS

The greatest shortcoming of the human race is our inability to understand the exponential function.

—Dr. Albert Bartlett

Anyone who believes exponential growth can go on forever in a finite world is either a madman or an economist.

—Kenneth Boulding

World oil demand has been increasing steadily at the rate of about 1.5 percent annually for the past several years. But according to the International Energy Agency (IEA), in 2007 it actually grew at a 2 percent rate.[1]

Not surprisingly, the global economy has expanded about the same amount at the same time. After all, most of our economic activity is rooted in the consumption of oil.

Now that it appears we're about at the peak of global oil production, how will the world's economies adapt?

GLOBAL DEMAND AND POPULATION

Global energy demand faces exponential growth. At current rates of growth, our 85 million barrels per day (mbpd) rate of oil consumption will grow to 120 mbpd by 2030,[3] and our need for natural gas and electricity will jump by 50 percent. Even so, we'd still have two billion of the world's population with little to no energy supply.[4]

At 6.4 billion and climbing, the world's population is expected to exceed 9 billion by 2050. Yet our known fossil fuel reserves are in decline, and alternative energy sources are not expanding rapidly enough to meet future demand.

— Chevron's "Will You Join Us?" Campaign[2]

The growth in energy demand is fundamentally based on two factors: increased industrialization and growing population. Compare the growth in human population with the growth in oil consumption, as shown in Figure 3.1.

Clearly, oil and population are closely correlated. More people means more transportation, more manufacturing, more food, more of everything, and almost everything in the modern world requires energy from oil.

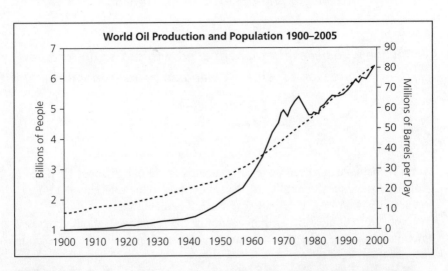

FIGURE 3.1 *World Oil Production and Population, 1900–2005*

Original: Paul Chefurka, Post to TheOilDrum.com, http://canada.theoildrum.com/node/2516.

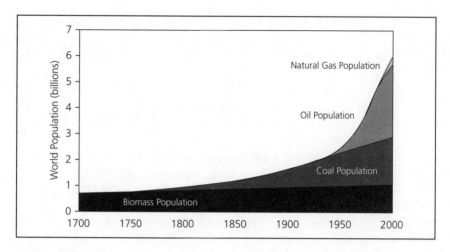

FIGURE 3.2 *Sum-of-Energies Model of World Population*

Source: Graham Zabel, Population and Energy, "Sum-of-Energies Model of World Population," 2000.

But what about the other sources of energy? Could they take up the slack to support a world population that continues to increase? Without oil and coal, which have been the primary sources of energy supporting the population boom over the past 100 years, it seems not. (See Figure 3.2.)

The chart comes from a thesis paper called "Population and Energy" by Graham Zabel, who explains the relationship as follows: "[T]he world's population would not be anything like the six billion that it is, if not for the discovery, commercialisation, and mass use of coal and subsequently oil and gas. Vast inputs of energy into modern society have led to vast increases in population."[5]

He estimates that natural gas will add approximately another half-billion people, but then—barring the development of some massive, as-yet-unknown alternative source of energy—population must decline.

Without the massive fossil fuel inputs of modern agriculture in the form of natural gas-based fertilizers, oil-based pesticides and herbicides, fuel to run big farm machinery, energy to run water pumps for irrigation, and other inputs, the world's output of food simply could not support the world's current population of some six billion people.

As Colin Campbell puts it: "It leads to the awful question, I mean just awful question, just how many people the planet can support without cheap oil. This is kind of a difficult subject, but the population of the world has gone up six-fold exactly in parallel with oil. So, whether it goes down six-fold in parallel with oil remains to be seen."

Perhaps the best way to estimate the carrying capacity of Earth without fossil fuel inputs is to look at the world's population before we started using fossil fuels en masse with the advent of the industrial revolution: about 1.5 billion people.

The problem, of course, is that we live on a finite planet with a finite amount of fossil fuel, but our population and our use of fuel have grown exponentially, and most prognosticators seem to expect the current trends to continue.

But even a child knows that no tree grows to the sky.

Perhaps the best-known critic of such pronouncements of endless growth is Dr. Albert Bartlett, now-retired professor of physics at the University of Colorado in Boulder. He has given his famous lecture on sustainability, population, and the exponential function over 3,500 times, and has spent a lifetime teaching about the mathematics of population growth and energy supplies. Both are examples of exponential growth rates, but he complains that very few people understand the implications of this "simple arithmetic" for even modest growth rates.

By way of example, he notes that if our current 1.3 percent per year rate of population growth "could continue, the world population would grow to a density of one person per square meter on the dry land surface of the earth in just 780 years, and then the mass of people would equal the mass of the earth in just 2,400 years."[6]

Here is Dr. Bartlett's classic example about bacteria populations:

Bacteria grow by doubling. One bacterium divides to become two, the two divide to become four, become eight, 16, and so on. Suppose we had bacteria that doubled in number this way every minute. Suppose we put one of these bacterium into an empty bottle at 11 in the morning, and then observe that the bottle is full at 12 noon. There's our case of just ordinary steady growth, it has a doubling time of one minute, and it's in the finite environment of one bottle. I want to ask you three questions.

Number one: At which time was the bottle half full? Well, would you believe 11:59, one minute before 12, because they double in number every minute.

Second question: If you were an average bacterium in that bottle, at what time would you first realize that you were running out of space? Well, let's just look at the last minute in the bottle. At 12 noon it's full, one minute before it's half full, two minutes before it's a quarter full, then an eighth, then a 16th. Let me ask you: At five minutes before 12, when the bottle is only 3 percent full, and 97 percent is open space just yearning for development, how many of you would realize there's a problem?

This has led to the oft-quoted question: Are humans smarter than yeast? How many of us realize that there is a problem right now, before the peak is a historical fact?

Applying his perspective to the question of oil production in a 1997 paper, Dr. Bartlett concluded: "My analysis, based on geological estimates of the total world resource of petroleum, suggests that world petroleum production will peak around the year 2004 and thereafter will start its inevitable decline toward zero."

It looks like that prediction is correct, plus a couple of years (because global reserve estimates have slightly increased since 1997).

Which leads naturally to the next question, put elegantly by Dr. Bartlett: "Think what it will mean to have declining world production of petroleum *and* an increasing world population that aspires to have increasing per capita consumption of petroleum."

What will it mean, indeed? How will we sort out our competing demands? What kind of future are we trying to attain, anyway?

As Bartlett points out, the name of the game is really sustainability: how many people can the planet's resources support? Putting a finer point on it, Bartlett defines the first law of sustainability as: "**Population growth and/or growth in the rates of consumption of resources cannot be sustained.** That's simple arithmetic. It's intellectually dishonest to talk about saving the environment, which is sustainability, without stressing the obvious fact that stopping population growth is a necessary condition for saving the environment and for sustainability."

It seems so obvious. And yet, so few data crunchers or policy makers seem to understand it. We must assume that they're capable of understanding the math, so why is this, if not for willful deception?

Perhaps it's the same reason that Dr. Colin Campbell has given for why oil reserves estimates have been overstated: because they are highly political estimates supplied by governments and oil companies.

"When I was the boss of an oil company I would never tell the truth," he said. "It's not part of the game."[7]

Or, as Upton Sinclair has famously remarked, "It is difficult to get a man to understand something when his salary depends on his not understanding it."

We bring up the relationship between energy and population for the simple reason that if global population continues to grow unabated, alternative energies must be developed, and developed soon enough to support the population. And as we'll see with China and India, this will be a huge investment opportunity for years to come.

CHINA AND INDIA

Just a decade ago, the rate of oil usage was mainly a function of the economic powerhouses of the United States, Western Europe, and Japan.

But not anymore.

With the world's developed economies having matured and settled down into 2 percent or lower growth rates, the growth in oil consumption is now being driven by the world's new powerhouse economies: China and India.

China

China's economy has been on a blistering tear, running at a 10 percent annual growth rate, with India right behind, at around 8 percent.[8] Compare this with 3.5 percent for the United States, 2.1 percent for Japan, and 1.7 percent for the European Union (2005 data).[9]

The growth of China's energy consumption is correspondingly spectacular. It is now the second-largest energy consumer in the world, after the United States, having become a net importer in 1995.

The EIA has estimated that the rate of China's energy demand growth would be 4 to 5 percent annually through 2015,[10] but in fact, in the first five months of 2007, China's oil consumption leapt 11.5 percent over the previous year.[11] In 2006, China had to import 47 percent of all the oil it used, and by 2015, it will need to import two-thirds.[12] China currently consumes and produces about 10 percent of the world's energy production.

Estimates of China's contribution to the growth of world energy consumption rates have varied:

■ In May 2006, OPEC estimated that China alone accounted for one-third of the increase in global oil demand.[13]

■ According to the McKinsey Global Institute, between now and 2020 developing countries will be responsible for 80 percent of the growth in world energy demand, with China representing 32 percent and the Middle East 10 percent.[14]

■ According to the EIA's current projections, 43 percent of the growth in oil demand from 2003 to 2030 will be attributable to non-OECD Asia (including China and India),[15] whose overall energy consumption will nearly double. The EIA also estimates that non-OECD electricity demand will nearly double by 2030.[16]

■ And according to Milton Copulos, China alone has accounted for 40 percent of the total increase in world oil consumption over the past several years.[17]

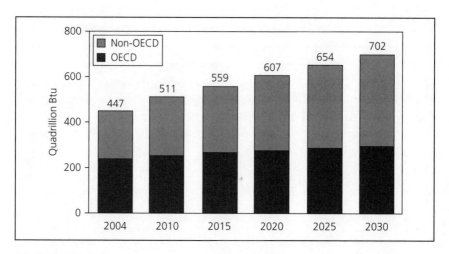

FIGURE 3.3   *World Marketed Energy Consumption by Region,*
2004–2030

Source: Energy Information Administration, International Energy Outlook 2007,
www.eia.doe.gov/oiaf/ieo/pdf/0484(2007).pdf.

The EIA's projection is shown in Figure 3.3.

However we characterize it, there is no doubt that China is currently the world's second-largest oil importer, after the United States,[18] and its appetite for energy is growing incredibly fast.

China's industrialization is a major cause for concern, because its population is so great. Consider the numbers shown in Table 3.1.

What will happen as China, with four times the U.S. population, increases its oil consumption per capita more than 10 times over as they strive for a First World standard of living?

China and Coal

China's rapid industrialization has also led to radically increasing its coal consumption. China uses more coal than the United States, the European Union, and Japan combined. And its coal use is growing at the rate of 14 percent a year, accounting for some 75 percent of the entire world's growth in coal demand.[19]

In fact, as coal consumption tapered off in most of the rest of the world, China's consumption grew 62 percent from 2000 to 2005, a major factor in the 50 percent growth of world coal consumption over the same period.[20]

Table 3.1 **United States and China Oil Usage Comparison**

	United States	China
Population (6.7 billion world total)	300 million	1.3 billion
Oil consumption per capita[a]	0.0688 barrels/day	0.0049 barrels/day
Percentage of world's oil use	26%	6%[b]
Percentage of world's population	4.5%	20%

[a]www.nationmaster.com/graph/ene_oil_con_percap-energy-oil-consumption-per-capita.
[b]www.mnforsustain.org/oil_peaking_of_world_oil_production_appendix.htm.

Several recent estimates say that China is now opening a new coal-fired plant *every three days*—plants big enough to satisfy all of the electricity needs of a city the size of San Diego.[21]

That coal is being consumed for one purpose: to generate electricity. China is building new coal-fired power plants so quickly that even the central government doesn't know about them all—in January 2007, it learned about 10 new ones that were built in Mongolia without the government's knowledge or permission.

And all of that coal is casting a shadow of soot around the world, depositing it in places like the West Coast of the United States and causing acid rain that poisons lakes, rivers, forests, and crops. It has been estimated that fully 77 percent of the black carbon emitted into North America's lower atmosphere comes from Asia.[22]

But that's not all. Coal emissions also carry mercury and other toxins. The burning of coal has been fingered as the reason why mercury concentrations are so high in tuna fish, leading to health advisories warning pregnant mothers and young children to limit their consumption of the fish to once a month, or avoid it altogether.

In China itself, the residents pay with their health for China's use of coal. A 2007 report by the World Bank and the Chinese government found that 750,000 people die prematurely in China each year, mostly due to air pollution in large cities, but also due to unclean water and other environmental hazards.

According to the *Financial Times,* the Chinese government forced the World Bank to remove nearly a third of the report, including the section on premature deaths, saying it could provoke "social unrest."[23]

However, the future of coal use in China is in doubt. According to a February 2007 report[24] prepared for European Commission Joint Research Centre, China has only 30 years' worth of hard coal reserves, which it is burning through rapidly. While China is currently producing about 2.2 billion tons of coal per year,[25] the report doubts whether it can maintain a rate over 2 billion tons per year past 2030 to 2040, leading to an increased use of nuclear power and low-quality sub-bituminous coal.

Car Crazy

Not surprisingly, much of the growth in China is due to the car.

A decade ago, there were hardly any privately owned cars in China. Now, there are more than 24 million of them, and China is the second-largest automobile market in the world.

And it doesn't stop there. From the seven million vehicles sold in China in 2006, one Shanghai auto analyst expects another 20 to 25 percent growth over 2007. By 2020, there could be more cars in China than there are in the United States today.[26]

China expects to add 120 million vehicles over the next decade, requiring 11.7 million barrels per day of new crude oil supplies.[27] (Again, that's more than the entire output of Saudi Arabia—just to fuel China's *new* cars.)

According to a June 2007 study by the Netherlands Environmental Assessment Agency, China's fossil fuel use has put it at the top of the list of CO_2-emitting countries for the first time. "China's 2006 carbon dioxide emissions surpassed those of the United States by 8 percent," it said in a statement. However, the agency notes that China's per capita emissions are still one-quarter of those in the United States.[28]

India

India's oil demand is likewise expected to increase by 28 percent over the next five years, to fuel its booming economy.[29] With a population of 1.1 billion people, an economic growth rate of 9 percent,[30] and a rapidly industrializing economy, its story is very similar to that of China. Its appetite for energy and cars is just as voracious, and its domestic energy resources are even more limited. Without further elaboration, it is clear that India's contribution to global energy demand is no more supportable than China's.

MAKING UP FOR DEPLETION

The current rate of global oil depletion is often cited to be around 2.5 percent per annum, but has been recently estimated by oil analyst Chris Skrebowski and others to be closer to 4 or 4.5 percent.[31] As we pass the global peak and go into terminal decline, the rate of depletion will accelerate.

To give an idea of how much this matters, at a rate of 4 percent, the world would need to add 3.3 million barrels per day of new capacity each year *just to keep world oil production flat.* At a rate of 5 percent per year, we would need 20 million barrels a day—about one-quarter of current global consumption—of *new* oil by 2015 just to stand still.

Discovering and producing that much more oil in eight years simply isn't plausible, and at any rate, even if we could keep oil production flat, it would still result in a global recession, since all economies depend on constant growth for their health.

As noted peak oil author Richard Heinberg puts it: "In 2006, according to the International Energy Agency, we'll need about one million-and-a-half barrels a day of new production capacity to meet new demand, and about 4 million barrels a day of new production capacity to offset declines, so in total, between 5-and-a-half million and 6 million barrels a day of new production capacity."[32]

That's nearly two-thirds of the total current oil production of Saudi Arabia, the world's top oil producer, which currently produces 8.6 million barrels per day.[33]

The year after that, we'd need the same amount of *new* capacity again.

In fact, according to the EIA's IEO2006 reference case, world oil demand will skyrocket from 80 mbpd in 2003 (85 mbpd in 2007) to 118 mbpd in 2030—and the reality could easily be higher than the reference case.[34]

That means we would need at least 33 mbpd of new capacity—almost a 40 percent increase from current production levels—to meet the projected increase in demand. That's like adding three new Saudi Arabias. But that would have to happen after we've made up for the depletion of mature fields, which could account for another 25 mbpd by then—another two Saudi Arabias!

There isn't another one Saudi Arabia, let alone another five.

Although EIA, BP's "Statistical Review of World Energy," and other reports can be forgiven somewhat for making such projections on the basis of sketchy data, suggesting that the world is going to discover another three Saudi Arabias' worth of oil in the next 23 years *and* compensate for the loss of two more is reckless and irresponsible.

U.S. DEPENDENCE

No study on energy would be complete without making a close examination of its number one consumer, the United States.

First a snapshot of the statistics:[35]

Population: 300 million, or about 4.5 percent of the world population.

Crude oil production: 5.1 mbpd.

Crude oil imports: 12.4 mbpd, of which 5.5 mbpd is from OPEC.

Finished petroleum product imports: 3.6 mbpd.

Total imports: 13.7 mbpd, or 66 percent of total consumption.

Total oil consumption: 20.7 mbpd, or about 25 percent of world consumption.

Being dependent on foreign sources for two-thirds of our total oil consumption is dangerous enough; but how reliable are our top sources of imports? (See Table 3.2.)[36]

Note that the top 16 suppliers to the United States provide fully 86 percent of our imports. We have serious concerns about nearly every country on that list, but the top five—accounting for 59 percent of our imports—deserve special mention.

Canada: Our number one source of imported oil is friendly, but passed its conventional oil peak in 1973. It now produces 3.3 mbpd, of which 1.2 mbpd is from tar sands.[37] It has some estimated 179 billion barrels of oil reserves, second only to Saudi Arabia, but less than five billion barrels are conventional crude.[38] The rest is in the form of tar sands, and as we will see, the expectations for radically increasing their production are probably overblown, and the sands production will likely top out around 5 mbpd, if it gets there at all.[39]

Overall, Canada will likely increase its production from the tar sands slowly, enough to allow it to maintain current levels of exports, but not enough to offset declines in U.S. imports from other sources.

Venezuela: After several years of renationalizing its oil assets, four of the major oil firms with stakes in Venezuela's operations—Chevron, BP, Total of France, and Statoil of Norway—have decided to remain there as junior partners. But ExxonMobil and ConocoPhillips have turned down President Hugo Chavez's offer to remain with a reduced stake, and have abandoned their operations there, seeking relief for their investments in the international courts. While Venezuela has been striking deals with China to provide oil development expertise, its hostile stance toward the far more experienced

TABLE 3.2 **Top 10 Exporters to the United States**

Rank	Exporter	U.S. Net Imports, 2006 (000s bpd)	% of Total
1	Canada	2,353	17%
2	Mexico	1,705	12%
3	Saudi Arabia	1,463	11%
4	Venezuela	1,419	10%
5	Nigeria	1,114	8%
6	Algeria	657	5%
7	Iraq	553	4%
8	Angola	534	4%
9	Russia	369	3%
10	Other Western Hemisphere < 1mbpd	1,966	12%
	Total	12,133	86%

Data source: EIA, 2006, U.S. Imports by Country of Origin, Total Crude Oil and Products, Annual Thousand Barrels per Day, http://tonto.eia.doe.gov/dnav/pet/xls/pet_move_impcus_a2_nus_ep00_im0_mbblpd_a.xls

"Other Western Hemisphere > 1mbpd" includes Virgin Islands, Ecuador, UK, Norway, Brazil, Netherlands and Columbia

Western oil majors makes it less likely that it will be able to expand production anytime soon. This is especially true considering that much of Venezuela's oil lies in a region called the Orinoco River basin, which contains heavy oil that is far more challenging to produce, and which requires advanced technology that only the Western majors have.

Venezuela's oil production is currently in decline.

Saudi Arabia: Saudi Arabia is usually the number one oil producer in the world, but is currently playing second fiddle (temporarily) to Russia. As we have discussed, it has the largest oil field in the world, the mighty Ghawar, and it is the only country with any significant spare production capacity.

The country is friendly to the United States—indeed, it is our largest customer for weapons—and it has historically acted as a friendly partner to us.

However, if Ghawar is indeed in decline—and if it isn't now, it will be soon enough—then, according to Matthew Simmons, the world is officially in decline. Being flush with cash from its oil sales, the country also has rapidly expanding domestic needs for oil as it embarks on a huge spree of building infrastructure.

By the end of 2006, Saudi Arabia was just barely keeping up with a 9 mbpd production rate, which it claims was intentional in accordance with OPEC production cuts. But some shrewd observers believe that due to the high water cut of its major field, Ghawar, the Saudis couldn't produce more than 9 mbpd if they wanted to, and their decline rate may be as high as 4 percent. It has also been estimated that by 2025, Saudi Arabia's domestic consumption is set to reach 5 mbpd—more than the total output of Ghawar.[40]

It is officially unknown if Saudi Arabia is in decline (and will no doubt remain so until the conclusion is all but indisputable), but all in all, it seems that our best hope would be for the Saudis to maintain their current level of exports to the United States for the near future, as it's unlikely that they will be able to increase them at all.

Mexico: Over half of the oil produced by Mexico comes from its giant Cantarell field, which is one of the top four oil fields in the world. It was discovered in 1976, and by 2003, with the help of an aggressive nitrogen injection program, it was the second fastest producing field in the world (after Ghawar), producing 2.1 mbpd.[41] But in 2004, in part due to the effects of the injection program, it entered into a catastrophic decline, which is now running at least 15 percent a year. (Its decline in 2006 was a whopping 28 percent.) At this rate, it will be producing only 1 mbpd by 2008.

Mexico's exports have taken the brunt of the drop in production, falling from 1.82 mbpd in 2005 to 1.53 mbpd in 2006. Its economy is booming (due to the exporting of U.S. jobs) and the country needs the energy. Mexico has already warned that it will be unable to fulfill some of its existing export contracts. Mexico's oil peak occurred in 2004.

Where does that leave the United States? Respected Mexican oil analyst David Shields has projected that Petróleos Mexicanos (PEMEX) will lose another 0.4 mbpd of production over the course of 2007, and will lose more than 1 mbpd by the end of 2008. The decline rate of Cantarell is expected to accelerate to 40 percent. In other words, give it a couple more years and our number two source of imports is kaput.

Nigeria: Although Nigeria is one of the few significant oil provinces in the world where oil production has yet to be fully exploited, attacks and kidnappings by indigenous rebel groups have crippled Nigeria's oil industry and stymied attempts to increase its production. Pipeline bombings, attacks on oil facilities, and kidnappings of foreign oil workers and their families have created a risky environment in which foreign oil companies are increasingly unwilling to participate. More than 200 expatriates have been kidnapped in the Niger Delta since the beginning of 2006. Most foreign countries with operations in Nigeria have called their citizens home, saying it's too unsafe to be there.

Subsequently, a July 2007 report by the United States Department of State entitled "Nigeria Energy Data, Statistics and Analysis—Oil, Gas, Electricity, Coal" states that as of April 2007, an estimated 587,000 barrels per day of Nigeria's crude production was offline due to all of the factors just mentioned, causing the country to lose an estimated $16 billion in export revenues since December 2005.[42]

In January 2007, due to constant attacks on its facilities by the rebel group Movement for the Emancipation of the Niger Delta (MEND), all of its oil refineries were shut down, forcing the country to import all of its refined products. In June, a general nationwide strike by the working class brought the oil industry to a standstill. In mid-July, Nigerian manufacturers issued a warning about the "imminent collapse of the textile industry," saying that 30 textile industries will be closed down and 30,000 jobs lost due to the loss of oil deliveries, and on July 16 over 4,000 workers in the United Nigeria Textile Limited (UNTL) were laid off due to a lack of fuel to run their mill.[43]

The situation shows no hopes of resolution as long as the proceeds from oil continue to enrich only a small oligarchy within Nigeria's hopelessly corrupt government, which ignores the basic human needs of its population. Most of the people live in squalor and fear, without access to clean water or other basic necessities. Over 70 percent of Nigerians, about 98 million people out of a population of 140 million, live in extreme poverty, on less than a dollar a day.

All of these factors are sure to breed further terrorism.

It is unlikely that the shut-in production in Nigeria can be restored, given these many issues. Therefore only its offshore production, which is more easily secured, might be expected to increase.

Expectations for Future U.S. Imports

All in all, the outlook for future oil imports to the United States is not good. Out of these top five suppliers, three are definitely past their peaks and the fourth (Saudi Arabia) may be near its peak.

For the world's largest consumer of oil, depending on imports for two-thirds of its supply, this is not a good position to be in.

INVESTMENT OPPORTUNITIES

The oil business is the biggest business in the world, and there are many ways to play it and many companies to invest in, including big blue chips like ExxonMobil (NYSE: XOM).

But we wouldn't touch most of them with a five-mile drilling rod.

By now, the reason should be clear: The big integrated oil companies, whose valuations largely rest on their reserves, have seen their best days in terms of exploration and production. Now they're focused on surviving and extracting the maximum value from their ever-shrinking reserves. They are presiding over the decline of a major industry, holding on to a mere 10 percent of the world's remaining oil reserves, and most of them (excepting BP) are making little to no investment in the renewable fuels of the future.

While in recent years the oil majors have been seeming to mint money as they recorded record profits quarter after quarter, those heady days are about to come to a crashing end. For the last several years, reserves replacement has consistently fallen short of investor expectations for most of the oil majors, taking their stocks down. Then at some point production flows will have to start to decline as well, taking them down another peg. Either way, investors will spook. Only then will the companies restate (that is, finally tell the truth about) their reserves numbers, as BP and Shell have already done, and they'll get whacked again.

Essentially, it looks as though oil majors are running a shell game here, no pun intended. The question is: When will investors figure it out?

One needs to look no further than the oil business' huge and rusting infrastructure to see that they are no longer investing in it as if it were a business with a future. And they have begun to prospect on Wall Street to prop up their declining reserves numbers far more aggressively than they are prospecting in the earth. But once their reserves numbers enter permanent decline, watch out! Dividends will dry up, and share buybacks will be the only thing standing between them and disaster. Perhaps this has something to do with the massive buyback of shares by the oil majors in recent years: to limit their exposure to market fluctuations and protect their earnings per share, in addition to simply believing that their stocks are currently too cheap.

We believe that the truly profitable part of the oil business is going to be not in owning reserves, but in providing essential oil and gas industry services. Let's have a look at some of them.

First is the heavy sour crude refiners, because as we have seen, there is mainly heavy sour left to produce.

The difference between the price of sweet and sour grades of crude is known as the sweet-sour spread. During the lows of oil prices in recent years, that spread was typically around $8, but at the highest points, it increased to as much as $20.

Therefore refiners who can process heavy sour grades of crude make more on the "crack spread," or the difference between the cost of the crude feedstock and the final refined products, than light sweet refiners do.

As "the price of oil" (light sweet crude) rises and the price of heavy sour stays low, the sweet-sour spread increases, and the crack spread increases. The heavy sour crude refiners make more money by simply continuing to do what they have always done.

In the United States, the heavy sour refining sector is dominated by Valero Energy Corporation (NYSE: VLO), a $37 billion company that is the largest independent oil refiner in the country, as well as a large independent oil retailer. After Valero, Tesoro Corporation (NYSE: TSO), a $6.7 billion company, is the next biggest heavy sour crude refiner. Since most of the crude oil that is yet to be harvested in the world is the heavy sour kind, and since the complex refining capacity in the United States is so limited, these companies are sitting in the catbird seat, optimally positioned to profit from the coming changes. With a much lower crude acquisition cost than their light sweet refining competitors, but the same retail value for their products, their profit outlook will be stellar in the long term.

And as long as there is Saudi oil to sell (which there will be for a long time yet) and consumers who want gasoline (ditto), Valero and Tesoro are going to make a pretty penny for every hour they operate their refineries. And their only downside exposure is force majeure and equipment failure, because their crack spread should remain high as long as demand for refined products is strong. However, we note that refining margins tend to be cyclical. In 2007, for example, margins rose to an historic high in the second quarter, then fell to the lower end of their historic range by the end of the year.

Next are the deepwater offshore drillers. Onshore drillers and shallow-water offshore drillers have seen their best days, and are scrambling to snatch the remaining crumbs, while the days of deepwater offshore drilling are only beginning to get interesting. Companies like Transocean Inc. (NYSE: RIG), a $32 billion offshore driller with 89 mobile offshore and barge drilling units, including 32 high-specification semisubmersibles and drillships (high-specification floating rigs), and Diamond Offshore Drilling, Inc. (NYSE: DO), a $15 billion company with a fleet of 44 offshore drilling rigs, are going to make out like bandits on the extreme drilling challenges of the future. Transocean already commands a daily rental rate of over $600,000 for its modern semisubmersible deepwater drilling rigs. These drillers will make money from whoever wants to rent their equipment, whether they drill dry holes or wet ones. And they have zero downside exposure (other than hurricanes, but as many deepwater rigs have left the Gulf of Mexico in the past two years, their exposure is limited).

Companies that provide oil well services and equipment are generally huge conglomerates with many business sectors, so not many of them are pure plays on oil. But for those with a taste for such stocks (and their less tasteful but common companions, defense technology), companies like the $113 billion behemoth Schlumberger Limited (NYSE: SLB), $33.7 billion Halliburton (NYSE: HAL), and $25 billion Baker Hughes Inc. (NYSE: BHI) should be safe and profitable investments.

For a speculative, unconventional take on the oil business, Sulphco, Inc. (AMEX: SUF) could be a good bet. This $532 million development-stage company is working on a sonic technology to upgrade heavy sour crude oil by exposing it to high-power ultrasonic sound waves. This process alters the molecular structure of the crude oil, making it less dense and viscous so that more light oil can be recovered from it during refining, as well as removing some sulfur and nitrogen to make the resulting fuel cleaner. The company's customers are crude oil producers and refiners. However, this is a highly speculative play, the company is still operating at a loss, and investors should examine the company carefully.

There are literally hundreds of public companies in the oil business, but investing in them wisely calls for a good understanding of the previous material, not just jumping on the XOM bandwagon.

CHAPTER

4

$480 A BARREL: THE TRUE VALUE OF OIL

We have to wake up. We are at the edge of a precipice and we have one foot over the edge. The only way to avoid going over is to move forward and move forward aggressively with initiatives to develop alternative fuels. Just cutting back won't work.

—MILTON R. COPULOS

CHEAPER THAN WATER

When you think about it, oil should be one of the most expensive commodities of all. It required millions of years to accumulate the carbon-based life-forms, millions of years to cook it, and over a hundred million years to transport it to its current location and preserve it in rare geological structures so it can be extracted today. Then it takes massive, expensive, technologically advanced equipment and highly specialized labor to produce and process the crude into usable forms.

And yet the retail price of oil is cheaper than the retail price of bottled water, when water falls freely from the sky and washes through surface rivers every day. At $90 per barrel, oil costs 14 cents a cup. At $3.20 a gallon, gasoline costs 20 cents a cup. And natural gas is even cheaper: At $8 per thousand cubic feet, it's equivalently priced to oil at $40 per barrel.

Fourteen cents a cup is about one-tenth the price you might pay for the same volume of water at your local convenience store. Even when purchased by the gallon, water is still often more expensive than gasoline.

Another way to put the true value of oil in perspective is by looking at its energy content.

A healthy, strong adult can exert about 100 watts of effort while working continuously, with peak output of about 200 watts. World-class athletes might achieve an output as high as 280 watts. So a strong human might produce about one kilowatt-hour per day over the course of a 10-hour day. For that same energy, you probably pay your local utility about 10 cents. But if you paid an adult a $7 minimum wage for the work, it would cost you $70.[1]

A strong man, working hard all day long, can do less work than an electric motor can with 10 cents' worth of electricity.

Therefore, electricity costs about one-1000th the equivalent value of human effort.

Oil is even cheaper. At 3,412 Btus in a kilowatt-hour, and 5.8 million Btus in a barrel of oil (see Appendix A), a barrel contains the equivalent of 18,000 man-hours of energy—approximately equivalent to 12 people doing manual labor full-time for an entire year—or about $126,000 worth of labor at $7 per hour.[2]

At $90 per barrel, oil is priced less than one-1,000th the equivalent value of human labor!

DRAINING THE NATIONAL COFFERS

How much of our nation's wealth goes to pay for oil? It's a difficult number to nail down accurately, but if all of our 21 million barrels per day consumption of crude oil were bought at the market price ($90/bbl as of October 2007), it would cost the economy $1.9 billion per day, or $690 billion per year.

But that's just for crude. The military costs are staggering.

According to noted peak oil author Michael Klare, U.S. military operations in Iraq and Afghanistan consume in total the equivalent of 16 gallons of oil a day for every American soldier. "Multiply this figure by 162,000 soldiers in Iraq, 24,000 in Afghanistan, and 30,000 in the surrounding region (including sailors aboard U.S. warships in the Persian Gulf) and you arrive at approximately 3.5 million gallons of oil: the daily petroleum tab for U.S. combat operations in the Middle East war zone."[3]

According to an April 2007 report by defense contractor LMI Government Consulting, the Pentagon might consume as much as 340,000 barrels (14 million gallons) every day—more than the total national consumption of Sweden or Switzerland.[4]

For the U.S. military, the cost of fuel is a major issue. The Air Force alone spends about $5 billion a year on fuel, seconded closely by the Navy and the Army.

The military's energy costs have doubled since 9/11. Costs are going up so fast and so high that they're worried about being able to afford weapons!

And the cost of having the U.S. military protect the oil supplies of the Persian Gulf—yes, even protecting the ones who want to blow us up—is around $44 billion per year.[5]

That's just the security costs.

We import about 800 million barrels per year of black gold from the Persian Gulf. Divided into $44 billion, that works out to slightly less than $55 a barrel—when oil is trading on the open market around $90!

If those protection costs weren't externalized onto the U.S. military (your tax dollars at work!) but priced on the world market at $90 a barrel, that would put our oil at around $145 a barrel. But the true price of oil—as we will discuss in a moment—is much higher than even that.

How much higher?

THE TRUE COST OF OIL

On March 30, 2006, Milton Copulos, the head of the National Defense Council Foundation (NDCF), presented an update of its 2003 report entitled "America's Achilles Heel: The Hidden Costs of Imported Oil" to the influential Senate Foreign Relations Committee.

Some of the senators were clearly stunned by his numbers.

The in-depth analysis attempted to calculate—perhaps for the first time—the true total economic cost of the nation's growing dependence on imported oil, including evaluating hundreds of thousands of documents over a year and a half, as well as rigorous peer review.[6]

He estimated that the supply disruptions of the 1970s cost the U.S. economy between $2.3 trillion and $2.5 trillion, but the cost of such an event today could be as high as $8 trillion—63 percent of our annual gross domestic product (GDP), or nearly $27,000 for every man, woman, and child living in the United States.

He said that the "hidden cost" of imported oil—including oil costs and defense expenditures—for 2006 is estimated at $825.1 billion, or almost twice the President's $419.3 billion defense budget request for that year. That would be equivalent to $5.04 for every gallon of gasoline from all imports, or $8.35 for every Persian Gulf gallon, bringing the "true cost" of a gallon of gasoline refined from Persian Gulf oil to $11.06.

That would make the "real cost" of filling up a family sedan about $220, and filling up a large SUV about $325.[7]

And those numbers don't even include the cost of treating injured veterans, only the operational costs of "shooting people and blowing things up, not to put too fine a point on it." But he did estimate that the cost of treating combat casualties runs about $1.5 million per soldier, sailor, and airman.

Prior to founding the NDCF, Copulos was the principal energy analyst for the Heritage Foundation. He was also a member of the National Petroleum Council for 12 years, and spent 18 months in the Reagan White House. He has advised about half a dozen U.S. Secretaries of Energy and briefed various Secretaries of Defense, along with two directors of the Central Intelligence Agency.

Looking at the long term, Copulos has no illusions about the fact that peak oil is going to put a serious cramp in our style.

"The simple fact is if you look at global demand and what's going to be required by 2025, there's not sufficient oil that could be discovered to take care of that. We simply can't meet demand from conventional sources. It's not possible.

"As a consequence, we could be faced with a Hobson's choice between economic collapse and global resource war if we don't do something and fairly quickly. The consequences of that sort of conflict would be incredible. We don't want to see that happen."

Add in the hidden costs, Copulos says, and a $75 barrel of oil really costs us about $480.[8]

GOVERNMENT SUBSIDIES

There is another entire set of hidden costs in the form of government subsidies to the oil and gas industries.

It's a surprisingly difficult thing to put a boundary around, because there are so many direct and indirect ways in which the government supports the oil industry, and every study has its own list of things to leave in and things to leave out.

For example, we found no studies that included the hidden subsidy of leasing public lands to oil companies for next to nothing, which in essence assigns zero value to the oil extracted from the ground, paying the public nothing for the loss of its natural capital.

But there are some subsidies that are more easily quantified. One 1998 study by the International Center for Technology Assessment (ICTA)[9] looked at petroleum industry subsidies, including the percentage depletion allowance and tax-funded programs that directly subsidize oil production and consumption, among other things.

It assessed up to $17.8 billion per year in tax subsidies, plus government program subsidies (such as vehicle R&D programs, highway construction, and environmental cleanup) of between $38 billion and $114.6 billion per year.

The ICTA study pegged health and social costs at an additional $231.7 billion to $942.9 billion per year, due to factors such as health issues resulting from pollution, loss of crop yields, and so on.

As for related costs, such as the direct and indirect costs of traffic delays, traffic accidents, subsidized parking, and the like, ICTA counted another $191.4 billion to $474.1 billion per year.

Adjusting the estimates to 2006 dollars and rounding, that makes a total of between $68 billion and $161 billion in government subsidies, between $283 billion and $1,152 billion in health and social costs, and between $233 billion and $579 billion in related costs.

All told, these subsidies amount to $584 billion on the low side and $1.9 trillion on the high side.

ENVIRONMENTAL COSTS

Burning fossil fuels has serious environmental costs as well as economic costs, from water and soil pollution, to loss of species, to loss of ecosystem services such as cleaning the water and air. And yet, nobody ever pays those costs directly. They are externalized onto the environment: you and me, and everything that lives around us.

The Union of Concerned Scientists reviewed some studies on this subject in a 1995 article[10] citing several estimates: "Delucchi (1995) estimates the total cost in 1991 of environmental externalities to be $54 billion to $232 billion. Human mortality and morbidity due to air pollution accounts for over three-quarters of the total environmental cost and could be as high as $182 billion annually. For the Los Angeles area, Hall et al. (1992) estimates that the annual health-based cost from ozone and particulate exposure alone to be almost $10 billion."

Taking the upper estimate, because it's extremely unlikely that their list of factors was comprehensive, and adjusting for inflation, call it a total environmental cost of $345 billion per year.

CLIMATE CHANGE COST

Then there are the costs of climate change owing to the production of CO_2 from burning oil and gas.

A 2006 study[11] by the UK's New Economics Foundation looked at these costs company by company, and concluded that the climate change costs far outweighed the oil companies' profits.

Using a government estimate that put the cost of environmental damage at $35 per ton of carbon dioxide, the researchers calculated the cost of emissions from BP's oil business from production all the way through to burning the fuel. They came up with a damage bill of $51 billion a year. But BP's profit was only $19 billion, putting the entire enterprise $31 billion in the red!

The same calculation put Shell $23 billion in the red.

Once you take into account the externalized costs, the oil business isn't even worth doing. Put another way, we are living off capital, not interest.

Given the United States' emissions of some 1,614 million metric tons,[12] and using the $35 per ton figure, that gives us a CO_2 bill of about $56 trillion a year—when our GDP is only $13 trillion.

NATURAL CAPITAL COSTS

Emissions and environmental destruction are not the only externalized costs of the fossil fuel economy. A value should also be assigned to the resource that is extracted—the "natural capital" that we inherited from the earth.

Historically, all leases on the public's natural resources—be they water, flora, fauna, or fossil—have been granted to producers for a tiny fraction of their value. Since "nobody" owned the resource before "somebody" came and exploited it, then there was no cost assigned—other than a token payment to the people in the form of a lease payment or a tax.

This has naturally led to the maximal production of all resources at the lowest possible cost. Indeed, that has been the desired outcome of our very economic systems.

Is this an intelligent way to run an economy, or to inform an energy market? Because the system doesn't yet know that all of our important resources are about to contract no matter the price, neoclassical economics has produced a highly unsustainable design for our infrastructure.

But a new kind of economics is now emerging, based on natural capital, or systemwide energy flows, such that nothing is ever externalized. From a pragmatic business perspective, Paul Hawken has written on the subject extensively in books such as *The Ecology of Commerce* (HarperCollins, 1993) and *Natural Capitalism* (Little, Brown, 1999), as have his co-authors Amory and Hunter Lovins.

Similarly, analysts from a diverse set of fields have addressed the problem by creating a theoretical framework called biophysical economics:

> *Biophysical economics is based on a conceptual model of the economy connected to, and sustained by, a flow of energy, materials, and ecosystem services.*[13]

Although the intellectual heritage of the idea goes back to the eighteenth century, a new crop of theories based on ecology and thermodynamics is attracting renewed interest for those who want to enable market-based solutions to the problems at hand.[14]

Professor Charles Hall has done some excellent work on the subject in many articles and books, such as *Quantifying Sustainable Development: The Future of Tropical Economies* (Academic Press, 2000), *Making World Development Work: Scientific Alternatives to Neoclassical Economic Theory* (University of New Mexico Press, 2007), and a new book, *BioPhysical Economics* (Hall, Klitgaard, in press). Professor Cutler Cleveland has also made enormous contributions to the field of "ecological economics" in such works as "Energy and the U.S. Economy: A Biophysical Perspective" (Cleveland et al., *Science*, 1984).[15]

Through the work of such theorists (and hopefully, a few economists), we hope that we can eventually correct our economic system, so that it can finally help us make informed, smart choices. When oil, which requires very unique circumstances and hundreds of millions of years to form, costs much more than water, which falls freely from the sky, we'll know we're on the right track.

CHAPTER

5

THE PENTAGON PREPARES FOR PEAK OIL

*In the future, energy security will be almost as
important as defense.*

—Tony Blair, former British prime minister

*Current debates over where and how to drill for oil in this
country soon may be rendered irrelevant by a nation
desperate to maintain its quality of life and economic
productivity. War over access to the diminishing supply
of oil may be inevitable unless the United States and
other countries act now to develop alternatives to
their dependence on oil.*

—Senator Mark Hatfield

Their reasons may differ, but environmentalists, security hawks, and Osama
bin Laden have a common cause: weaning the United States from fossil fuels
and reducing our exposure to the Middle East.

For environmentalists, global warming is the chief concern, caused by the burning of fossil fuels—essentially, carbon that was sequestered underground for hundreds of millions of years and is now being put back into the atmosphere.

For bin Laden, the presence of American armed forces in the Muslim holy lands is intolerable. As he has stated in numerous speeches, he wants the U.S. occupation of the Middle East ended. And let's face it—our military forces wouldn't be over there if the region's main export were broccoli.

For security hawks like James Schlesinger, John Deutch, George Shultz, James Woolsey, and Frank Gaffney, it's a matter of security. For them, imported oil brings danger, and domestic renewables bring security.

These men are former CIA heads, statesmen, defense and energy analysts, and policy makers. They're all veterans of government, each of them having spent decades in a variety of key roles, under both Republican and Democratic administrations. And all are old friends and colleagues of other prominent neoconservative defense hawks such as Dick Cheney, Paul Wolfowitz, and Richard Perle.

These "green hawks" have now been joined by various military brass, the Council on Foreign Relations (CFR), the Pentagon, statesmen, and security-oriented think tanks. While their recommendations are many and varied, their objectives generally come down to these four:

1. Reduce dependence on oil.

2. Reduce CO_2 emissions.

3. Staunch the bleeding.

4. Invest heavily in renewables.

Let's review these more closely.

REDUCE DEPENDENCE ON OIL

In October 2006, a task force within the Council on Foreign Relations published a 90-page policy paper entitled "National Security Consequences of Oil Dependency."

It was a serious piece of work, and a stunning departure from the policy statements made by the President and other political leaders. The CFR, as you may know, is a hugely influential organization comprising the elite of the elite, one of the true power centers of government and business everywhere.

The report was startlingly frank about the futility of seeking energy independence, the absolute necessity of energy conservation, and the pressing need for investment in R&D for alternative energy and next-generation vehicles.

In other words, it was a prescription for facing the peak oil challenge.

The CFR's task force was chaired by two former CIA directors, James Schlesinger and John Deutch.

Here are just a few choice excerpts from the report:

- [T]he U.S. government has failed to pay sufficient attention to energy in its conduct of foreign policy or to adopt a consistent approach to energy issues.

- The issues at stake intimately affect U.S. foreign policy, as well as the strength of the American economy and the state of the global environment. But most of the leverage potentially available to the United States is through domestic policy. Thus, the Independent Task Force devotes considerable attention to how oil consumption (or at least the growth in consumption) can be reduced and why and how energy issues must become better integrated with other aspects of U.S. foreign policy.

- The challenge over the next several decades is . . . to begin the transition to an economy that relies less on petroleum. The longer the delay, the greater will be the subsequent trauma. For the United States, with 4.6 percent of the world's population using 25 percent of the world's oil, the transition could be especially disruptive.

- The voices that espouse "energy independence" are doing the nation a disservice by focusing on a goal that is unachievable.

- The central task for the next two decades must be to manage the consequences of dependence on oil, not to pretend the United States can eliminate it.

- [W]hile reducing U.S. oil imports is desirable, the underlying problem is the high and growing demand for oil worldwide.

The task force also debunked these widely held "myths" about energy:

Myth #1: The United States can be energy independent.

Myth #2: Cutting oil imports will lower fuel prices.

Myth #3: Large Western companies like ExxonMobil, BP, Shell, and Chevron control the price of oil.

Myth #4: There's plenty of low-cost oil ready to be tapped.

Myth #5: Renewable energy and nuclear power can quickly reduce dependence on oil and gas.

We generally agree with the task force, which pointed to the importance of renewable energy in a long-term strategy.

Unsustainable in the Long Term

Another Pentagon-commissioned study by defense consulting firm LMI came to complementary conclusions. It said that the dwindling availability of oil, plus its rising costs, makes the U.S. military's operations "unsustainable in the long term."[1]

The report sees our dependence on unfriendly oil-producing nations as a key vulnerability.

LMI says that it is "imperative" for the Department of Defense (DoD) to "fundamentally transform" everything it does, immediately—not just weapons systems, not just base operations, not just the designs of war machines, but *everything. Immediately.*

The study, titled "Transforming the Way DoD Looks at Energy," was commissioned by the Pentagon's Office of Force Transformation and Resources, an office established to help execute former Secretary of Defense Donald Rumsfeld's ambition of transforming the U.S. military.

That office is a pretty rarified environment, for the military. This isn't some jarhead operation. They do experimental "skunk-works" projects. They publish policy papers on "highly adaptive, self-synchronizing, dynamically reconfigurable demand and supply networks that anticipate and stimulate actions to enhance capability or mitigate support shortfalls" and other things that mere mortals cannot understand.

In short, they try to anticipate the challenges of the future. And they are turning their attention to the security of oil supply for good reason.

For one thing, the sheer scale of the military's dependence on oil is absolutely immense.

The Department of Defense is the largest single energy consumer in the country and the single largest oil-consuming government entity in the world.

The Defense Department consumed 132.7 million barrels of oil in 2005[2]; that's nearly 2 percent of all oil used by the United States.

And thanks to its incredibly oil-thirsty machines, the military also has the unfortunate need to burn a lot of fuel just to move more fuel.

More than half of all the cargo moved by the military is just fuel. And 80 percent of the material transported on the battlefield is fuel. That's a lot of effort, just to move fuel around.

And, as we discussed in Chapter 4, the military costs associated with oil and natural gas are immense—around $44 billion per year just for the Persian Gulf.

And they say that renewable energy is too expensive compared to oil.

It sure is, if you externalize (i.e., don't count) most of the costs.

Given what we know from the preceding peak studies of fossil fuels, the outlook for such a fuel-dependent military is not only unsustainable, but indeed, desperate.

What kind of future will there be for the U.S. military, when loss of imports and spiraling costs cut off its air? It's no wonder that the defense community is worried, and looking into every possible alternative. Even alternatives such as—get this—kite and solar power assisted propulsion for Navy vessels! Those were among the options suggested by a 1996 study prepared for Congress on how the Navy might reduce its use of oil.[3]

A Growing Thirst

The third factor is probably the most worrisome of all. Former U.S. Secretary of Defense Donald Rumsfeld's push to reduce the military's footprint by closing far-flung bases and transforming it into a network of small, agile task forces has had an unfortunate consequence: Everything now has to travel greater and greater distances.

This means a growing, not declining, thirst for liquid fuels.

According to the LMI report,

The U.S. military will have to be even more energy intense, locate in more regions of the world, employ new technologies, and manage a more complex logistics system. Simply put, more miles will be traveled, both by combat units and the supply units that sustain them, which will result in increased energy consumption.

Consider this fact: A single contemporary U.S. Army heavy division (10,000 to 25,000 soldiers plus artillery and support) uses more than twice as much oil on a daily basis as an entire World War II field army!

Combined with the nonstop advancement of war machines, this trend has led to a *16-fold increase in the amount of fuel consumed per soldier per day since World War II.*

And according to the report, the trend has been sharpening: In 2006, the fuel intensity per soldier was double that of the previous year!

No wonder the report pulled no punches in its recommendations. This is a serious and urgent situation.

The authors admit that the necessary changes won't be easy, and would "challenge some of the department's most deeply held assumptions, interests, and processes."

But the U.S. military has no choice but to learn to love being green.

Now, the Pentagon is looking for ways to stop using oil entirely by 2050.

In March 2007, the Pentagon's message was echoed by President Reagan's national security adviser, Robert McFarlane, another green hawk. He is deeply concerned about the eventuality of a successful attack on Saudi oil facilities, such as the one foiled by Saudi security in April 2007.[4]

One such attack could triple the cost a barrel of oil overnight, he warned.

Like us, McFarlane believes that renewable energy technologies, such as cellulosic ethanol and solar energy, could make up a substantial offset in oil consumption in a relatively short period of time.

"The solution is within our reach. We have to get busy," he admonished.

But our vulnerability extends beyond oil to other sources of energy. Indeed, the recent trend toward switching from oil to natural gas for some uses is running into new limitations.

Apparently recognizing that the North American natural gas supply is past its peak and dwindling, a recent Army study explored availability and cost scenarios for natural gas, warning, "Current Army assumption is that natural gas may cease to be a viable fuel for the Army within the next 25 years based on price volatility and affordable supply availability."

Woolsey and Shultz

Perhaps the most outspoken of these ex-officials is James Woolsey, former director of the CIA under President Bill Clinton. He's been traveling the world since 9/11 to champion renewable energy and educate the public about the intimate relationship between oil dependence and terrorism. (He also walks the talk, driving a hybrid and powering his farm with solar.)

He has had leadership roles in two nonpartisan groups, the Energy Future Coalition and the National Commission on Energy Policy, comprising experts in business, labor, the environment, and national security, who are actively lobbying to reduce our reliance on fossil fuels and increase conservation, fuel economy, and renewable energy.

In 2005, Woolsey co-authored a paper with George Shultz entitled "Oil and Security,"[5] which they published via their antiterrorism lobbying group, the Committee on the Present Danger. It was a remarkably clearheaded assessment of both our oil addiction and our best options going forward.

George Shultz, of course, was the U.S. Secretary of Labor from 1969 to 1970, the U.S. Secretary of the Treasury from 1972 to 1974, and the U.S. Secretary of State from 1982 to 1989. You might say he's a man who knows a thing or two about the world.

Their report was candid about recognizing that our whole transportation infrastructure is completely wedded to oil-based products, and that only alternatives that can work with that infrastructure are tenable and worth pursuing.

Hydrogen, for example, would need an entirely new infrastructure, from the source all the way to the destination, so they write it off as impractical—a very sound bit of analysis that has been heard all too little amid the clamor of pie-in-the-sky promises about "the hydrogen economy."

Woolsey and Shultz also offered a clear-eyed picture of the global oil supply. They nimbly sidestepped the phrase *peak oil* but admitted that demand growth from China and India, combined with the fact that enhanced oil recovery and deepwater drilling cannot change the basic oil production curve, means that we will continue to be—quite literally—over a barrel, and beholden to Middle East oil producers who sit atop most of the world's remaining oil reserves.

REDUCE CO$_2$ EMISSIONS

The Pentagon has also realized that the flip side of the peak oil threat is another significant threat: global warming.

In 2004, a leaked Pentagon report worried that rapid climate change may well set off global competition for food and water supplies and, in the worst scenarios, spark nuclear war.

In April 2007, a top panel of 11 retired military brass from all branches of the military, including five admirals and four generals, released a report that came to similar conclusions. Entitled "National Security and the Threat of Climate Change," it was commissioned by the Center for Naval Analyses, a nonprofit government-funded think tank.

Though initially several of the authors were skeptical of the topic, they spent months meeting with climate scientists, business leaders, and other experts, and found the experience "very sobering."

Their conclusion? "Climate change is a national security issue."

The report says that the security consequences of climate change should be fully integrated into national defense strategies, and "the intelligence community should incorporate climate consequences into its National Intelligence Estimate."

In other words, they insist that we stop pretending that climate change and defense are separate issues, and start working on them together. (To those issues we would also add peak oil.)

In addition to the Pentagon's 2004 report on climate change, in March 2007, the U.S. Army War College sponsored a two-day conference on the subject titled "The National Security Implications of Global Climate Change."

So seeing military brass join the green hawks movement is hardly a surprise.

But it's the first time we've ever heard a military expert connect global warming with the so-called global war on terror: "Climate change can provide the conditions that will extend the war on terror," said retired Admiral T. Joseph Lopez, former commander-in-chief of U.S. Naval Forces in Europe and of Allied Forces, Southern Europe.

Why? Because it's a "threat multiplier," exacerbating the conditions that tend to breed terrorist groups in volatile parts of the world, like water and food shortages.

For example, the report notes, nearly half the world gets about half of its drinking water from melting snow and glaciers that are quickly disappearing.

The authors point out that migrations of environmental refugees, strained border relations, and resource conflicts will make it hard for states to meet the basic needs of their residents, which will lead in turn to security problems.

But the climate change threat affects us all, as report author Vice Admiral Richard Truly admits: "It's going to happen to every country and every person in the whole world at the same time."

The Army's former chief of staff, General Gordon Sullivan, dismissed the Bush administration's position (that more certainty about the human causes of global warming is needed before taking action to reduce greenhouse gases) for the same reasons we do here: the precautionary principle.

"People are saying they want to be perfectly convinced about climate science projections," he said. "But speaking as a soldier, we never have 100 percent certainty. If you wait until you have 100 percent certainty, something bad is going to happen on the battlefield."

The report also showed that the commanders were wisely taking a long-term view of the problem. Said retired Marine Corps General Anthony C. Zinni, former commander of U.S. forces in the Middle East, "We will pay for this one way or another. We will pay to reduce greenhouse gas emissions today, and we'll have to take an economic hit of some kind. Or, we will pay the price later in military terms. And that will involve human lives. There will be a human toll."

Emissions in the Developing World

Some observers in the Western world point to the industrialization of China and India and other developing countries as the biggest part of the global warming challenge going forward, because it's their growth that is primarily driving demand and increased greenhouse gas emissions. In 2006, China became the largest emitter of greenhouse gases, in part due to its heavy reliance on coal to drive manufacturing industries. Two-thirds of China's energy comes from coal.[6]

Of course, this conveniently ignores the fact that the developed world was mainly responsible for the emissions created thus far, and that it is hypocritical to outsource polluting industries to China and then turn around and blame China for exacerbating global warming. We have outsourced a great deal of our manufacturing capacity to China, to take advantage of its cheap labor markets and its loose regulatory environment. In short, we can have things made more cheaply in China because they'll tolerate poor working conditions and environmental damage where the United States will not.

There is also the fact that on a per-capita basis, China spews about 10,500 pounds of CO_2, whereas the emissions of the United States are four times that, at 42,500 pounds per person.[7]

Consequently, Asian business leaders have objected to being singled out as the primary polluters. "This is green imperialism," complained Nor Mohamed Yakcop, Malaysia's deputy finance minister, at a World Economic Forum in June 2007. "Companies that are polluting in China are owned by American, European, Japanese, and others. They are benefiting from the cheap labor, from the resources, and at the same time accusing China of pollution," he said.[8]

It's a fair point. Clearly, the blistering growth and equally skyrocketing emissions of Asia are the direct result of demand from the Western buyers of their goods. The United States is China's biggest customer by far.

Perhaps that explains why the net CO_2 emissions of the United States and China have increased only slightly in the last 10 years, while the U.S. share has decreased and the Chinese share increased. (See Figure 5.1.)

A June 2007 study by two Carnegie Mellon researchers of the embodied emissions in US international trade addressed this issue directly. Not surprisingly, it found that when it comes to emissions, there is no free lunch. Researcher Christopher L. Weber explains: "Over the last decade, the United States' share of global carbon emissions has gone down and China's has gone up. However, if you count not by who makes the goods, but by who consumes the goods, the United States' share of responsibility has stayed constant or even gone up. However, these emissions are not counted because they've been outsourced to other countries."[9]

The honest assessment is simple: If you buy the item, then you are responsible for the consumption of energy and resources that went into making it, and the emissions that resulted.

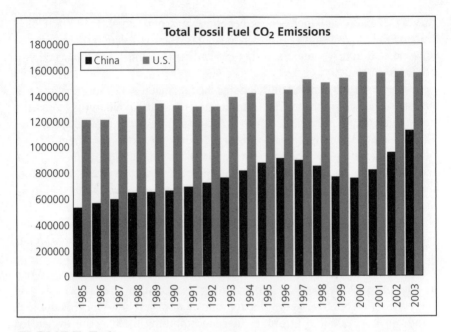

FIGURE 5.1 *Carbon Dioxide Emissions from Fossil Fuels for the United States and China, 1985–2003*

Source: EIA, International Energy Annual 2005, Table H.1CO$_2$.

Nor Mohamed was right to call for a framework of shared responsibility. "There should be no hypocrisy. Let's take the hypocrisy out of the equation," he said. "Treat it as a global problem . . . the world has to play a role rather than take the issue in a very adversarial or biased basis."[10]

As a friend of ours, cleantech business analyst Brian Fan, remarked: "The ultimate culprit is American consumer culture that is responsible for most consumption in the world. At the end of the day, the culture of consumption must change."

STAUNCH THE BLEEDING

As we mentioned in Chapter 3, at $90 a barrel, the United States consumes about $690 billion worth of crude oil per year. Of that, about $181 billion per year—half a million dollars each day—goes to OPEC countries that are mostly dictatorships and oligarchies who are hostile to us.

The funding that has supported Islamic radicals and terrorists is coming mainly from those countries.

According to prominent neoconservative defense hawk Frank Gaffney, this makes reducing oil imports "a national security imperative."[11]

Without stopping the flow of dollars to those countries, we are literally feeding the enemy with one hand and fighting him off with the other.

And as Woolsey and Schultz have pointed out, much of that cost is deficit spending. The United States borrows about $13 billion per week, principally from Asian states, to finance its debt-fueled consumption, and $2 billion to $3 billion per week of that is just to pay for imported oil.

That's right: Two to three billion *per week,* just for oil, and some of it goes directly to those who strap explosives to themselves and set them off in public places from Baghdad to Jakarta.

And that bottomless hole of deficit spending ultimately leads to the devaluation of the U.S. dollar, which in turn leads foreign countries to reduce their exposure to dollars, leading to further devaluation.

INVEST HEAVILY IN RENEWABLES

It should be obvious that if a tiny fraction of the $44 billion we spend every year on oil security in the Persian Gulf were spent instead on R&D for clean, renewable energy sources, it would take us a long way toward advancing those technologies and making them economical and scalable.

Indeed, a fraction of it is being spent on those things. In April 2007, the Air Force broke ground on what will be the largest solar farm in North America.

The 15 megawatt power plant will occupy 140 acres of Nellis Air Force Base, outside of Las Vegas. It will generate about 25 million kWh annually, providing about 25 percent of the electric needs of the base, where more than 12,000 people work and over 7,000 live.

The Air Force expects to save $1 million a year on electricity bills, while helping to fulfill its commitments to deploy more renewable energy.

"It allows the Air Force to show its leadership in applying renewable energy and new technology to reduce our needs to use traditional forms of electric power," says operations flight chief Major Don Ohlemacher.

Colonel Michael Bartley, commander of the 99th Air Base Wing at the base, agrees. "The Nellis solar power plant is the start of the way ahead for future DoD and community partnership. . . . The base will benefit from the energy produced, the environment benefits from using clean solar energy, and we may even test state-of-the-art security measures at the site. This is a good thing for everyone."

The Air Force is not alone in its pursuit of renewable energy. All four branches of the military have already begun to explore greater efficiency and renewable energy.

In addition, the Department of Energy has offered over half a billion dollars in co-investment for biofuel refineries, which will help provide a desperately needed additional supply of liquid fuels.

With strong political support and serious investment dollars from the likes of the DoD and the CIA, there is no doubt that renewable energy is going to get a big push from defense.

POLICY RECOMMENDATIONS

When you boil it all down, America's green hawks have essentially issued marching orders to the federal government:

■ Invest heavily in R&D, *without regard for return on the investment*, in all kinds of energy alternatives and efficiency technologies, ASAP.

■ Fully integrate climate change into our national security and defense strategies.

■ Commit to a stronger national and international role to help stabilize climate changes.

■ Increase efficiency of oil and gas use.

■ Switch from oil-derived products to alternatives.

■ Encourage supply of oil from sources outside the Persian Gulf.

The Woolsey/Shultz paper also offered some specific guidance on how to transition from our current energy paradigm to a more sustainable one:

■ *Improve fuel economy.* In Europe, the average economy of private vehicles is 42 miles per gallon, nearly double the U.S.'s 24 mpg, largely due to the Europeans' reliance on efficient, next-generation, clean-burning diesel engines. Woolsey and Shultz also see a bright future for hybrid cars (as do we!).

They point to the work done by Amory Lovins et al. at the Rocky Mountain Institute, which demonstrated that by building car bodies out of super-strong and super-lightweight carbon fiber instead of metal, with advanced engine designs and aerodynamic contours (so-called hypercars), we could double the efficiency of today's hybrids, achieving 100 mpg or better.

- *Encourage cellulosic ethanol.* Woolsey and Shultz don't pay any attention to corn-based ethanol, perhaps because they know that it runs quickly into competition for food production and has a very low EROI or energy returned on energy invested (EROEI). (We discuss EROI in more detail in Chapter 6.)

  They believe that biofuels will play a role, but probably a minor one. And they believe—quite correctly, we think—that liquid fuels produced from coal, tar sands, or oil shale will remain bit players in the overall fuel mix.

  But they project that at least half of U.S. oil demand could be displaced by cellulosic ethanol from switchgrass grown on unused land in the Conservation Reserve Program soil bank, and that the fuel could be produced for as little as 67 to 77 cents a gallon when the industry is mature.

- *Push for plug-in hybrid electric vehicles (PHEVs).* Since most personal vehicle trips are under six miles, and since driving a car on batteries charged by grid power is less than half the price of driving on a tank of gasoline, hybrid cars with enhanced battery packs that can be charged up overnight from the grid could put a major dent in our liquid fuel demand.

  Accordingly, Shultz and Woolsey would make R&D on battery technology a top priority, as well as increased investment in the grid to make it more reliable and secure.

- *Increase federal R&D investment in new energy technologies*, including higher fuel efficiency innovations, plug-in hybrids, ethanol, synfuels, and advanced nuclear designs.

With the contribution of modern diesels, flexible-fuel vehicles, hybrids, and plug-in hybrids, they believe that we could achieve a substantial reduction in our oil imports, and do it fairly quickly.

And by putting some of these technologies together, they say, à la Lovins' hypercars, "the reduction could be stunning." For example, a PHEV with next-generation lithium batteries, constructed with carbon fiber, charged overnight from the grid (preferably from domestically generated renewable energy), and running on E-85 cellulosic ethanol or biodiesel, could squeeze 1,000 mpg from the petroleum it uses.

SOLAR FOR CHINA?

In 2005, Woolsey testified before the House Armed Services Committee on the proposed takeover of Unocal by China Oil, along with Frank Gaffney, the president of the Center for Security Policy and a prominent neoconservative who championed the Iraq war, and Richard D'Amato of the U.S.-China Security Review Commission.

It was probably the most unflinching, candid talk about energy, peak oil, security, trade deficits, and China anyone in the U.S. government had ever uttered on television (C-SPAN).

Their top recommendation?

To heavily invest U.S. tax dollars in renewable energy production in China!

Why? Because the Chinese have a chance to build their burgeoning economy on renewables from the beginning, whereas we are trapped by our fossil-fueled infrastructure, and they will only compete with us for those diminishing resources as they continue to industrialize.

It will literally be cheaper and better to invest in renewable energy for China than it would be to compete with China for oil, gas, and coal and contend with the consequences of their emissions.

Considering the size of their population, and how far they have yet to go in industrializing their economy, China simply cannot attain first-world status using the same energy sources that got the United States there.

PART

II

MAKING MONEY FROM THE FOSSIL FUELS THAT ARE LEFT

It should be clear by now that the fossil fuels we have left should be stewarded carefully, with a preference for maximizing their long-term production rather than their short-term profits.

How we produce our remaining resources is critical. If we produce them too quickly, not only will we strand a portion of the oil and gas that could have been harvested, but we will not have enough time to deploy alternative energy sources. So how we produce our energy over the next decade might have disproportionate implications for the bigger energy picture over the next five decades. Since land-based production is well exploited already in North America, we will have to expand offshore production.

It also seems inevitable that we will increasingly turn to unconventional sources of natural gas, including imported liquefied natural gas (LNG), and unconventional ways of exploiting our coal and natural gas reserves. Due to the immediacy of peak oil, we will need these alternative sources of hydrocarbons to give us a bridge to a future powered by renewables.

CHAPTER

6

TWILIGHT FOR FOSSIL FUELS

*My father rode a camel. I drive a car. My son flies
a jet airplane. His son will ride a camel.*

—POPULAR SAYING IN SAUDI ARABIA

*There has been a paradigm shift in the energy world whereby
oil producers are no longer inclined to rapidly exhaust their
resource for the sake of accelerating the misuse of a precious and
finite commodity. This sentiment prevails inside and outside of
OPEC countries but has yet to be appreciated among the major
energy-consuming countries of the world.*

—SADAD AL-HUSSEINI

We are not just facing the twilight years of oil—we're facing the twilight of *all hydrocarbons*. In the same way that we have burned through the cheapest and best oil, we have also burned through the cheapest and best deposits of natural gas and coal—the last two great sources of fossil fuels. The deposits that are left are of progressively lesser quality, and quantity.

There is no doubt, though, that those who do possess some of the remaining fossil fuels are sitting on a gold mine. Those assets will only appreciate as time goes on, and investing in their production will continue to be a very profitable business.

Let's take a look at their potential.

NATURAL GAS

Natural gas is actually a mix of gases (mostly methane and propane) and natural gas liquids. Like oil, it initially comes out of the ground easily because it is under pressure, but as the field matures, the field must be repressurized (usually by injecting CO_2 gas) in order to maintain the pressure to extract the natural gas.

In the early days of oil production, natural gas was considered a hazard more than a fuel, and was routinely burned off or *flared* onsite. Only in recent decades have we captured such sources of natural gas to be processed into fuels. Oil depletion is one reason why natural gas production has become more important—as we discussed in Chapter 2, most of the anticipated increase in "oil" production (defined as "all liquids") between now and the global peak will come in the form of natural gas liquids and condensates.

Natural gas production is mostly a landlocked business. We import only 19 percent of the natural gas we use, and 86 percent of that comes by pipeline from Canada and Mexico, both of which are past their gas production peaks.

Natural Gas Reserves

The world's large remaining reserves of natural gas are even more concentrated than those of oil, being heavily dominated by just three countries: Russia, Iran, and Qatar. (See Table 6.1.)

Natural gas production, however, is a different story. The industry is far more advanced in older producers, such as the United States and Canada, than in other parts of the world that hold larger reserves. For example, Qatar is third in reserves, but 18th in production, and Venezuela is 9th in reserves, but 24th in production. (See Table 6.2.)

However, the actual reserves of domestic natural gas that we still have in North America are relatively abundant, and could provide at least a temporary bridge of liquid fuels to the future. We could transform some of those gas reserves into liquid motor fuels via the Fischer-Tropsch process. Legendary oil investor T. Boone Pickens has said that he sees a definite future in that idea.

TABLE 6.1 Natural Gas Reserves, Top 10 Nations

Rank	Region/Country	Gas Reserves (Trillion Cubic Feet)	Percent of Total
1	Russia	1,680	27%
2	Iran	974	16
3	Qatar	911	15
4	Saudi Arabia	240	4
5	United Arab Emirates	214	3
6	United States	204	3
7	Nigeria	182	3
8	Algeria	162	3
9	Venezuela	152	2
10	Iraq	112	2
	World total	6,183	

Source: Oil & Gas Journal, last updated January 1, 2007. As reported by www.eia.doe.gov/emeu/international/reserves.xls with these data notes:

PennWell Corporation, *Oil & Gas Journal* 104.47 (December 18, 2006). Data for the United States are from the Energy Information Administration, U.S. Crude Oil, Natural Gas, and Natural Gas Liquids Reserves, 2005 Annual Report, DOE/EIA-0216(2005) (November 2006).

Peak Natural Gas

In many ways, the story of natural gas is similar to that of oil.

Gas production in North America topped out in 2002, and has been declining ever since. This is despite a tripling of producing gas wells since 1971—from

TABLE 6.2 Natural Gas Producers, Top 20 Nations

Rank	Region/Country	Dry Gas Production (Billion Cubic Feet)	Percent of Total
1	Russia	22,386	23%
2	United States	18,591	19
3	Canada	6,483	7
4	United Kingdom	3,389	3
5	Netherlands	3,036	3
6	Iran	2,963	3
7	Norway	2,948	3
8	Algeria	2,830	3
9	Indonesia	2,663	3
10	Saudi Arabia	2,319	2
11	Malaysia	2,205	2
12	Uzbekistan	2,114	2
13	Turkmenistan	2,068	2
14	United Arab Emirates	1,635	2
15	Argentina	1,585	2
16	Mexico	1,464	1
17	China	1,439	1
18	Qatar	1,383	1
19	Australia	1,308	1
20	Egypt	1,150	1
	World Total	98,530	

Source: EIA, International Energy Annual 2005, Table 4.1: World Natural Gas Production, 2004. Data sources for that table: www.eia.doe.gov/emeu/iea/4source.html.

approximately 100,000 to more than 300,000—the inevitable result of mature gas basins reaching the end of their productive lives.[1] (See Figure 6.1.)

The onset of the U.S. production peak was in 2001, and production is now declining at the rate of about 1.7 percent a year, as shown in Figure 6.2.

This is despite a record level of drilling and the application of advanced technology, as shown in Figure 6.3.

And the same is true for Canada, as shown in Figure 6.4.

In short, we're drilling more than ever, production is still declining—and now gas drilling rigs have been making an exodus from Canada.

Current supply and demand forecasts indicate that a serious shortfall in natural gas supply is looming, possibly by as much as 11 trillion cubic feet (Tcf) per year by 2025, or *about half of our current usage* of 22 Tcf per year.

At the same time, demand for natural gas is rising steadily along with demand for electricity, but drilling can't make up for depletion, let alone additional demand. Therefore we must turn to imports.

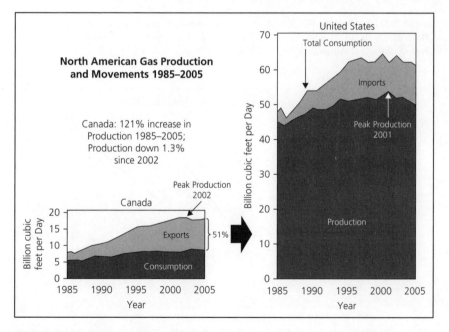

FIGURE 6.1 *North American Gas Production, 1985–2005*

Source: J. David Hughes, Geological Survey of Canada, Presentation to ASPO/Boston, "Natural Gas in North America: Should We Be Worried?" www.aspo-usa.com/fall2006/presentations/pdf/Hughes_D_NatGas_Boston_2006.pdf.

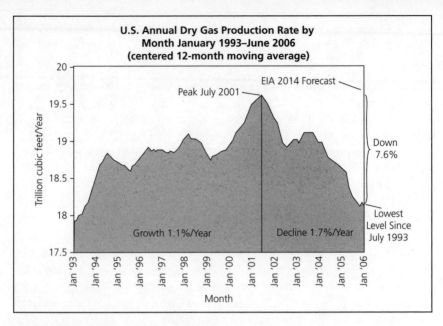

FIGURE 6.2 *U.S. Gas Production Rate, 1993–2006*

Source: J. David Hughes, Geological Survey of Canada, Presentation to ASPO/Boston, "Natural Gas in North America: Should We Be Worried?"www.aspo-usa.com/fall2006/presentations/pdf/Hughes_D_NatGas_Boston_2006.pdf.

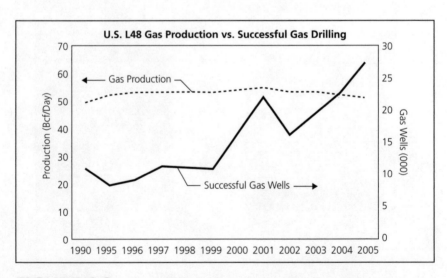

FIGURE 6.3 *U.S. L48 Gas Production versus Successful Drilling*

Source: U.S. Department of Energy, www.fossil.energy.gov/programs/oilgas/publications/naturalgas_general/ng_supply_overview.pdf.

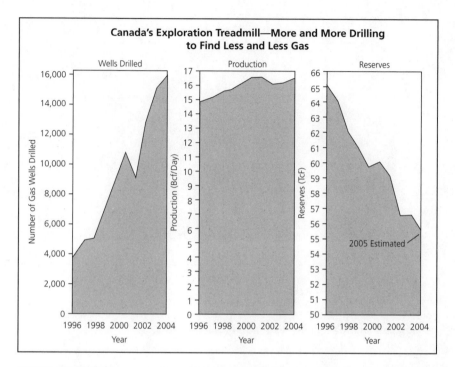

FIGURE 6.4 *Canada's Gas Production versus Wells and Reserves*

Source: J. David Hughes, Geological Survey of Canada, Presentation to ASPO/Boston, "Natural Gas in North America: Should We Be Worried?" www.aspo-usa.com/fall2006/presentations/pdf/Hughes_D_NatGas_Boston_2006.pdf.

J. David Hughes, a research geologist with the Geological Survey of Canada and an expert on natural gas in North America, explains the trend this way:

"U.S. gas production peaked in about the second quarter of 2001 and has been going down and remained flat since that time. Canada's gas production hit a plateau in mid-2001. It maintained that plateau until mid-2002. And then, despite drilling a record number of holes, production went down about three and a half percent.

"We drilled another record number of holes in 2004, and production has stayed pretty much flat. So you've got no production response from all that extra drilling."[2]

His assertion is amply demonstrated graphically. Looking at the total of North American gas production, we can see that it has been flat to slightly

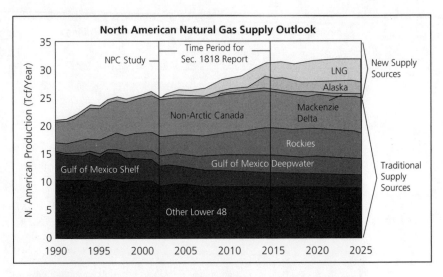

FIGURE 6.5 *North American Natural Gas Supply Outlook*

Source: U.S. Department of Energy, www.fossil.energy.gov/programs/oilgas/
publications/naturalgas_general/ng_supply_overview.pdf.

declining since 2000, and that any increase in demand will have to be satisfied
by imported liquefied natural gas (LNG) and gas from Alaska and the Arctic.
(See Figure 6.5.)

However, it is less than certain that the pipelines required to bring the
stranded gas of Alaska and the Arctic to market will be available by the time
the gas is needed, due to numerous pockets of resistance to the projects.

Like oil, the new wells are tapping smaller and less productive resources
every year, indicating that the best prospects have already been exploited and
that we're now relying on infill drilling and unconventional sources. (See
Figure 6.6.)

And like oil, there is a quality issue as well. It appears that we have
already burned through the best and cheapest natural gas—the high-energy-
content methane that comes out of the ground easily, at a high flow rate. We're
now getting down to smaller deposits of stranded gas and the last dregs of
mature gas fields, and we're producing gas that has a lower energy content.

Making matters worse, there has been an exodus of drilling rigs from
Canada over the past year, as they are called away to work for higher day rates
on more productive wells elsewhere.

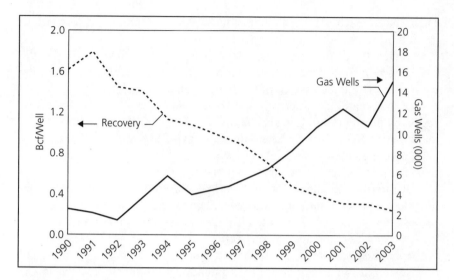

FIGURE 6.6 *Gas Recovery per Well versus Gas Wells Completed,*
Western Canada Sedimentary Basin

Source: U.S. Department of Energy, www.fossil.energy.gov/programs/oilgas/publications/
naturalgas_general/ng_supply_overview.pdf.

And because it's difficult to store, there is little storage or reserve capacity in our nation's web of gas pipelines. We have only about a 50-day supply
of working storage of natural gas in the United States.[3] So there isn't much
cushion in the system. The whole system operates on a just-in-time inventory
basis, and so the market pricing does, too.

In short, the natural gas market does not price in the possibility of long-
term shortages or a sharp drop-off in production from mature fields.

So the supply outlook in our neighborhood is not good.

This leaves natural gas imported from overseas as our remaining option.

Liquefied Natural Gas

In order to import natural gas by sea, it must be turned into liquefied natural
gas (LNG). To do this, it must be carefully cooled to minus 260 degrees
Fahrenheit, at which point it condenses into a liquid. It then must be kept
under controlled temperature and pressure to stay liquefied, with some of it
"boiling off" along the way, and transported in super-insulated, very expensive, pressurized tanker vessels, of which there are only so many in the world.

Then when it reaches its destination, it must be slowly warmed back up before it can be sent through a pipeline to the end user.

Obviously, all of this requires significant inputs of energy. The whole LNG process, from cooling to transporting to regasification, consumes the equivalent of 15 to 30 percent of the energy in the original gas.[4]

Of the natural gas imported into the United States, 86 percent is transported by pipeline from Canada and Mexico. Only 14 percent is imported in the form of LNG, primarily from Trinidad, Egypt, Nigeria, and Algeria.

Imports account for only about 19 percent of U.S. natural gas consumption. The remainder—81 percent—is produced domestically.

Due to domestic depletion and the inherent limits of transport by pipeline, the long-term future of natural gas usage for North America will have to come in the form of LNG imported from producers with large reserves of natural gas, such as Qatar and Russia. At the current time, it seems unlikely that the geopolitical standoff with Iran over its nuclear development program will be resolved anytime soon such that it might be a hospitable investment climate. So we can probably rule out Iran as a major source of LNG, at least for North America.

The trend toward LNG is clear, however. According to natural gas analyst Keith Kohl, between 2001 and 2006 U.S. total natural gas imports from Canada and Mexico have declined roughly 3 percent, while during that same period LNG imports rose by 145 percent.[5] Regardless of where we get it from, we definitely have a growing appetite for natural gas.

LNG Demand

For the past three years, imports, like domestic production, have been pretty flat, while consumption spikes up sharply during the winter, and less sharply during the hot summer months. (See Figure 6.7.)

Now let's look at the cost of gas imports over the past 30 years, as shown in Figure 6.8.

In inflation-adjusted dollars, the cost of imported natural gas reached an all-time high in 2005, and has remained in the upper range of historical prices ever since.

And thanks to declining domestic production, imports are becoming an ever-larger part of the supply. (See Figure 6.9.)

In short, every year we're needing more imports, but getting about the same amounts and paying more for them. This trend shows no signs of abating, because we can increase neither domestic production nor imports.

That leaves the prognosticators at the Energy Information Administration (the U.S. government's official energy data keeper) with a real quandary:

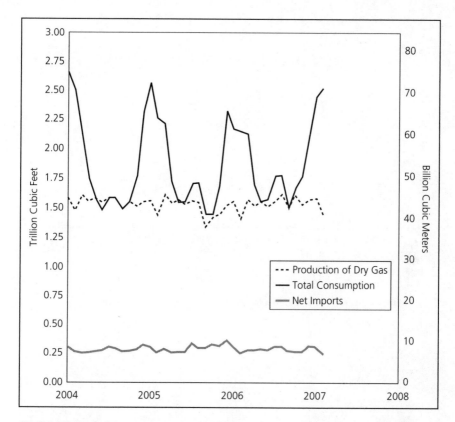

FIGURE 6.7 *Production, Consumption, and Net Imports of Natural Gas in the United States, 2004–2007*

Source: EIA, *Natural Gas Monthly,* April 2007, www.eia.doe.gov/oil_gas/natural_gas/ data_publications/natural_gas_monthly/ngm.html.

How can we tell a positive story about this? Where can we make up the loss in North American gas production?

The EIA's answer? You guessed it: production from Alaska and a 580 percent increase in LNG. (See Figure 6.10.)

That projection simply isn't realistic, and Figure 6.11 shows why.

To cover the projected gas shortfall of 10 to 11 Tcf per year in the United States alone, we would need to *double* (or, after competition sets in, *triple*) the world's current LNG capacity.[6]

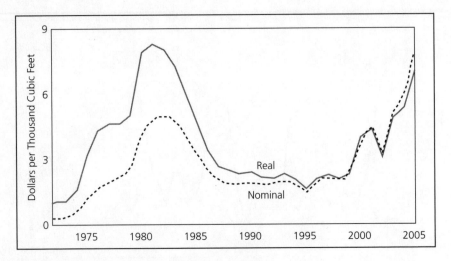

FIGURE 6.8 *U.S. Cost of Gas Imports, 1970–2005*

Source: EIA, *Annual Energy Review 2005*, Figure 6.7.

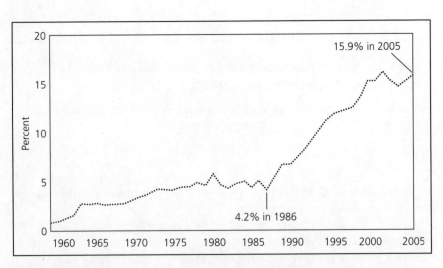

FIGURE 6.9 *U.S. Net Imports as Share of Consumption, 1958–2005*

Source: EIA, *Annual Energy Review 2005*, Figure 6.3.

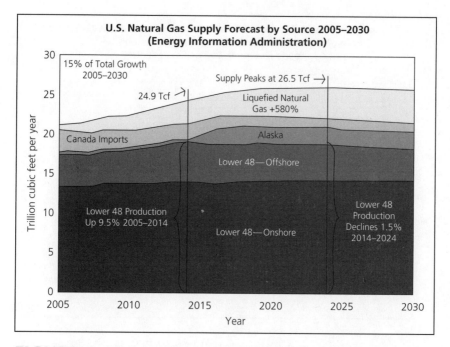

FIGURE 6.10 *U.S. Natural Gas Supply Forecast by Source, 2005–2030*

Source: J. David Hughes, Geological Survey of Canada, Presentation to ASPO/Boston, "Natural Gas in North America: Should We Be Worried?" www.aspo-usa.com/fall2006/presentations/pdf/Hughes_D_NatGas_Boston_2006.pdf.

According to David Hughes (in whose debt we remain for his work on this subject and some of these charts), expanding North American LNG capacity to 11 Tcf per year would require:

- Two hundred new LNG tankers, each with capacity of three billion cubic feet (bcf).

- Thirty new North America–based receiving terminals, each with capacity of one bcf per day.

- Some 56 new foreign-based 200 bcf/year liquefaction trains.

- Capital investment in the order of $US100–200 billion.

- Time to build total capacity = 10 to 20+ years.

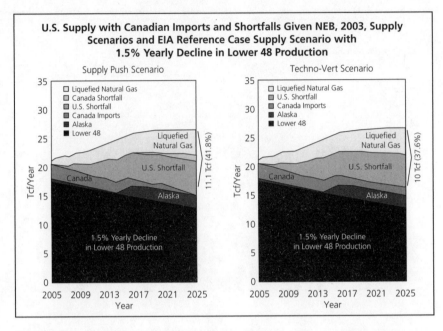

FIGURE 6.11 *U.S. Natural Gas Supply with Canadian Imports and Shortfalls, 2005–2025*

Source: J. David Hughes, Geological Survey of Canada, Presentation to ASPO/Boston, "Natural Gas in North America: Should We Be Worried?" www.aspo-usa.com/fall2006/presentations/pdf/Hughes_D_NatGas_Boston_2006.pdf.

Considering that the current effort to site several new LNG terminals near San Diego has been stymied by not-in-my-backyard (NIMBY) pressure, and that the rest of the country seems equally uninterested in hosting a new LNG terminal (think "big fat terrorism target" because an LNG tanker blowing up is roughly equivalent to a nuclear explosion)—well, let's just say that we wouldn't bet anything but play money on that expectation.

Limits to LNG

Many LNG plants, both for import and for export, have been announced worldwide, but it remains to be seen which ones will materialize, and when. Most projects have online dates of 2010 and beyond, and there are troubling signs emerging in 2007.

In February, ExxonMobil announced that the costs of its much-anticipated, $15 billion LNG project in Qatar were running out of control, and so it decided to scrap the project altogether.

"Right now, everyone around us is postponing and delaying projects," Qatari oil minister al-Attiyah said.

And yet about one week later, PricewaterhouseCoopers released a report saying that LNG will deliver 31 percent of global gas by 2010, a doubling of the production level in 2005. About two-thirds of that production was to come from Qatar. (Presumably the report was already finished by the time the ExxonMobil news came out.)

Likewise, a large LNG import facility planned for Louisiana has been shelved over NIMBYism. A large import facility that was planned for just off the shore of Long Beach, California, was given the thumbs-down by various regulatory agencies. And attempts to begin LNG export facilities in other parts of the world have run into a wide array of hurdles, not unlike those for new oil projects: skyrocketing costs, shortages of basic materials like steel and cement, and a lack of drilling and production equipment.

Getting Real about Gas

Here's what we think is realistic:

Canada's production has been falling for several years, and can't fill the supply gap.

Mexico is no help, either.

And LNG can't ride to the rescue.

What options does that leave us with?

The bottom line: When it comes to natural gas, we're on our own.

Although new drilling in the Gulf of Mexico (and eventually in Alaska) will produce some additional gas, it won't be nearly enough to change the basic production picture.

That leaves one remaining option: switching fuels. Since gas for heating is not easily substituted, we need alternatives to gas-fired electrical power plants.

Given the constraints on building new coal and nuclear plants, we are convinced that the most likely candidates for filling the electricity supply gap are renewable sources like wind and solar.

"A window of opportunity now exists to push for a cleaner and more efficient generation portfolio that will have significant impact on the energy sector and the environment for the next 40 to 50 years," said Claude Mandil, former Executive Director of the Paris-based International Energy Agency (IEA).[7]

It is a window that is yawning wider every year, as we reach the end of the line for natural gas–fired power plants.

Methane Hydrates

A more remote potential source of natural gas exists in the form of methane hydrates, also known as methane clathrates and methane ice. This form is essentially ice, with a lot of methane trapped in it. Extremely large deposits of methane hydrates have been found under the sediments of the ocean floor and in structures of sandstone and siltstone where the surface temperature is below 0°C. These deposits are believed to have formed when natural gas migrated upward from its source rocks and came into contact with cold sea water.[8] It has been estimated that the United States possesses 317,700 trillion cubic feet of natural gas in this form,[9] equivalent to 56 trillion barrels of oil,[10] or about 23 times the total amount of oil that will ever be recovered worldwide. One deposit in Alaska is estimated to contain 590 trillion cubic feet of natural gas locked in hydrates, equivalent to 104 billion barrels of oil. Worldwide, it is estimated that the planetary endowment of sedimentary methane hydrates could be 7 times as large as the currently known reserves of conventional natural gas in the low estimate.[11]

However, despite their enormous potential, it is suspected that most deposits are too widely dispersed to make production economic. There are currently no viable technologies for extracting methane hydrates, although research is under way. One research and development project in Japan is aiming for commercial-scale extraction by 2016,[12] and China has announced plans to spend $100 million over the next 10 years to study hydrates.[13]

Gas to Liquids

One promising alternative to liquid fuels from oil is liquid fuels from gas, otherwise known as gas to liquids (GTL).

Building GTL plants on a commercial scale will require a good deal of investment, but the technology is well developed, and it can produce a clean-burning liquid motor fuel that is compatible with our existing infrastructure—a crucially important factor that is missing in many alternative fuel scenarios.

Gas to liquids has another advantage, in that it can make use of small pockets of stranded gas that aren't economical or accessible enough to be produced by standard methods and distributed by pipeline. In Alaska alone, the United States currently has 104 trillion cubic feet of stranded gas, plus a pipeline with some 1.1 million barrels per day of excess capacity that could carry the liquid fuel produced from the stranded gas to the lower 48 states.[14]

At this point, the United States' nearest hope for a fresh natural gas supply is the Mackenzie Gas Project, a proposed 1,220-kilometer natural gas pipeline system along the Mackenzie Valley of Canada's Northwest Territories to connect its large gas fields with North American markets via an existing pipeline in northwestern Alberta. The project is slated to cost $7 billion and could transport as much as 1.2 billion cubic feet per day of gas. However, sky-rocketing costs, resistance from "first nations" (Canada's preferred term for aboriginal native tribes) whose lands the pipeline would cross, and uncertainty about the possibility of shipping through the Arctic where there used to be ice have conspired to delay the long-awaited project.

Investment Opportunities

Natural gas, like oil, is largely the province of big oil companies. A goodly number of players are trying to exploit hard-to-reach, stranded natural gas. Of these, only a few are large, stable, *pure play* companies that are well positioned to profit from future production of natural gas.

EnCana Corporation (NYSE: ECA) is the largest independent natural gas producer and gas storage operator in North America, and the largest producer and landholder in western Canada. With a $45 billion market capitalization, it is truly a blue-chip play on domestic natural gas. EnCana also has oil operations, and specializes in producing unconventional, hard-to-reach oil and gas deposits. Its assets are highly concentrated in four key North American growth platforms, including western Canada, offshore fields on Canada's east coast, the Rocky Mountains, and deepwater Gulf of Mexico. In addition, it has two important international growth platforms, in Ecuador and in the UK's central North Sea.

Chesapeake Energy Corporation (NYSE: CHK) is another good choice for investing in North American natural gas. With a $15 billion market cap and a stalwart stock performance, it should be a relatively safe path to profit. The company owns interests in approximately 34,600 active oil and natural gas wells, of which 28,100 are primarily natural gas wells, and produces approximately 1.5 billion cubic feet of natural gas per day. With approximately 8.4 trillion cubic feet of onshore natural gas reserves in New Mexico, Texas, Oklahoma, Louisiana, Arkansas, Kansas, Kentucky, Ohio, West Virginia, and New York, Chesapeake has an excellent position in the North American gas market.

Southwestern Energy Company (NYSE: SWN) is a $6.6 billion natural gas and oil exploration and production company, primarily focused on natural gas. It currently has operations in Texas, Arkansas, and the onshore Gulf Coast.

COAL

Coal is by far the dirtiest form of fossil fuel we use, but it's also the most readily usable fuel that we still have in abundance. It has been widely assumed that the United States has 496.1 billion tons of demonstrated coal reserves,

27 percent of the world total,[15] and thus is often called "the Saudi Arabia of coal." Our coal endowment has been estimated to be a 250-year supply, but as we shall see, that's probably a severe overstatement.

Peak Coal

This startling realization was announced in March 2007 by a German consultancy called the Energy Watch Group.[16] The researchers scrutinized the world's coal resources and concluded that the United States does not have anywhere near its claimed 250-year supply of coal.

Indeed, they claimed that, in terms of energy content, the United States passed its peak of coal production in 1998 and has less than 244 billion tons of reserves in total!

In the same way that we have burned through the world's best sources of oil and natural gas, we have burned the best sources of coal. High-Btu "black coal" (also known as anthracite) is rapidly being depleted. Although in some places, like the United States, the actual *volume* of coal produced is still going up each year, the energy content of that coal is declining. In terms of energy content—which is the only metric that really matters—we are past peak coal in the United States as well, and costs of transporting coal with a lower and lower energy content are going up relentlessly.

The best coal—anthracite (with 30 megajoules of energy per kilogram, or 30 Mj/kg) from Appalachia and Illinois—has been in decline since 1950. Our supposedly vast reserves are mainly of lower-quality bituminous coal, which peaked in 1990 and contains 18 to 29 Mj/kg, and subbituminous coal and lignite ("brown coal"), delivering a mere 5 to 25 Mj/kg.

For comparison purposes, the group translated the energy content of the coal produced into tons of oil equivalent. In terms of *volumes of stuff mined*, they found that growth in U.S. coal production can continue for about another 10 to 15 years. But in terms of *energy*, which is the only metric that really matters, U.S. coal production peaked in 1998 at 598 million tons of oil equivalent, and fell to 576 million in 2005.

What's worse, in a replay of the well-worn debate about oil reserves, it turns out that the global reserve numbers for coal have also been vastly overstated. The information we've had is decades old and unreliable, and modern reassessments by nice, transparent countries like Germany and the UK have resulted in 90 percent reductions!

The reserve numbers from Asia are particularly suspect, some dating back to the 1960s. China hasn't reduced its reported reserve numbers in 15 years, even though we know it has produced some 20 percent of its reserves since then.

In fact, for the past 20 years, *all* major coal-producing nations that have updated their reserve numbers have adjusted them downward. And in the past 25 years, the global total reserve estimate has been cut by 60 percent.

This is, most emphatically, not a growth scenario.

In terms of world energy consumption, coal provides about one-quarter of the total. Electricity production is 40 percent powered by coal. Two-thirds of the steel industry relies on it for fuel, and that coal must be the high-energy kind.

In terms of world coal consumption, China uses 36 percent, the United States 10 percent, and India 7 percent.

In terms of coal production, China is the largest producer, and will hit its peak "within the next 5 to 15 years, followed by a steep decline." The United States is the second-largest producer at 30 percent, and will likely peak between 2020 and 2030.

Total global reserves: about 909 billion tons. A little more than half of that is the good, high-energy stuff, and the rest is low-grade. About 90 percent of all coal in the world is in just six countries: the United States, which has the most, plus Russia, India, China, Australia, and South Africa.

Figure 6.12 is the group's chart of possible worldwide coal production.

Based on this scenario, the group estimates that the absolute peak of global coal production will likely be around 2020, approximately 10 years, maybe less, after the global peaks of oil and gas!

Their conclusion was echoed by a 2007 study by the National Academy of Sciences. The researchers looked at recent updated surveys from the United States Geological Survey (USGS) and determined that some of the old assumptions were wrong.

"There is probably sufficient coal to meet the nation's needs for more than 100 years at current rates of consumption," the academy study says. "However, it is not possible to confirm the often-quoted assertion that there is a sufficient supply of coal for the next 250 years."[17]

Apparently, the 250-year estimate was based on a USGS study from the 1970s, which assumed that 25 percent of the known coal could be recovered with current technology and at current prices. But now the USGS believes that only 5 percent is recoverable with today's technology and at current prices. Further, the 100-year forecast is based on our current consumption rate of about 1.1 billion tons a year, but by 2030, due to users switching over to coal from other fuels, the rate of coal consumption could be 70 percent higher than it is today, in which case that "100-year" supply could be depleted much more quickly.[18]

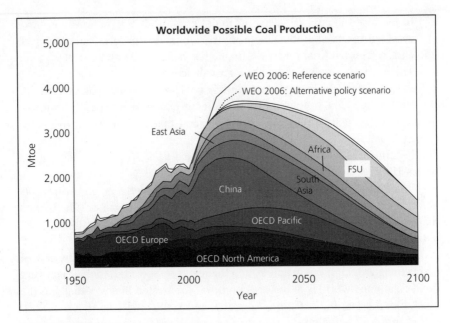

FIGURE 6.12 *Worldwide Possible Coal Production*

Source: Energy Watch Group, *Coal: Resources and Future Production,* March 2007.

Carbon Emissions and Sequestration

Depending on how quickly the world acts to deal with global warming, however, the problem of carbon emissions may inhibit the growth of coal consumption before pure supply constraints. If the potential costs of climate change are deemed too great, we may decide to deploy more renewables instead, despite their higher initial cost. Indeed, we ardently hope that we will.

This raises the question of using carbon capture and storage (CCS), also known as "clean coal" technology, or carbon sequestration. In this process, carbon dioxide is removed from the emissions of power plants using a variety of methods. Then—in theory—it can be safely injected into abandoned oil and gas wells for storage underground, or even stored on the ocean floor, where it would safely remain due to the immense pressure of the water above.

Captured carbon dioxide can even be profitable, by using it to maintain pressure in productive oil and gas wells or by cleaning it and selling it to the beverage industry for use in carbonating beverages.

However, we should bear in mind the scale of quantities we're talking about. According to Jeremy Gilbert, the former chief petroleum engineer for British Petroleum, the world currently produces about 36 billion tons per year of CO_2 emissions, but CO_2 used for well injection is only about 30 million tons per year.[19]

Coal champions argue that because the technology has existed for years to capture a significant portion of the emissions of coal plants instead of discharging them into the air, we can look forward to a major expansion of coal consumption in clean coal plants.

Indeed, CCS technology has been available for years, but it has failed to really catch on because it is deemed to be too expensive. Before we assume that it will become a common feature of coal-burning plants in the future, we must ask ourselves what will be different in the future so that the cost of CCS will come to be considered acceptable.

There is another cost attached to CCS that is almost never mentioned: that of energy. An interesting and detailed study by oil industry analyst Rembrandt Koppelaar of ASPO-Netherlands looked at the energy cost of CCS, and compared that to the aforementioned Energy Watch Group study that predicted peak coal around 2020 to 2030, with a gentle slope past the peak. Koppelaar determined that adding CCS technology shifted the peak of coal forward five years, to 2015–2025, and significantly sharpened the slope of the decline. (See Figure 6.13.)

We can therefore imagine a scenario in which we push for increased coal usage due to peak oil and peak natural gas, but we do it responsibly by requiring CCS technology on every coal plant—only to move up the peak of coal.

Coal to Liquids

Although observers such as the Energy Watch Group and the National Academy of Sciences may be alert to the foreshortened future of coal, public policy makers are still proceeding on the assumption that the United States has a 250-year supply and are pushing for accelerated development of liquid fuels from coal. Coal to liquids (CTL) technology, they argue, could give us a bridge to the future and span the chasm between demand and declining liquid fuels from oil.

The process to do this was developed by two German researchers, Franz Fischer and Hans Tropsch, in the 1920s. Germany has negligible oil resources, but abundant supplies of coal. In 1939, after their access to overseas oil imports was cut off during World War II, the Germans invaded Russia, in large part to gain access to its oil production facilities. When the war deprived them of that source as well, they turned to the Fischer-Tropsch (F-T) process for another source of liquid fuels.[20] From 1938 to 1943, synthetic fuel output

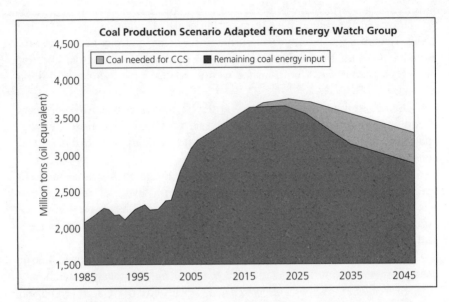

FIGURE 6.13 *Coal Production Scenario with Energy Input Costs for Carbon Dioxide Capture and Storage (CCS)*

Source: Chart by Rembrandt Koppelaar, http://europe.theoildrum.com/node/2733.
Source of production scenario: Energy Watch Group, www.energywatchgroup.org/files/Coalreport.pdf.

grew from 10 million barrels to 36 million, and reached more than 124,000 barrels per day from 25 plants, about 6.5 million tons total in 1944. These "synfuels" provided more than 92 percent of Germany's aviation gasoline and half of its petroleum during World War II.[21]

In the F-T process, coal, a hydrocarbon containing little hydrogen, is gasified under pressure and heat in the presence of water and a catalyst to produce hydrogen and carbon monoxide. Those products in turn are refined into synthetic fuels. Consequently, the synfuels are clean and relatively free of sulfur and other compounds that must be removed from oil-derived gasoline and other fuels at great expense and effort.

Since the United States has the world's largest coal resource, the F-T process has received more attention in recent years as a source of alternative fuels. But building a CTL plant is no small matter. The first commercial-scale CTL plant in the United States is being built by a partnership of Peabody Energy Corporation, the top coal producer, and Rentech, Inc., a firm that specializes in CTL technology. The plant is expected to cost a whopping

$1 billion and produce roughly 400,000 barrels of liquid fuel per year, as well as about 545,000 tons of nitrogen fertilizer.[22]

An investment of that magnitude takes decades to produce a return, so development of the industry has been sluggish. But new support in Congress promises to make CTL a viable part of the U.S. energy mix. A package of inducements has been proposed that would include $30 billion in loan guarantees for coal-to-liquid (CTL) plants; a $0.51 per gallon tax credit bounty for CTL fuels through 2020; automatic subsidies if oil prices drop below $40 a barrel; and permission for the Air Force to sign 25-year contracts for almost a billion gallons a year of coal-based jet fuel, guaranteeing a market for it.

Coal and Global Warming

There is a downside to CTL production, too: It's a greenhouse gas nightmare, emitting twice the volume of greenhouse gases as ordinary diesel per unit of volume when you burn it. Plus the very process of producing CTL fuels emits *another* ton of carbon dioxide for every barrel of liquid fuel.

The *New York Times* offers the infographic shown in Figure 6.14.

When coal is burned in a power plant, the emissions are even worse, containing soot, caustic ash, mercury, and other toxins, in addition to the greenhouse gases. According to the Oak Ridge National Laboratory, U.S. coal-burning power plants emit over 2,000 tons of radioactive uranium and thorium into the atmosphere every year.

Coal industry boosters invariably point out that the technology exists to sequester the carbon emissions that result from CTL production as well as coal-burning plants. And this is true. However, it has yet to be commercially installed. At this point, we must view "clean coal" strictly as a sound bite. In the real-life coal industry, it doesn't yet exist.

In all fairness, though, Rentech claims that its aforementioned new plant will capture emissions of carbon dioxide. The company is also evaluating prospects for selling the captured gas to beverage companies and oil producers.

Investment Opportunities

Among North American coal producer stocks, only two really stand out.

Peabody Energy Corporation (NYSE: BTU) is the largest by far, with an $11 billion market capitalization. It has majority interests in 40 coal operations located throughout the United States and Australia, but their production is primarily low-sulfur coal from the Powder River Basin in Wyoming. This is their primary strategic advantage, as the low-sulfur bituminous coal is desirable, and accessible by rail.

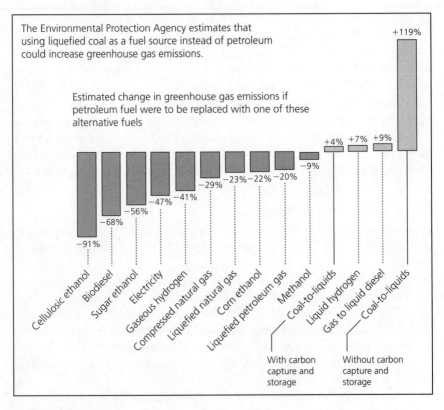

The Environmental Protection Agency estimates that using liquefied coal as a fuel source instead of petroleum could increase greenhouse gas emissions.

Estimated change in greenhouse gas emissions if petroleum fuel were to be replaced with one of these alternative fuels

+119%

+4% +7% +9%

−9%

−29% −23% −22% −20%

−47% −41%

−56%

−68%

−91%

Cellulosic ethanol
Biodiesel
Sugar ethanol
Electricity
Gaseous hydrogen
Compressed natural gas
Liquefied natural gas
Corn ethanol
Liquefied petroleum gas
Methanol
Coal-to-liquids
Liquid hydrogen
Gas to liquid diesel
Coal-to-liquids

With carbon capture and storage

Without carbon capture and storage

FIGURE 6.14 Change in Carbon Emissions from Substituting for Petroleum

Source: The *New York Times.*

Arch Coal, Inc. (NYSE: ACI) is the other, a $4 billion company that produces coal from 21 mines in Virginia, West Virginia, Kentucky, Wyoming, Colorado, and Utah. It also has equity interests in coal production in Illinois. The company sells almost all of its coal to electric power plants, steel producers, and industrial facilities. In 2006, it fueled approximately 6 percent of all electricity generated in the United States. Like Peabody, Arch Coal is primarily focused on low-sulfur coal production, but the company has also been taking equity interests in private CTL companies.

CTL is another way to invest in coal. Companies like the United States' Rentech, Inc. (AMEX: RTK), a $355 million company, and South Africa's Sasol Limited (ADR) (NYSE: SSL) a $24 billion company, have significant CTL operations using the Fischer-Tropsch process.

DIMINISHING RETURNS AND RECEDING HORIZONS

Whether we're talking about crude oil, natural gas, or coal, the trend is the same: Every year, we're paying more (and expending more effort) for less and less energy.

While it's true that there are still vast deposits of hydrocarbons under the ground, particularly of tar sands and oil shale, the quality of those hydrocarbons is getting worse, the cost to extract them is going up, and the energy inputs needed to convert them into usable energy are going up.

Energy journalist Roel Mayer has termed the phenomenon the Law of Receding Horizons, which states that as the price of a commodity like oil goes up, the cost of producing it goes up, too, keeping that magical break-even point for some marginal energy project always just out of reach. Why does this happen? Because energy from oil is used all along the way in building a new facility and running it.

It's a classic case of diminishing returns, and has been amply observed in the oil and gas sectors.

For example, the cost of light sweet crude more than tripled from $28 a barrel at the end of 2000 to over $90 today. Over the same period, in part due to the increasing cost of fuel, the cost of finding new oil has doubled from $10 to $12 per barrel in 2000 to $20 to $25 per barrel today.[23]

The same trend has held for the cost of finding new natural gas reserves, which rose 127 percent between 2000 ($1.13) and 2006 ($2.56).

This is particularly true for oil shale, which has seemed to be on the verge of profitability for decades.

James D. Hamilton, a professor of economics at the University of California, San Diego, who has followed the oil shale story for some three decades, explains: "It's remarkable that for over thirty years, the claim has always been that the projects would become economical if the price of oil went up just a little higher. I've watched oil prices go up, and then it turns out the projects still won't fly."[24]

In the energy business, the standard joke is: "Shale oil—fuel of the future, and always will be."

Indeed, in 1946, where today's I-70 traverses Colorado's oil shale–rich lands, you could have seen a billboard suggesting that you "Get In On The Ground Floor" of real estate there, to capitalize on the impending shale oil rush. And it's still not too late, because to this day there is still not a single production-scale oil shale facility.

The dynamic that Hamilton has observed still holds true today. Several years ago, shale oil was supposed to be economical as long as crude stayed above $30 a barrel, but when crude passed $30 to hold firmly above $60 a barrel, the projects still weren't cost-effective.

In June 2007, Shell withdrew one of its three permits to test a new in situ method for oil recovery from shale, saying that costs had "significantly escalated" and that "We are being more cautious and more prudent."[25] Reportedly, the new break-even point was moved up to $90[26] a barrel, but here we are with crude around $90 a barrel, and so far nobody is saying that shale oil makes economic sense.

Another good example is the Kashagan oil field in Kazakhstan. Situated on the western coast of the Caspian Sea, it's the largest new oil field discovery in over 30 years, with a potential production of 1.5 million barrels per day. That would make it one of the top four most productive oil fields in the world. (Only the three largest of the world's 4,000 oil fields produce more than 1.5 mbpd, and as we have seen, they are either in decline or suspected of being in decline.)

Consequently, production from Kashagan has been eagerly anticipated by cornucopians, who have expected it to make up for the depletion of the world's mature fields.

But in February 2007, the Italian oil group operating the field, Eni, announced that the start-up cost of the project was going to be almost double the initial estimate, at $19 billion versus $10.3 billion. And that's just to get the initial phase of the project going through 2011, when it will produce 300,000 barrels per day.

It's also going to take about three years longer than previously anticipated, beginning production around 2010, and won't hit its 1.5 mbpd production peak until 2019.

Since it appears that we may already be at the peak of global production, the Kashagan cavalry will show up just in time to clear the bodies off the battlefield.

Ironically, one of the causes of the receding horizons problem is the very success of the oil and gas industry. Record oil revenues being raked in by oil-producing countries of the Middle East are causing a boom in building and expanding their infrastructure. This in turn has led to a global shortage of contractors, raw materials, equipment, and qualified labor—and ultimately to higher prices for all the world's big construction projects, including the oil and gas industry's own. It's the snake eating its own tail.

In some cases the price of oil itself is stifling oil projects. For example, at Shell's Alberta oil sands project, the cost of producing a barrel of oil, after a planned 100,000 bpd expansion, will be six times higher than the cost when the project first started. That announcement in 2006 had investors fleeing for the exits, and mercilessly took down the stocks of the companies involved—no doubt slowing down those projects as well.

The aforementioned report by the Energy Watch Group on the impending peak of global coal production put it bluntly: "the present and past experience does not support the common argument that reserves are increasing over time as new areas are explored and prices rise."

The overriding theme is clear:

- Cost overruns are the norm, not the exception, and they're typically running over by 2× or more.

- Foreign oil companies are taking some serious hits in their far-flung projects and are adopting defensive postures. They will not be rushing out to the frontiers of Africa and the Caspian to develop the world's last major sources of untapped oil and natural gas anytime soon.

- The fossil fuel cavalry, if they ever leave home at all, won't be arriving in time to delay the peak or avert shortfalls.

Can we trust our expectations for future oil and gas production? How eager do we think Big Oil is really going to be to drill more aggressively between now and five or 10 years from now, when we're clearly past the global oil peak and they're basically powerless to do anything about it?

It seems likely that the problem of receding horizons is going to plague many of the much-anticipated supply-side solutions to the oil crisis. When it becomes clear that oil shale is never going to pay off and that oil sands have a necessarily limited future, what will that do to other unconventional oil development plans?

The importance of this point is more than academic. Archaeologist Joseph Tainter has argued, in his seminal book *The Collapse of Complex Societies* (Cambridge University Press, 1988), that complex societies tend to collapse because their strategies for energy capture are subject to the law of diminishing returns.[27] Will we fail to recognize this and become a new chapter in Tainter's study, or will we learn from experience and find ways to adapt to a world of diminishing energy?

ENERGY RETURN ON INVESTMENT

In addition to rising costs, there is another problem facing the future of fuels, and that is the energy return on investment (EROI), also sometimes referred to as energy returned on energy invested (EROEI). The concept was originally developed by systems ecologist Dr. Charles Hall, who was studying the energy balance of fish migrations (Hall, 1972), and who later applied the concept to oil production, with Dr. Cutler Cleveland and others (Hall and Cleveland, 1980; Cleveland et al., 1984; Hall et al., 1986, among others).

In the early days of U.S. oil production, the EROI was around 100—you got about 100 times as much energy out of the oil you produced from the well as you had to invest to get it. EROI is sometimes expressed as a ratio, for example 100:1.

EROI is a particularly important metric for oil and gas production. As we have seen from the earlier studies, early in a field's life, oil flows through the field and gushes up the well bore under its own pressure. But after some quantity of the oil has been produced, the pressure gradually drops until it has to be generated from above, to maintain the flow. And after the easy-to-get oil has been produced, getting the remaining oil out requires the injection of water, CO_2, or other substances to force oil out of the pores in the rock and make it flow to the well bore, where it has to be lifted to the surface. Clearly, the older the field is, the more energy one has to invest to recover the oil.

Now, as we get into lower and lower quality hydrocarbons, the EROI is falling, too. Oil and gas extraction in the United States now gives an EROI of about 17;[28] the EROI of synthetic crude from Canadian tar sands may be as low as 5; and for oil shale, it is perhaps 2 or 3.[29]

The EROI of ethanol from corn, by comparison, has been variously estimated between 1.2 and less than 1, which is why it's not workable as a true substitute for oil-based fuels. In a 2003 article in the scientific journal *Nature* by five of the world's top academic authorities on EROI calculations, the authors explain the problem this way: "An EROI of much greater than 1 to 1 is needed to run a society, because energy is also required to make the machines that use the energy; feed, house, train, and provide health care for necessary workers; and so on."[30]

More recent preliminary results from Charles Hall and his colleagues suggest that the EROI for extracting known oil globally is about 20:1 but falling fairly rapidly; that the EROI for finding new resources of oil today might be as low as 3:1; and that if the EROI of an energy project isn't at least about 5:1, it may not be a net source of energy to society because you must also pay for the production and maintenance of the infrastructure to use that oil.[31]

GLOBAL WARMING

Aside from practical and economic considerations, there is another reason why we must wean ourselves off of fossil fuels, and that is global warming.

The balance of scientific consensus holds that emissions of carbon dioxide (and other noxious gases) that result from the burning of hydrocarbon fuels is a major contributor to global warming. Burning fossil fuels is essentially a process in which carbon, which has been sequestered underground for millions of years, is put back into the atmosphere, from which it was originally taken by organic life-forms eons ago.

While the debate on the role of greenhouse gases in global warming is far from over, there is enough consensus that they are a major contributor to prompt wiser heads to apply the precautionary principle: "If an action or policy might cause severe or irreversible harm to the public, in the absence of a scientific consensus that harm would not ensue, the burden of proof falls on those who would advocate taking the action."[32]

In other words, where business-as-usual advocates would like to avoid the expense of limiting greenhouse gas emissions and force those who argue for it to prove conclusively that the emissions are responsible for global warming, the precautionary principle puts the burden of proof on those who would continue to emit them instead.

In the past few years, a growing body of scientific work and a growing chorus of expert observers have argued that the potential effects of global warming are so catastrophic that we have no choice but to aggressively begin controlling greenhouse gas emissions.

NASA's top climate change scientist, James E. Hansen, the longtime director of the agency's Goddard Institute for Space Studies, is one such expert.

"With another decade of 'business-as-usual' it becomes impractical to achieve the 'alternative scenario' (in which warming is held to less damaging levels) because of the energy infrastructure that would be in place," he says. " 'Business-as-usual' would be a guarantee of global and regional disasters."[33]

The United Nations' Intergovernmental Panel on Climate Change is another such body, established to assemble and coordinate scientific study of climate change around the world. To much fanfare, the panel issued three major reports in 2007, making the case that greenhouse gas–caused global warming is indeed an extremely serious problem deserving of immediate attention and efforts to control it.

A proper treatment of the subject is beyond the scope of this book, but global warming has emerged as one of the key motivators of policy change that has begun to steer humanity away from using fossil fuels and toward renewable energy sources that emit less, or no, greenhouse gases.

CHAPTER

7

TAR SANDS: THE OIL JUNKIE'S LAST FIX

The worst thing that could happen is to confuse ourselves and the public with too much spin about unlimited energy supplies at cheap prices, alternative fuels on a global scale, or energy independence in a matter of years. That kind of thinking simply dilutes our focus, defers the tough solutions that are needed today, and sets us all up for more future shocks and economic disruptions.

—SADAD AL-HUSSEINI

TAR SANDS

With oil and natural gas on the wane, and coal to liquids (CTL) still in a nascent stage, the immediate question is clear: Where are we going to get tomorrow's liquid hydrocarbon fuels?

The obvious answer would be tar sands.

It has been estimated that worldwide, the deposits of tar sands amount to approximately 2.5 trillion barrels, making them among the largest hydrocarbon deposits in the world, greater even than the total amount of oil that might ultimately be produced.

However, the economically recoverable portion is significantly less. In Alberta, Canada, the world's most productive tar sands resource by far, estimated reserves of oil from mined tar sands stand at about 35 billion barrels (a little over one year's worth of world petroleum consumption), and at about 140 billion additional barrels that could be produced in situ.[1]

What Are Tar Sands?

Tar sands, also sometimes called "oil sands" to make them seem more appealing, are a black, tar-like combination of clay, sand, water, and bitumen.

Bitumen isn't really oil; we know it as asphalt, when it is mixed with gravel to make road surfaces. It's a semisolid, degraded form of oil that does not flow at normal temperatures and pressures, making it difficult and expensive to extract.[2]

In order to get some usable hydrocarbons out of tar sands, we use one of two processes: strip mining and in situ processing. The oil that is produced is heavy oil, which must be processed in a complex refinery.

Virtually all of today's tar sands production is done by strip mining. One must really see some video to get a sense of the scale of these operations, for they are truly mind-boggling. First the trees are clear-cut and the topsoil overburden is removed. Then huge shovels dig the sands and load them into the largest dump trucks in the world. Then the tar is mixed with steam and solvents, and spun in giant vats to make the bitumen rise to the top. The contaminated wastewater is dumped in huge ponds and the tailings are dumped into valleys.

In one type of in situ (meaning "in place" in Latin) method, pipes force steam deep underground to melt the bitumen out of the sand, and then another pipe lifts it to the surface. This has the advantage of not creating the vast deposits of contaminated water and tailings that the open-pit process does.

There are several variants of in situ methods, including steam-assisted gravity drainage (SAGD) using horizontal wells; cyclic steam stimulation (CSS) using a vertical well; vapor recovery extraction (VAPEX) using solvents rather than heat; toe-to-heel air injection (THAI), a patented and as yet commercially unproven method that uses hot air to begin combustion of the tar sands underground, which then melts the bitumen; and primary or cold production (used where the bitumen will flow from reservoirs without the addition of heat or solvents).[3]

In situ projects are considerably faster and cheaper than building a mine and extraction plant, and as we have noted, in situ production holds the far greater promise for total extraction. However, there are many technical hurdles to be overcome with in situ production, such that it will likely not be a significant contributor for a long time to come. There are no such commercial-scale facilities at present.

Tar Sands Production

As we know from studying the examples of oil and natural gas, "It's not the size of the tank which matters, it's the size of the tap."[4] How much production can we really get from the tar sands, and how much does it help to offset oil depletion?

One of the most authoritative analysts on tar sands is Professor Kjell Aleklett of Uppsala University in Sweden, who is also the president of the Association for the Study of Peak Oil and Gas (ASPO). In his comprehensive June 2006 paper on the subject, "A Crash Program Scenario for the Canadian Oil Sands Industry,"[5] Aleklett considered how much production might be achieved from the Canadian tar sands (primarily the Athabascan region of Alberta).

Under a short-term crash program scenario, he believes that the Canadian tar sands could grow from their current production rate of around 1 mbpd to a plateau of 3.6 mbpd around 2018[6] and stay flat until production drops off around 2040. This projection is more or less in line with that of the IEA. Production is currently increasing at the rate of about 8 percent per year.[7]

Under a long-term crash program scenario, he determined that production could reach a maximum of 5 mbpd by 2030, but that a shortage of natural gas would limit it. (Other forecasts seem to center on a ~3.5 mpbd maximum rate.)

But even at that maximum, the tar sands would account for a mere 4 percent of *current* global oil consumption, or about 2.5 percent of the IEA's forecast of 120 mbpd by 2025. That's about the same amount of oil that will be lost due to oil field depletion less than two years after the global peak. In fact, it wouldn't even be enough to offset the combined decline of crude oil production from the North Sea and Canada.

Limits to Tar Sands

Producing oil from tar sands requires an enormous amount of effort, energy, and water. About one-quarter of the energy contained in the oil produced is burned in the form of natural gas to produce and upgrade the oil into synthetic crude. Depending on a host of factors, the total net energy gain for tar sands production is in the range of 5 to 10 percent, which makes it of questionable merit at any price.

Due to the significant energy inputs needed to harvest tar sands, it's expensive, costing between $18 and $23 per barrel to produce.[8] Until 2000, when the price of oil finally rose above that level, tar sands development made no economic sense.

There are three main choke points to tar sands development: energy, water, and labor.

The first problem is energy. Typically, tar sands are produced using natural gas to heat the steam that drives the bitumen out of the sands. It takes a lot of gas to do this, over 1,000 cubic feet of gas—about $8 worth—to produce one barrel of bitumen,[9] which still requires substantial energy inputs to upgrade it to a usable fuel.

At the current production level of about 1 mpbd, the tar sands operations consume about 4 percent of Canada's natural gas supply. So quadrupling production would consume fully 16 percent of the supply, and completely max out the gas market. Nearly all estimates for tar sands operations over the next 10 years exceed the projections for available amounts of natural gas!

If tar sands production were to be scaled up to 3 mpbd by 2025, the energy input would be between 1.6 and 2.3 billion cubic feet (bcf) of natural gas per day, which is approximately the *entire* planned capacity of the proposed Mackenzie Valley gas pipeline (1.9 bcf per day) from northern Canada, or about one-fifth of all of Canada's anticipated daily gas production.[10]

Aleklett puts it bluntly: "The supply of natural gas in North America is not adequate to support a future Canadian oil sands industry with today's dependence on natural gas."[11]

Therefore, he says, the only way to scale up production significantly from tar sands is to build dozens of nuclear plants to generate the heat needed to create the steam.

But even if that were possible (and as we shall see, it may not be), would there be enough water?

According to Dr. David Schindler, a University of Alberta biologist considered Canada's top water expert, perhaps not. In his May 2007 paper, "Running out of Steam? Oil Sands Development and Water Use in the Athabasca River Watershed," he contends that the main source of water for the Athabascan tar sands, the Athabasca River, cannot support expanded production: "[P]rojected bitumen extraction in the oil sands will require too much water to sustain the river and Athabasca Delta, especially with the effects of predicted climate warming." If that amount of water were used, he warns, it would threaten the water security of two northern territories, 300,000 aboriginal people, and Canada's largest watershed, the Mackenzie River Basin.[12]

Aleklett identified another little-discussed geological limitation to tar sands development: the poor concentration of energy-rich sands. Only 20 percent of the resource consists of big, easy-to-produce open-pit mines. The rest are smaller deposits that would be uneconomical to mine because of the large percentage of non-oil-bearing sand that would have to be processed. Therefore the only (purportedly) economical way to harvest the smaller deposits is using in situ methods.[13]

As if to reinforce the point, in March 2007 a Canadian parliamentary committee called for a hold on plans to build some 20 new nuclear reactors to increase Alberta's oil sands production through 2015, until the full consequences of building the reactors are known.[14] Undoubtedly, this will mean another delay in meeting the oil sands output projections.

Finally, there is a pipeline capacity constraint. The existing Alberta pipeline system will be fully utilized by mid-2008, and the proposed expansions—if they are built on time—will also be maxed out between 2009 and 2011. At that point, the pipelines will support a maximum of 3.5 mbpd of flow. There are no known plans for additional expansion beyond that capacity—probably because the developers agree with Aleklett's assessment. Without building a whole slew of new nuclear reactors, it won't be possible to increase oil production beyond that rate, anyway. The risk-averse approach would be to wait and see if the nuclear plants will in fact be built, then figure out where to get the water, and *then* consider expanding pipeline capacity.[15]

Environmental Concerns

There are some significant environmental concerns with tar sands as well.

For one thing, it requires an enormous amount of natural gas and diesel fuel to mine (or harvest in situ) the bitumen and refine it into synthetic crude.[16] Therefore, its carbon footprint is atrocious, even worse than that of coal.

For another, a massive amount of water is needed: typically two to four times as much water as the amount of oil extracted.[17] David Schindler says the amount of water now used for tar sands is enough to sustain a city of two million people every year.

Once the water has been used, it is toxic with contaminants, so it cannot be released into the environment. Some of it is reused, but huge amounts of it are pumped into vast settlement ponds to be retained as toxic waste.[18] These ponds are the largest bodies of water in the region, and some of the world's largest man-made ponds overall, with square miles of surface area. It may take 200 years for the smallest particles to settle down to the bottom of this toxic brew, which also contains very high levels of heavy metals and other health-threatening elements.

The contaminated wastewater not only is a great loss to the local environment and the wildlife that would otherwise live on it, but also presents a long-lasting contamination threat to groundwater and to wildlife that try to use it.

The end result of a tar sands mining operation is devastating: mountain-tops removed, valleys filled in, the topsoil amiss, and a massively disrupted ecosystem.

Given the very low EROI for tar sands, it's abundantly clear that if all the environmental costs were taken into account and not externalized, tar sand development would be a nonstarter.

That is what we call the oil junkie's last fix: an act of sheer desperation to stave off that inevitable day just a little longer, that day when we are forced to realize that the fossil fuel game is truly over. No more rabbits in the hat, ever.

In the July 2006 issue of *Rolling Stone*, Al Gore called the tar sands "crazy," a huge waste of energy and an eyesore on the landscape of Western Canada. "For every barrel of oil they extract there, they have to use enough natural gas to heat a family's home for four days," Mr. Gore told the magazine. "And they have to tear up four tons of landscape, all for one barrel of oil. It is truly nuts. But you know, junkies find veins in their toes. It seems reasonable, to them, because they've lost sight of the rest of their lives."[19]

Investment Opportunities

Nearly $100 billion in commitments has already been announced for future tar sands projects. With that kind of money flowing in, there will be important investment opportunities in tar sands, no matter what their net energy may turn out to be.

The vast majority of the tar sands are located in the Athabasca region of Alberta in Canada, and there are about a dozen companies with investments in the area, but given the relatively early stage of the sector's development, and the many uncertainties that surround its future, it's hard to say which will be the most profitable. But here are a few suggestions.

Suncor Energy Inc. (NYSE: SU), at $42 billion market capitalization, is the largest of the tar sands companies. It is an integrated Canadian company with end-to-end operations in crude oil and natural gas. It has both tar sands mining and in situ development in the Fort McMurray, Alberta, area where the Athabascan tar sands are located.

Another major player in the Athabascan area is Western Oil Sands, Inc. (TSE: WTO), a $5.6 billion Canadian company with a 20 percent interest in the Athabasca Oil Sands Project (AOSP). The other partners in the joint venture are Shell Canada Limited, with a 60 percent interest, and Chevron Canada Limited, with a 20 percent interest, but neither subsidiary is publicly traded apart from its parent company.

A final significant tar sands project is the 46,170-acre Fort Hills Project in the Athabasca region. The partners in this project are $28 billion Petro-Canada

(TSE: PCA) with a 55 percent interest, $2.5 billion Canadian company UTS Energy Corporation (TSE: UTS) with a 30 percent interest, and $19 billion Teck Cominco Limited (NYSE: TCK) with a 15 percent interest.

OIL SHALE

The United States has the largest resources of oil shale in the world, estimated at between 500 and 2,600 billion barrels—potentially more oil than the entire world will ever harvest. Oil shale is a bit misnamed, because it doesn't hold oil, but rather kerogen, a precursor to oil, with a hydrogen-to-carbon ratio of around 1.2 to 1.

Oil shale is much younger than tar sands. The latter have some oil that has already been expelled from the kerogen. Oil shale hasn't been cooked enough to break down its hydrocarbons into liquids, so processing it means that they must be cooked first. This process is called "retorting."

However, surface methods produce unacceptable loads of tailings and emissions and require the removal of enormous amounts of surface material. This is not only expensive, but also extremely disruptive to the environment.

Therefore, an in situ process is being tried. But the in situ process for harvesting oil shale is considerably more difficult than that for tar sands. First the shale would be heated underground so that a semiliquid goo can be extracted that can be processed into lighter fuels.

A widely watched in situ oil shale demonstration project is Shell's test project in western Colorado. From a technical standpoint, the project is as impressive as it is challenging.

An electrical element is buried in the ground to heat the rock to 600 to 700 degrees Fahrenheit for three to four years and cook the kerogen. But that would open the possibility of having the liquid hydrocarbons leak into the surrounding water table, so to prevent that, the engineers are sinking chillers around the perimeter of the area to create a "freeze wall" around the heated kerogen.

Obviously, there is a significant cost to investing all the energy needed to do this freezing and heating for a period of years. Still, Shell has estimated that each unit of primary heat to drive the process yields 3.5 units of fuel.

But in what has become a common occurrence on the cutting edge of the energy business, the original expectations now look to have been overestimated.

In 2005, Shell expected its in situ oil shale project to reach commercial production by 2010, producing perhaps one mbpd by 2015, and five mbpd by 2030. The company stated that it was economically feasible as long as oil was priced at $20 to $30 a barrel.[20]

But in May 2007, with crude oil in the mid-$60s, they weren't so sure anymore.

"We still have a plethora of questions to answer," said Terry O'Connor, the spokesman and vice president for Shell Exploration and Production Co., in his keynote speech at the Grand Junction Economic Partnership annual meeting.

And in June, Shell withdrew its mining permit application to begin testing its in situ process in Colorado, saying that drilling the test freeze wall took longer than expected due to some geological problems, and that the costs had increased substantially. "We want to further mature the containment method and further develop the heater technology prior to doing the demonstration project on federal acreage," said a Shell spokesperson.[21]

Now they're saying that the decision on whether the process is commercially viable won't be made until early in the next decade—the time at which they expected it to go into commercial production only two years previously.

Numerous questions about the viability of oil shale production remain, including:

- Can the technology really be scaled up on a sustainable basis to commercial production levels?

- Will the freeze wall approach really protect groundwater from contamination?

- Is there enough available water to harvest and process oil from shale in that very water-constrained part of the country?

- Does the balance of energy inputs and energy outputs really come out positive?

- Will the industry have a positive or a negative effect on the local economy and environment?

According to Andrew Gulliford, author of *Boomtown Blues* (University Press of Colorado, 2003), a history of the oil shale boom and bust on the Western Slope of Colorado, Shell is wise to take a cautious approach to the oil shale project. "I think it's extremely rare; it's an untested technology," Gulliford said of Shell's freeze wall. "It has incredibly large environmental and energy costs that are as yet unknown. The goal is to avoid air pollution, so the goal is to avoid moving lots of rock. But that technology is not in any way understood or proven."[22]

Investment Opportunities

At this point in development, we cannot recommend any investment angles on oil shale.

PART

ENERGY
AFTER OIL

Clearly, if by 2025 the world will be past the peaks of oil, gas, and coal, it is hard to imagine how we will meet our future energy needs, particularly if we expect demand to continue to grow. As we will see, switching much of the load to nuclear power may not be as feasible as expected, since we may soon be at peak nuclear as well.

So where can we find the energy we need?

First, it's helpful to put the problem in perspective. According to noted peak oil author Richard Heinberg (*The Party's Over*, *Powerdown*, and *The Oil Depletion Protocol*):

> *Oil, natural gas, and coal together supply over 87 percent of total world energy, which stands at about 400 quadrillion BTUs, or "quads," per year.*

Therefore, compensating for a realistically possible 2.5 percent annual decline in all fossil fuels averaged over the next 20 years would require developing almost 10 quads of energy production capacity from new sources each year (this assumes no growth in energy demand). Ten quads represent roughly 10 percent of total current U.S. energy production. By way of comparison, today's total installed world wind and solar generating capacity—the result of many years of investment and work—stands at less than 1 quad.[1]

As of 2004, electricity generation from solar, wind, geothermal, biomass, and waste *combined* accounted for a mere 2.1 percent of global electricity generation.[2]

How can we possibly make up 10 quads of new energy production each year, just to meet current demand?

Most immediately, because peak oil is fundamentally a liquid fuels problem, we can expand our production of biofuels such as biodiesel and ethanol, as a transitional strategy. Every gallon of fuel we can grow domestically instead of importing it from a foreign supplier is a win on all levels—economically, politically, environmentally.

But, as we discussed earlier, we must take care to ensure that every gallon of biofuel we produce has an acceptable EROI, does not seriously impinge on the food supply, and does not result in net environmental damage. Therefore, cellulosic ethanol and biofuels from high-yield, less food-oriented crops will be preferable to corn and soybeans, the primary biofuel feedstocks today.

Because two-thirds of our petroleum use goes to transportation, we can make a significant dent in our consumption by switching to biofuels and higher-efficiency vehicles. "Flex-fuel" vehicles that can run on fuel blends containing 85 percent ethanol (so-called E85 fuel) or on straight gasoline will enable us to use more domestically grown fuel. Hybrids will help to reduce gasoline consumption due to their greater efficiency. And the new plug-in hybrids, which can be charged up directly from the grid, will stretch a gallon that much farther, as well as give us a way to use renewably generated electricity for transportation.

An excellent potential exists in switching freight transport from trucks to rail. As we shall see, rail is far more fuel efficient than trucking, and trucking is a major component of our petroleum consumption. Rail also offers the possibility of running high-speed trains on pure electricity, which when fully deployed, could radically reduce our consumption of all liquid fuels.

As for the other third of our petroleum consumption that is not used for transportation, nearly half is used for heating. This portion could be reduced relatively easily by building more energy-efficient homes with less heat loss—something that is quickly becoming de rigueur in the building industry—and by using shallow geothermal heat pumps to provide some of the necessary heat.

Apart from biofuels, however, most of our alternative energy technologies produce electricity. Solar, wind, geothermal, hydro, and biomass-burning power plants all produce electricity. So in the long run, it seems a foregone conclusion that electricity will be our preferred form of energy.

In this part we examine these alternatives in detail, and explore the possibilities of each one.

CHAPTER

8

THE RENEWABLE REVOLUTION

*Contrary to public perceptions, renewable energy is not
the silver bullet that will soon solve all our problems.*

—Jeroen van der Veer

Until just a few years ago, renewable fuels were rarely discussed anywhere outside of energy industry and environmental circles. They simply weren't a significant part of the industry. Consider the primary energy mix for the United States shown in Figure 8.1.

The mix for the world isn't terribly different. (See Figure 8.2.)

Note that the vast majority of the renewable energy slice is hydropower and power generation from biomass and waste (such as biosolids from water treatment plants, methane gas harvested from landfills, even burning cow dung).

The portion provided by solar and wind energy—what most people think of when they think about renewable energy—is a fraction of 1 percent of the total mix.

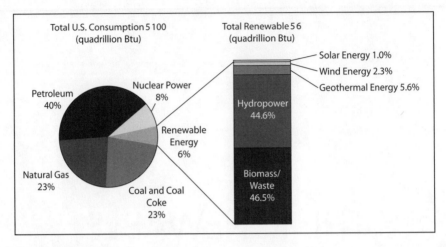

FIGURE 8.1   *United States Energy Sources, 2004*

Source: Energy Information Administration. www.eia.doe.gov/neic/brochure/renew05/
renewable.html.

But according to a recent report, all forms of renewable energy combined could meet up to half the United States' electricity needs and 40 percent of its transportation fuel by 2025. Wind would supply 40 percent of the renewable energy mix, with the rest comprising solar, geothermal, biomass, and water.[1]

Achieving that much growth that quickly would probably be the greatest business growth story of all time.

But it seems inevitable. According to New Energy Finance, a research company, global investment in renewable power generation, biofuels, and low-carbon technologies rose from $28 billion in 2004 to $71 billion in 2006—a 75 percent annual growth rate!

Since 2004, the solar photovoltaic (PV) market has grown by an average of 41 percent a year, and wind power has grown by 18 percent a year.[2]

Thanks to growing fears about global warming and the risks inherent in being totally dependent on foreign oil, consumers are increasingly becoming educated about energy issues, and are demanding more investment in renewables. State renewable portfolio standards (RPSs), which specify a portion of the overall energy mix that must be supplied from renewable sources, have been rapidly proliferating and as of June 2007 are now in place in 24 of the states.[3] Most of them are agnostic about how the power is generated—be it wind, solar, geothermal, or something else—and geothermal power easily satisfies the criteria, due to its many advantages. With most states targeting

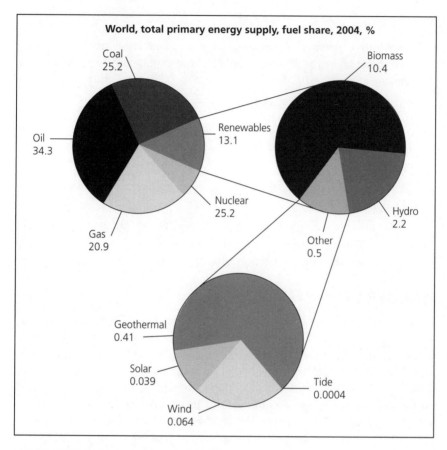

FIGURE 8.2   *World Total Primary Energy Supply, Fuel Share, 2004, Percent*

Source: IEA Key World Energy Statistics © OECD/IEA, 2006, p. 7.

roughly 20 percent by 2020, there is an enormous need to be satisfied by renewable energy technologies.

OIL AND GAS EXECUTIVES WANT RENEWABLES

A telling perspective on the enormous growth potential of renewables—and the flagging production of oil and gas—came from an April 2007 survey by tax firm KTMG of 553 individuals who probably know the score better than anyone else: financial executives from the U.S. oil and gas industry.

The results were pretty astonishing.

- Twenty-five percent of respondents wanted at least three-quarters of government funding for energy put into renewables, and 44 percent would allocate at least half.

- Eighty-two percent cited declining oil reserves as a concern.

- Sixty percent said the trend of declining oil reserves is irreversible, and 70 percent said that the emerging markets will only intensify the problem.

- Thirty-three percent said their next personal car will be a gas-sipper, such as a hybrid.[4]

It seems unlikely that financial executives in the oil and gas industry would make such statements if they didn't believe wholeheartedly in the peak oil problem, and the importance of renewables as part of the solution.

WORLD BANK FINANCING

The World Bank, being an entity that seeks to provide assistance to the developing world, has long sought renewable energy solutions as part of its mission. After all, energy inequity leads directly to economic inequity, with all its attendant social problems. Also, it is clear that the effects of global warming will disproportionately fall upon the poor, as they are often located in the places that are most vulnerable to problems like flooding, and they have few options for relocating. The World Bank's goals include such things as helping countries transition to a low-carbon economy, and giving 47 percent (currently 25 percent) of African households access to energy by 2030. But what has always held these projects back is capital. Investment needed in sub-Saharan Africa alone to meet the aforementioned target will be some $4 billion.

Realizing that private sector investment for such projects had declined significantly in recent years, the World Bank developed a 2003 Infrastructure Action Plan (IAP) to ramp up investment in energy and carbon emissions control, and encourage co-investment from the private sector, world governments, and other concerned bodies. Over the three years since the plan was initiated, the Bank has invested $7 billion in energy projects, and its commitment is growing.

In April 2007, the World Bank published a report, "Clean Energy for Development Investment Framework: The World Bank Group Action Plan," in which it reviewed the progress so far. Renewable energy projects have proven themselves cost-effective and highly desirable solutions for the developing world, and the governmental and regulatory environment has become supportive.

For the next three-year period of 2006–2009, the Bank expects to increase its funding for energy projects by 40 percent to $10 billion in such areas as renewables, energy efficiency, and transportation. It is also lending for low-carbon projects around the globe, to the tune of $3 billion in 2006. It believes that further investment will make it possible for these developing economies to support their own local markets for energy and carbon control, where today they lack a certain critical mass to do so.[5]

BIOFUELS

The most direct and obvious substitutes for liquid fuels from oil are biofuels—biodiesel and ethanol.

Biodiesel

Biodiesel is made from vegetable oils or animal fats—everything from waste cooking grease to vegetable oil to blue-green algae.[6] It is produced via a process called transesterification, which is the reaction of a triglyceride (fat/oil) with an alcohol to form esters and glycerol.

When treated with alcohol, the base product is converted into a fuel that is just as effective as diesel, but with additional benefits.[7] Biodiesel is 100 percent biodegradable, reduces carbon emissions by 75 percent, and produces fewer particulate matter, carbon monoxide, and sulfur dioxide emissions than petroleum diesel ("dino diesel"). It's also safer to store and transport.[8]

Soybean oil is currently the most economical base for biodiesel production, but biodiesel can also be made from rapeseed, canola oil, mustard, jatropha, palm oil, or algae.[9]

Start-up companies in Philadelphia[10] and New York[11] are making a business out of something biodiesel home brewers have been doing for years: making it from waste grease from fast-food restaurants. Restaurants are usually happy to give it away, since their only alternative is to pay handsomely to have the nasty, gunky stuff hauled away as toxic waste!

Best of all, transesterification requires far less energy than making ethanol from corn.[12]

While biofuels are a new development in modern times, the reality is that they predated fuels made from petroleum! Peanut oil was the original fuel for the first diesel engine, built in 1897. Rudolf Diesel was a champion of the common man, and wanted a fuel that could be grown locally, giving smaller industries, farmers, and common folk a chance to compete with the big industries that had monopolized energy production.

One of the advantages to biodiesel is that it can be used in a standard diesel engine without modification, either as a 100 percent biodiesel fuel (called B100) or mixed with regular dino diesel (a typical blend of 20 percent biodiesel is called B20).

Biodiesel may even gain market share more quickly than ethanol because, unlike ethanol, it can be used in any diesel engine without modifications, and needs no special infrastructure to deliver, store, and sell it.[13]

Biodiesel production is taking off in the United States, headed for a 16-fold increase, from 25 million gallons in 2005 to 400 million gallons in 2030, according to the EIA. Biodiesel production tripled from 2004 to 2005. The number of biodiesel refineries has more than tripled since 2004, and newer plants are being designed with much larger production capacities—up to 100 million gallons per year, compared to today's average of 30 million.[14]

The demand is equally strong in Europe, where, according to recent Frost & Sullivan research, approximately 224 million gallons per year of biodiesel will be needed to meet the European Union's portfolio standard of obtaining 5.75 percent of transport fuels from biodiesel.[15]

At present, most of the publicly traded companies that produce biodiesel are outside the United States, but several up-and-coming companies here are expected to go public in the next year or so.[16]

Biodiesel from Algae

One of the most promising sources of biodiesel feedstock isn't a plant at all, but rather the simple aquatic organisms called algae—the same organisms, ironically, that became much of the crude oil we use today.

Algae can capture light energy through photosynthesis and create something like vegetable oil. Certain species of algae have a high oil content—some over 50 percent—and very high growth rates, and so are ideal for biodiesel production.

Algae has several advantages over oilseed crops. For one, it can be grown almost anywhere with sunlight, in closed tubes or open ponds; it doesn't need soil. For another, the only inputs it needs are sunlight, water, a little power to run the operation, and carbon dioxide, which it takes from the atmosphere.

Because algae take CO_2 from the atmosphere, biodiesel from algae can be a true carbon-neutral fuel.

Algae could also be a key element to capturing the CO_2 emissions of power plants that burn fossil fuels. One company, Israel's Alga Technologies (Algatech), is doing just that, by locating its algae-growing units alongside the smokestacks of power plants. No only could this capture all the emissions of the power plant, but it could also provide a fuel source for the power plant, making the whole operation self-contained.

So how much biodiesel can we make from algae? According to Solix Biofuels, another aspiring producer of algae-based biodiesel, the numbers add up as follows.

In order to replace all the petroleum-based transportation fuel in the United States, we would need about 140 billion gallons of biodiesel a year.

To produce that much biodiesel from soybeans, you would need about three billion acres of fertile land. To produce it from canola, you'd need more than one billion acres. But we only have 434 million acres of cropland in the United States, most of which we need to grow food.

Producing it from algae, though, could theoretically be done on just 95 million acres of infertile land.[17]

However, as there are no commercial-scale algal biodiesel plants in existence yet, and all the companies working on it are tiny start-ups, we must take such estimations with a good grain of salt. Such estimates have historically proven overblown, sometimes by an order of magnitude or more. Before we go putting a lot of our eggs in the algal biodiesel basket, we will need to see proven performance in working, commercial-scale systems.

Investment Opportunities

Most biodiesel producers are still relatively young companies, and their best days are still ahead. So investors should take a cautious approach to investing in these stocks and look at them as speculative plays. Of the many biodiesel start-ups, however, only a few are publicly traded, and they're all micro-caps.

Allegro Biodiesel Corp. (OTC: ABDS) is a producer and distributor of biodiesel fuel. Its operations are based in Louisiana, and it primarily uses soybean oil as a feedstock. Allegro began biodiesel fuel production and sales in April 2006, and as of the end of 2006, had a production capacity of 12 million gallons per year.

GreenShift Corporation (OTC: GSHF) is a tiny company with a penny stock. It holds a license agreement with Ohio University for its patented bioreactor process for growing blue-green algae using the exhaust gas streams from fossil-fueled power plants.

Valcent Products Inc. (OTC: VCTPF) is another very small company that has developed a vertical bioreactor for growing a species of algae that yields a large volume of high-grade vegetable oil, which is easily blended with dino diesel. The company also holds various patents for related technologies. In July

2007, it announced a joint venture with the SGC Group of Portugal, to build their first commercial "Vertigro" plant near Lisbon, Portugal.

Ethanol

Ethanol is simply alcohol—the same stuff you drink in an alcoholic beverage. Because alcohol for human consumption is tightly regulated, the law requires that industrial alcohol have impurities added that will make you sick if you drink it.

Making ethanol is a lot like making whiskey. Sugar is dissolved out of sugar cane or sugar beets, or converted from starchy crops like corn, wheat, and barley.[18] The sugar is then fermented with yeast, which produces ethanol and carbon dioxide.[19]

In the United States, the sugars are mostly produced from corn, the dominant U.S. crop by far. However, sugar-bearing crops such as sugar beets and sugar cane are even more productive feedstocks. The oft-cited ethanol success story of Brazil, which obtains 40 percent of its motor fuel from domestically produced ethanol, is due to its extraordinarily productive sugar cane crop (which, unfortunately, doesn't grow nearly as well elsewhere).

Ethanol can also be produced from the fermentation of various types of plant matter and biowaste to create cellulosic ethanol. More on that later.

Ethanol hits the road in three different concentrations today:

1. Pure ethanol, usable only in specially modified engines.

2. E85, a combination of 85 percent ethanol and 15 percent gasoline. A new car can be equipped to run on either regular gasoline or E85 for about $100.[20] About five million of these flex-fuel vehicles are already on the road in the United States.

3. E10, an octane-boosting mix of 10 percent ethanol with regular gasoline. This combination is usable in any gas-powered vehicle and is already in wide distribution as a substitute for MTBE, which was phased out in 2006 by federal mandate.[21]

On a straight volumetric basis, though, ethanol has only about two-thirds the energy content of an equivalent volume of gasoline, so it takes about one-third more ethanol to move a vehicle the same distance.

E85 fuel is not yet widely deployed. In 2006, only about 1,200 out of the 170,000 gas stations in the United States offered E85, or less than 1 percent. But experts believe that E85 will have to be available at around 10 percent of all stations before it will be eagerly adopted by the public.[22] For example, California has 257,318 flex-fuel vehicles but only two public stations with

E85, and New Jersey has 116,512 flex-fuel vehicles without a single station selling E85. Consequently, "more than 99 percent of the flex-fuel cars run on regular gasoline because E85 is rarely available to the everyday driving public."[23]

Big Oil has actively resisted the expansion of the E85 market. According to the *Wall Street Journal*, oil companies make it difficult to deploy E85 pumps at gas stations. For instance, franchises may be required to purchase all the fuel they sell from the oil company, but if the oil company doesn't sell E85, which is most often the case, then the stations can't either without obtaining an exception from the oil company. There are other restrictions as well, such as prohibiting payment by credit card.[24]

Still, the number of E85 pumps has increased 500 percent in three years and is on track to continue its rapid expansion, thanks to government and ethanol industry grants that each provide up to $30,000 to install ethanol pumps.[25]

Corn Ethanol

Initially driven by government subsides, the U.S. corn ethanol industry has sprung up like a weed. Even though the EROI of corn ethanol is widely considered to be too low to be worthwhile, at about 1.2, government subsidies and high oil prices have conspired to produce a robust domestic corn ethanol industry. Ethanol from corn constitutes over 90 percent of all biofuels produced in the United States today.[26]

But according to Lester Brown of the Earth Policy Institute, the growth spurt is increasingly due to its profitability:

"Investment in crop-based fuel production, once dependent on government subsidies, is now driven by the price of oil," Brown writes. "With the current price of ethanol double its cost of production, the conversion of agricultural commodities into fuel for cars has become hugely profitable. In the United States, this means that investment in fuel distilleries is controlled by the market, not by the government."

Indeed, the productive capacity for biofuels in the United States will easily shoot past the federal Renewable Fuels Standard for 7.5 billion gallons per year (bgy) by 2012. A. G. Edwards projects U.S. ethanol capacity will be about double that by 2009, at 13 to 14 bgy.[27]

Cellulosic Ethanol

Ethanol can also be produced from many kinds of organic matter that contain cellulose, the basic building material of all woody plant fibers. Appropriate feedstocks for cellulosic ethanol include wood chips, rice and wheat straw, and other waste materials that are currently expensive and difficult to dispose of.

Therefore, cellulosic ethanol production can be expanded without competing with food crops for land and water, and without the large inputs of fertilizer and pesticides used in commercial food farming, making the feedstocks much more abundant and much cheaper than food grains.

One promising method is to make cellulosic ethanol from feedstocks such as switchgrass, a perennial grass that is native to the United States, and miscanthus, a grass native to Europe that can grow to 14 feet tall.[28] Such grasses can actually improve the environment in which they are grown, by reducing soil erosion and chemical and water use, while at the same time providing habitat for wildlife. And because it can be grown with very little in the way of fossil fuel inputs, taking all of its carbon from CO_2 in the air, it can produce a nearly carbon-neutral biofuel.

A recent University of Minnesota study found that high-diversity grasslands can even remove carbon from the atmosphere and sequester it in soils and roots, and at the same time produce 238 percent more energy than monoculture crops![29] Clearly, the subject deserves intensive further study.

One of the major hurdles to large-scale production of cellulosic ethanol is the fact that nature designed cellulose *not* to break down easily. Currently, one approach to this problem is using high-tech, chemically engineered enzymes, which can break the cellulose down chemically into fermentable sugars. Unfortunately, high-tech chemical engineering also means high-priced, small-batch enzymes. At this point in time, there are no commercial-scale producers of these specialty enzymes.

Another approach is similar to coal-to-liquids production, using heat to gasify the cellulosic matter, then hydrogenating the gas to turn it into synfuels, including ethanol and synthetic gasoline and diesel. Commercial-scale production using these methods is not yet a reality, however, and it remains to be seen what the EROI of the process will be at commercial scale.

But the race is on to build the first commercial plant in the United States to convert wood into ethanol. In Georgia, Range Fuels, Inc. will soon begin building a plant to gasify wood and turn the "syngas" into ethanol. This plant is expected to produce 20 million gallons of ethanol per year starting in 2008.[30]

And in Michigan, the Mascoma Corporation is planning a commercial ethanol plant that will make the fuel from wood chips and other nonfood agricultural products. The plant will use an enzymatic approach to derive sugars from the biomass and ferment them into ethanol. The time line for the project is unknown, but the governor wants the bragging rights to the first commercial-scale wood-to-ethanol plant in the country, so development is expected to proceed apace.[31]

The world's first commercial wood-to-ethanol plant, which uses fermentation technology developed by Verenium Corporation, was unveiled in 2007 in Osaka, Japan. The plant is expected to produce 370,000 gallons of ethanol per year. Verenium is also building a demonstration-scale plant in Louisiana that will produce 1.4 million gallons of ethanol per year, which should be built by the end of 2007.[32]

In Florida, ethanol developers are planning to build a plant that will convert citrus peels into ethanol. Citrus Energy LLC and FPL Energy, LLC will build a commercial-scale ethanol facility on the grounds of a Florida citrus processor that is expected to produce four million gallons of ethanol per year.[33]

Although intensive study and pilot projects in recent years have reduced the cost of producing cellulosic ethanol from $5.66 a gallon in 2001 to $2.26 in 2005, conventional ethanol from corn still costs anywhere from one-third to one-half less, according to the U.S. Department of Energy. So further research and government support are still crucial to developing a truly viable, commercial-scale cellulosic ethanol industry.[34]

Limits to Corn Ethanol

Like any other fuel, corn ethanol has its limits. As soon as we start producing it at commercial scale, we run straight up against food supply.

Corn is used in an amazing array of foodstuffs. According to Michael Pollan, author of *The Omnivore's Dilemma* (Penguin Press, 2006) and *The Botany of Desire* (Random House, 2001), every single thing on the McDonald's menu is in some way made from corn, in the form of either high-fructose corn syrup or cornstarch or corn oil or corn-fed beef, or any of 13 different ways.[35] In the United States, corn is the main feed for beef, poultry, egg, dairy, and hog production, and high-fructose corn syrup sweetens everything from cereal to soft drinks.[36] So when the price of corn goes up, it drives up the prices of food and beverages across the board.

But corn production also affects the prices of all other grains, because good corn-growing land isn't unlimited. Growing more corn for ethanol cuts into the available land for growing other things, and drives up their prices as well, even as the price of the remaining corn for food goes up.

Then there is the problem of the sheer volume of gasoline we consume. A study published in the Proceedings of the National Academy of Sciences says that even turning *all* of America's corn into ethanol would meet only 12 percent of our gasoline demand.[37]

Consider this statistic: To produce enough ethanol to fill the tank on a big four-wheel-drive SUV, you would need enough grain to feed one person for an entire year.[38]

Robert Hirsch has famously quipped that making ethanol from corn is a process by which a certain amount of energy in the forms of natural gas and diesel fuel are used to create an equivalent amount of energy in the form of ethanol, with the primary output being money from government subsidies.[39]

The need for food production will continue to limit the growth of the corn ethanol industry, despite our desire for domestically grown fuels. In the United States, we used about 27 percent[40] of the 2007 corn crop to make about 5.9 billion[41] gallons of ethanol, which accounted for just 4 percent of the 145.2 billion[42] gallons of gasoline we consumed.

The U.S. Department of Agriculture further projects that in five years, ethanol production will consume almost a third of the U.S. corn crop, leading to higher costs for everything from animal feed to meats.[43]

Consider this: One of the objectives of the Energy Independence and Security Act of 2007 is to quintuple the domestic ethanol production to 36 billion gallons per year by 2022.[44] If we scaled that linearly and continued to produce almost all of the ethanol from corn, as we do now, then we would need 162 percent of the 2007 corn crop to meet that 36 billion gallons per year target, which would offset only one-quarter of our current gasoline usage. And we would have less than nothing to eat.

Consequently, most analysts agree that corn ethanol production in the United States will top out somewhere around 15 billion gallons per year.

Another little-recognized fact is that corn is very susceptible to changes in temperature, and it appears that the warming of the earth over the past two decades has significantly impacted corn production.

According to U.S. government scientists, a rise of about 0.7 degrees Fahrenheit between 1980 and 2002 reduced the annual yields of the world's major cereal crops—wheat, corn, and barley—by a combined 40 million metric tons.[45]

Then there is the matter of fuel consumption. According to author Michael Pollan, a half gallon of fossil fuel is required to produce a bushel of corn.[46] If biofuels are to provide any sort of relief from imported oil, they cannot require such enormous inputs of fossil fuels.

Clearly there are limits to corn ethanol. But what we can achieve with cellulosic ethanol remains to be seen.

Limits to Biofuels

Aside from the specific limits on corn ethanol, there is another, larger issue that applies to all feedstocks, and that's demand.

We are suffering under the tyranny of the automobile. We are simply consuming so much fuel that at some point the decline of oil supply cannot be made up by anything else.

Fatih Birol, chief economist for the IEA, affirmed this in a June 27, 2007, interview with the French newspaper *Le Monde*.[47] Noting that Europe, the United States, and Japan are all greatly increasing their biofuel production, but that the expectations are overblown and will not help the greenhouse gas emissions problem, he explained:

> *Some of these policies are not based on a solid economic rationale: The biofuels will remain very expensive to produce. But even if these policies succeed we think that the biofuel portion of total hydrocarbons will only be 7 percent in 2030. To reach that 7 percent, one would need an agricultural area equivalent to the surface area of Australia, more than that of Korea, Japan, and New Zealand. Therefore, for these economic and environmental reasons, 7 percent of the total production of fuels is a very, very optimistic figure.* The agricultural fuels will never replace the oil of OPEC, *as some hope for it. Their contribution will remain minor. (Emphasis ours)*[48]

Again, the problem is scale. Fundamentally, nowhere in the world is there enough unneeded, arable land and water to grow the requisite feedstock for the immense volume of biofuels we will need, no matter which feedstock you choose, and the energy returned on energy invested (EROEI) is so low that in most cases, it's simply not worth doing. As Dr. Tad Patzek of the University of California, Berkeley, one of the top experts on the feasibility of biofuels, has said:

> *[The] vision is to capture in real time most of net growth of all biomass in the US, while at the same time mining soil, water, and air over 72 percent of our land area, including Alaska, Hawaii, and Puerto Rico. This biomass would then be devoured to feed our inefficient cars. We would have little food production, as well as little wood for paper and construction. In effect, the new brave US economy would be dedicated to feeding cars, not people. This vision has been enthusiastically embraced by some in the US science and industrial establishment.*[49]

According to Patzek, the EROI figures in the oft-cited Department of Energy/U.S. Department of Agriculture (DOE/USDA) report of 2005 are "laughable," requiring impossible crop yields and impossible levels of residue recovery; he adds sardonically, "To utilize all residues, I suggest to also process fresh corpses into biofuels."[50]

The International Monetary Fund (IMF) warned about the limits to ethanol from corn and biodiesel from soybeans in its Spring 2007 World Economic

Forecast, indicating that cellulosic ethanol is the only biofuel that would make sense in large-scale production:

> *While on a small scale biofuels may be beneficial by supplementing fuel supply, promoting their use to unsustainable levels under current technology is problematic, and long-term prospects for biofuels depend heavily on how quickly and efficiently second-generation substitutes (such as plant waste) can be adopted. Many energy market analysts also question the rationality of large subsidies that benefit farmers more than the environment.*
>
> *While new technology is being developed, a more efficient solution from a global perspective would be to reduce tariffs on imports from developing countries (for example, Brazil) where biofuels production is cheaper and more energy efficient.*[51]

We are already seeing some of the unintended effects of the shift to biofuels, as farmers all over the world switch to feedstock-producing crops. For example, in Mexico, there were riots in early 2007 over the rising cost of tortillas, the number one staple food. The cause of the rise was the increasing cost of corn from the United States due to the expansion of the corn ethanol industry. Consequently, Mexican farmers set as much as 35 percent of their fields of blue agave ablaze, in order to make room for growing more profitable corn. The loss of blue agave production then caused a spike in the price of its end-product, tequila.[52]

Similarly, a May 2007 study by the United Nations showed that the push to replace food crops with biofuel feedstock crops is having other unintended consequences all over the world. Seventeen countries have made large commitments to growing biofuel feedstocks such as palm oil trees, corn, and soybeans, and global production of biofuels is doubling every few years. But this has led to deforestation, erosion, nutrient loss, severe loss of animal habitat, increasing poverty, and the subjugation of family farmers to big international corporations.

Worse, the burning of forests to make room for crop fields is releasing so much carbon into the atmosphere that it negates the lower emissions of biofuels.[53]

Investment Opportunities

Of course, just because something doesn't make sense—like trying to run a nation of 210 million vehicles on biofuels—doesn't mean that it won't be attempted, or that there won't be profits made along the way.

The enormous federal subsidies for corn ethanol production—approximately $7 billion in 2006,[54] or the equivalent of $1.50 per gallon—combined with ever-increasing Renewable Fuel Standards, which mandate the production of increasing amounts of biofuels, ensure that there be a market for ethanol and biofuels, even if they're made from corn.

The Andersons (NASDAQ: ANDE) is the top producer of corn ethanol in the United States and is a good pure-play approach to betting on ethanol. Pacific Ethanol (NASDAQ: PEIX), VeraSun Energy (NYSE: VESA), and Aventine Renewable Energy (NYSE: AVR) are other popular ethanol stocks.

Companies that process grains are also good ways to play biofuels. Grain-processing giant Archer Daniels Midland Company (NYSE: ADM) controls about 20 percent[55] of U.S. ethanol production. SunOpta (NASDAQ: STKL) and MGP Ingredients (NASDAQ: MGPI) are also good choices for smaller stocks with broader markets, including organic foods.

Grain futures—even cropland!—are also ways to play the biofuel boom. In June 2007 wheat futures hit an all-time high, and corn futures hit their all-time high in February 2007 and then revisited those levels in June.[56] Likewise, the price of good Iowa farmland has reached new record highs for the past four years.

CHAPTER

9

ENDLESS ENERGY: HERE COMES THE SUN

I'd put my money on solar energy. . . . I hope we don't have to wait till oil and coal run out before we tackle that.

—Thomas Edison

Of all the energy sources available to us, the Sun is still our largest source by far, dropping 970 trillion kWh worth of free energy on us every day. Enough solar energy strikes the United States each day to supply its needs for one and a half years. The amount of solar energy striking the Earth every minute is greater than the amount of fossil fuel the world uses in a year![1]

In a sense, all energy forms on Earth come from the Sun.

As we have seen, all fossil fuels are the product of organic life-forms on Earth that ultimately drew their energy from the Sun. Algae and plants harvested their energy via photosynthesis, and after accumulating and being cooked for millennia, became the substances that we know today as oil, coal, gas, shales, tar sands, and so forth—what Thom Hartmann has called the "last hours of ancient sunlight."

Likewise, modern solar energy technologies harvest the Sun's energy waves. Photovoltaic (PV) cells make electricity from photosensitive materials that respond to the visible light spectra of sunlight. Solar thermal technologies, such as solar hot water systems and concentrating solar power (CSP) systems, directly capture heat from infrared light spectra.

Wind energy comes from the uneven heating of the planet as it spins through the day and night, being warmed and cooled by the Sun.

Hydropower depends on rain, which is the result of the Sun warming the surface of the planet and causing evaporation.

Even nuclear energy owes its origin to a long-dead sun somewhere. About 6.6 billion years ago, our uranium was formed in a supernova explosion—the colossal collapse of a star. The heat at the core of our planet is the result of uranium, thorium, and potassium decaying, causing convection and continental drift.

Therefore, even geothermal energy ultimately comes from a sun.

In fact, just about the only kind of energy we use that doesn't derive from the sun is tidal energy, which is generated by the gravitational pull of the moon.

A SHORT HISTORY OF SOLAR TECHNOLOGIES

Modern attempts to harvest the sun's energy directly date back to the 1870s, and the first known solar motor company was founded in 1900.

The first documented design was a concentrating solar power (CSP) device, which focuses the heat of the sun using lenses or mirrors to drive thermal engines or generators. In the 1870s, CSPs were used to drive steam engines, which in turn were used to do something else, usually pump water (although they were also used to make ice, in order to impress investors and astonish the public).

Today, CSP plants have been radically improved, and are already generating more than 354 megawatts of power in California alone. And when the sun isn't available, they can be switched over to run on natural gas.[2]

The most familiar kind of solar equipment is solar hot water systems, which provide domestic hot water and/or pool heating. Solar hot water experienced an explosion of popularity in the 1970s, thanks to generous federal and state incentives made available under the Carter administration. Unfortunately, the flood of money, directed at a less than fully developed technology and market, led to a Wild West atmosphere in much of the industry. A goodly number of badly made systems were installed, which functioned for a while and then quit, usually sitting ugly and useless on the roof for many years longer than they worked (if at all). The experience gave the solar industry a black eye, from which it has only recently begun to recover.

But recover it has, and how! Today's solar hot water equipment is dramatically improved, and well tested after three decades of experience in the field. With the return of rebates, tax credits, and other incentives, the solar hot water industry is experiencing a rebirth. In some areas, it is even a required part of the home's construction.

The next most common application of solar energy is photovoltaics (PV), in which photons of light are converted into electricity in a semiconductor, not unlike a computer chip. The first PV chip was made in 1883, using a semiconductor made of selenium and gold.

In 1954, the modern age of PV arrived, when Bell Lab engineers discovered—quite accidentally—that silicon doped with certain impurities was very sensitive to light. Since then, the technology has been steadily improved. Today's everyday silicon cells boast efficiencies as high as 24 percent, and the race for higher efficiency, lower cost, and greater durability is on.

The exponential growth of the market caught cell makers by surprise, and for the past three years the industry has suffered from shortages of refined silicon. But this only led to two things, both good for the business: First, the silicon refining and chip manufacturing segments received a big influx of investment to address the supply crisis. Second, it led to the accelerated development of thin-film solar cells, which can use no silicon at all and have the potential to be mass-produced for a fraction of the cost.

There is also a new breed of solar heating devices that are coming to market, which directly absorb the sun's radiation to heat air and water. They are most often used for large commercial buildings, such as hotels or breweries. One of the largest systems like this heats the million-gallon swimming pool built for the 1996 Atlanta Olympics, saving an estimated $12,000 per year.[3] However, innovative, small rooftop designs are also gaining popularity in the residential market, helping to heat homes passively and without greenhouse gas emissions.

THE SKY'S THE LIMIT

With the advent of higher oil and gas prices beginning around 2000, more consumers and businesses began looking for clean, green, domestic alternatives, causing a boom in the solar industry. Annual growth rates of 35 percent or more drove the global market to $11 billion and climbing.

But demand for solar power has actually been on a steady climb, growing about 25 percent every year for the past 15 years, and about 30 percent per year for the past three years. That's exponential growth!

In fact, in 2006 the growth rate of installed PV in the United States was a whopping 33 percent over the previous year,[4] and worldwide the increase was 50 percent. The growth of PV cells worldwide has been even greater: a six-fold rise since 2000, and 41 percent growth in 2006 alone.[5]

Even so, it currently accounts for less than 1 percent of worldwide electricity consumption. So the sky is the limit for the solar industry. Some estimates say it could produce as much as 20 percent of worldwide electricity consumption in as few as 35 years, which would be an amazing growth story.

What seems certain, however, is that China will become a dominant player in the solar arena. With its immense capacity to manufacture silicon-based electronics quickly and cheaply, making solar products is an easy reach for China. In 2006, China passed the United States to become the world's third largest producer of the cells, after Germany and Japan—the latter two being the two most solarized nations in the world.

And they're not done yet.

"To say that Chinese PV producers plan to expand production rapidly in the year ahead would be an understatement," said Travis Bradford, president of the Prometheus Institute, in May 2007. "They have raised billions from international IPOs to build capacity and increase scale with the goal of driving down costs. Four Chinese IPOs are expected to come to market this month alone."[6]

PHOTOVOLTAICS TAKES CENTER STAGE

Of the four types of solar energy systems, PV is by far the largest and has the most rapidly growing market. Three major factors are fueling the new solar energy boom: lower costs, improved performance, and grassroots momentum.

The latest figures show that global production of solar cells skyrocketed 45 percent in 2005, and players from every level are piling on.

Naturally, as the industry grows, costs are coming down.

The price of solar power has fallen to less than 4 percent of what it was in the 1970s.[7] It is already economically competitive in states where electricity is expensive, including Hawaii, Massachusetts, and New York, and states with good solar exposure and lots of land, like California, Nevada, and Arizona.[8]

As costs continue to drop for PV equipment, it is rapidly closing in on cost parity in all markets.

Production costs of PV solar cells are dropping 8 percent per year in Japan—currently the world's largest exporter of solar technology—and 5 percent per year in California.[9] In Japan, the cost of PV is now so low, and the equipment so ubiquitous, that the Japanese are phasing out their incentive program altogether—the most successful such program in the world.

In Germany, solar incentives are so attractive that PV makes good economic sense for anybody with a decent site. The guaranteed price paid to a solar generator by a utility is 54 to 57 cents per kWh, but the price of buying grid power is only 20 cents per kWh, so customers are effectively getting paid to install solar!

Consequently, their solar industry has been red-hot in recent years, consuming over half of the world's entire output of solar modules. Germany accounted for 960 megawatts of new installations in 2006, or 55 percent of the world's installations, where the United States installed only 140 megawatts, or 8 percent.[10]

We may assume that as the market there becomes saturated and costs continue to fall, Germany, like Japan, will be able to phase out its incentives altogether. At some point in the relatively near future, the solar industry there will be able to support itself, providing clean green and worry-free power at a price that is competitive with grid power generated from other sources.

The cost reductions of recent years are promising. When solar PV first started taking off in the 1970s, the price of a watt of capacity was around $20; in 2004 that had dropped to $2.70. Likewise, wind power has dropped from $2 per kWh to 5 to 8 cents now. With coal-fired power currently running about 2 to 4 cents per kWh, clean energy is rapidly closing the gap on dirty energy.[11]

In fact, according to a new study by the Worldwatch Institute in Washington, D.C., and the Prometheus Institute in Cambridge, Massachusetts, the cost of PV will decrease 40 percent by 2010, just two years from now![12]

Better Performance

At the same time as costs of PV are coming down, the technology itself is being improved.

Much of the energy absorbed by solar cells is wasted as heat, but recent research is dramatically improving PV efficiency.

Ten years ago, the best solar cells available had efficiency levels of only 12 to 15 percent (14 percent is generally considered the minimum profitable performance for standard silicon solar cells).[13] Today's commercially available solar cells are 14 to 24 percent efficient. And new, experimental multi-junction solar cells, which combine different types of photosensitive materials that respond to different wavelengths of light, have achieved efficiencies of up to 40 percent.[14]

That number is likely to climb even higher as big companies like BP, Solar World, and Applied Materials pour billions of dollars into solar research and development (R&D).

Applied Materials, the world's largest producer of chip-making equipment, sees a bright future for solar. CEO Mike Splinter estimates that the PV manufacturing equipment sector will triple from about $1 billion today to more than $3 billion by 2010. "I don't see any reason that Applied Materials can't capture between 15 percent and 20 percent of this total capex over that period, and grow a business that is profitable at $500 million," he says.[15] And the company's vice president, Dr. Charles Gay, wrote in a January 22 editorial, "In some regards the industry has reached a 'tipping point' where the demand, infrastructure, and number of manufacturers have reached a high enough level that makes large-scale production viable, and in fact facilitates still more growth."[16]

Silicon Solar

Traditional solar modules are made with photovoltaic cells made from silicon. The silicon is "grown" in ingots and either sliced into thin wafers to make monosilicon cells or sliced into thin chips that are then assembled into polysilicon cells.

Making solar cells is a very high-tech process, the first stages of which are essentially the same as for making computer chips. In furnaces, silicon is melted down and refined to 99.9999 percent purity so that it will make a good conductor.

Then the silicon is applied to a substrate to make a wafer. Traditional silicon solar cells are built up from layers of silicon wafers that have been doped with other substances, which is what causes them to produce electricity that can be harvested by a wire running through the cells.

Then the wafers must be baked in furnaces as hot as 1,350 degrees Centigrade. While they're baking, and then while being unloaded from the furnace, many factors must be carefully controlled: oxygen, moisture, and airborne particles.

The materials involved are delicate and must be handled carefully, the temperatures are dangerously high, and the whole process must be done in a "clean room" environment so the product will be free of any contaminants.

Consequently, making silicon solar cells is an expensive process, and one that can only produce relatively small batches of finished product for a relatively great expenditure of effort.

The PV industry used to rely on the scraps from the semiconductor (computer chip) industry for its feedstock, as it started to take off during a slump in the computer industry. But the latter's recovery has led to a chronic shortage of refined silicon for PV, which has led in turn to a shortage of solar modules in some parts of the world, particularly the United States.

The industry has responded, increasing global production of solar cells in 2006 by 33 percent over 2005, for a total of 2,204 megawatts. And the production of polysilicon increased by 16 percent.[17]

But another approach to the silicon shortage problem is to not use any at all. Indeed, because highly refined silicon is so expensive to make—about 45 percent of the cost of solar cells—that also represents the greatest potential for cutting the cost of PV.[18]

Thin Film Advances

So-called thin-film PV devices are based on other mixtures of elements—most notably copper indium gallium selenide (CIGS)—applied to plastic, even organic, substrates. Such innovations have the potential to make solar so cheap and cost-effective that it can be deployed anywhere, from the first world to the developing world. Already, Kenya buys more than 30,000 small panels each year for as little as $100 each.[19]

While thin-film solar is considerably cheaper than traditional polysilicon solar, it has also suffered from low efficiency. Most of the thin-film products brought to market in the past 10 years had only 4 to 5 percent efficiency—less than half that of their traditional counterparts—so they took up more than twice as much space to achieve the same output. If you wanted to use thin-film solar, you needed the same amount of money but twice the surface area—not a recipe for huge success.

But intensive research over the past two years or so is changing all that. Exciting innovations in PV are cropping up everywhere. Researchers in the Materials Sciences Division of Lawrence Berkeley National Laboratory recently made an unexpected discovery that could enable solar cells to convert the full spectrum of sunlight—from the near infrared to the far ultraviolet—into electricity.[20]

Some commercially available thin-film solar cells have achieved efficiency levels as high as 9 percent, putting them within competitive reach of traditional silicon modules but at a lower cost.

Other solar cell manufacturers such as Arise Technologies are taking a different approach, combining both traditional polysilicon and thin-film PV wafers in a hybrid cell with 18 percent efficiency—right at the top end for commercially available solar cells—and are actually bringing those products to market this year.

Another player in the thin-film space is Nansolar, a privately held Silicon Valley company that is building its first manufacturing plant, which will churn out a kind of solar foil in long rolls using a modified printing press. If successful at commercial scale, the process could slash PV production cost to one-tenth of what it is today, and on a rapid production line.[21]

The ultimate goal of this technology, however, is what is known as building integrated photovoltaics (BIPV), which incorporates PV directly into roofing and other materials, eliminating solar panels entirely. So BIPV modules not only produce power, but also function as a roofing membrane, just like composite asphalt shingles. Some models, like those made by Open Energy Corporation, integrate very well aesthetically with composite shingles, making the solar portion hardly noticeable.

Solar roofing tiles are already being installed on some new homes, but their popularity far exceeds their availability. However, with initiatives like California's Million Solar Roof campaign, which requires solar to be offered as a standard option for new homes, BIPV has a guaranteed market. Thanks to the steady demand outlook, manufacturers now have the green light and the confidence to invest the hundreds of millions of dollars it will take to scale up the production of BIPV modules to commercial levels.

GRASSROOTS MOMENTUM

With escalating energy costs, increasing environmental concerns, and a need to secure more energy options, many states haven't waited for the federal government to jump-start solar energy programs, opting to establish their own incentive programs instead.

It's a win-win-win: The states win because it means increasing their clean, green, local production, often a requirement of their renewable portfolio standards; consumers win, because they get tax breaks and the cost insurance of solar; and solar manufacturers win because the incentives provide the security of demand that is crucial to persuading a large electronics company to pony up a cool couple hundred mil for a new manufacturing plant.

California, New Jersey, and Pennsylvania have some of the strongest incentive programs in the country, and there are more than 20 states with their own incentive legislation in the works.[22] In August 2006, California governor Arnold Schwarzenegger signed legislation making solar panels a standard option for new-home buyers by 2011.[23] California has also joined

Germany and Japan in the hope of adding 3,000 megawatts of residential rooftop capacity by 2018.[24]

Corporate America has recognized the good economic sense of solar power and is making large investments for its corporate campuses. Rolling blackouts in 2001 quickly led Google, Microsoft, and Yahoo! to investigate solar energy as an option for powering large server installations.[25]

Google recently announced that it will build a 1.6-megawatt solar installation on its corporate campus—the largest on any corporate campus in the United States, and one of the largest on any corporate site in the world.

INVESTMENT OPPORTUNITIES

The solar PV sector has gotten quite crowded over the past five years or so, and now offers a good selection of investing candidates. A comprehensive treatment of them would be beyond the scope of our present purposes, but here is a small selection to begin your investing in this red-hot sector.

Amtech Systems (NASDAQ: ASYS) is a good choice for capitalizing on the shortage of refined silicon, because the company manufactures equipment for making semiconductors and solar cells. In 2007, it boasted an $18.2 million order backlog, including $9 million in solar orders alone.[26]

MEMC Electronic Materials, Inc. (NYSE: WFR) is a similar play on the silicon shortage, as it designs, manufactures, and sells silicon wafers. The company offers wafers in a variety of sizes and categories, and also sells "intermediate products, such as polysilicon, silane gas, partial ingots, and scrap wafers to semiconductor device and equipment makers, solar customers, flat panel and other industries."[27]

Energy Conversion Devices (NASDAQ: ENER) is a full-service energy solutions company serving the alternative energy generation, energy storage, and information technology markets. It holds nearly 1,000 patents in basic material compositions, product applications, and manufacturing processes, and has produced innovations in optical media, digital memory, solar energy, battery technology, and solid hydrogen storage. The company is truly a one-stop shop, offering design, engineering, installation, commissioning, maintenance, and financing, bringing their customers plug-and-play, custom, turnkey solutions. Energy Conversion Devices invented the nickel-metal hydride battery (and receives licensing fees on every such battery made today) and sells a popular thin-film, flexible, BIPV solar roofing membrane that has been attracting $100 million sized orders.

First Solar, Inc. (NASDAQ: FSLR) has fast become the solar darling of the stock market, rising steadily from its initial public offering (IPO) in

November 2006 at $28 to over $170 one year later. The company is a manufacturer of thin-film solar material, which it makes into low-cost solar modules on high-throughput, automated production lines that operate in one continuous flow, able to turn a panel of glass into a PV module in under three hours using a minimum of the semiconductor material. First Solar is currently building its third manufacturing plant, and has already signed long-term sales contracts to deliver 264 megawatts of its modules between 2009 and 2012 to customers who are eager to tie up their supplies in a red-hot, seller's market.

SunPower Corporation (NASDAQ: SPWR) is one of the oldest dedicated players in the solar PV game, but it's also one of the best solar companies in the country, with a high-quality product, hands-on installation experience, and vertically integrated manufacturing. SunPower's unique edge in the market is its A-300 solar cell. It's a high-performance, monocrystalline cell with a minimum 20 percent efficiency—as much as 50 percent more power per square foot than conventional solar cells, making it the highest-efficiency commercially available solar cell on the market. With a stock price that has more than doubled in the past year and a $5 billion market capitalization, SunPower has become a true blue-chip investment in the solar sector.

Akeena Solar, Inc. (NASDAQ: AKNS) is a decent play on the PV installation market. Akeena targets the residential and small commercial market segments, which account for about 65 percent of the U.S. PV market. The company offers a full suite of solutions for those grid-tied segments, including systems with or without battery or generator backup, and a variety of monitoring systems. With 86 percent revenue growth from 2005 to 2006 and expectations of another 125 percent growth in 2007, this is an aggressive company that should return good rewards for the speculative investor.

Open Energy Corporation (OTC: OEGY) is a small speculative solar stock, a micro-cap with a stock priced under a buck. But don't let that fool you. Open Energy has been landing million-dollar deal after million-dollar deal to supply builders with its SolarSave® Roofing Tile. This BIPV solar module not only produces power, it is also a strong and durable roofing membrane and blends in so well with regular composite asphalt shingles that you can hardly tell the difference between them when installed side by side. Open Energy has been striking key marketing and distribution agreements with top solar gear distributors, builders, and roofing product manufacturers, something that other solar manufacturers with BIPV products have so far been unable to do in any significant way. Open Energy seems poised to become a major player in the nascent BIPV sector.

Xantrex Technologies (TSE: XTX) designs, manufactures, and sells inverters, the components of energy systems that transform raw direct current (DC) power generated by systems like wind turbines and solar PV arrays into high-quality alternating current (AC) power, which they can feed back onto the grid. With a $340 million market capitalization, it's a good-sized and stable company whose products should continue to enjoy high demand for many years to come.

CHAPTER

10

PRESSURE COOKER: TAPPING THE EARTH'S HEAT

The peak of oil and gas discoveries came during the 1960s and this must be followed by a peak in production. While some believe that we are already at the peak at 85 million barrels per day (mbpd), industry experts consistently express doubts of ever getting above 100 mbpd, which is forecast to happen within the next decade. If steps are not taken to manage demand, it will soon outstrip supply and a return to the scenes during the oil crises of the 1970s can be expected. . . . We must reduce our demand and develop our rich natural and sustainable energy resources.

—COLIN CAMPBELL

Geothermal power—using the enormous heat generated in the earth's core by the radioactive decay of unstable elements—could prove to be the cleanest, greenest, and most abundant source of energy we have ever used. Literally beneath our feet is a white-hot, seething mass of magma that generates temperatures of up to 9,000 degrees Fahrenheit.

Geothermal energy is so sustainable that the first modern site, established in Lardarello, Italy, in 1904, is still producing power.[1] The existing plant has been in operation since 1913, interrupted only once: by a World War II bomb.[2]

The potential is absolutely enormous. According to a 2006 study by the Massachusetts Institute of Technology (MIT), there are over 100 *million* quads of accessible geothermal energy worldwide—when the entire worldwide consumption of energy is only 400 quads. That's enough to meet the world's total current energy needs for 30,000 years!

The recoverable share of that heat energy found beneath American soil alone is 13 million quads—the power equivalent of 149 million Titan II nuclear warheads, or 130,000 times our current annual energy consumption![3] There are more than 100 undeveloped known sites with good geothermal potential in the United States alone.

The MIT scenario is based on the use of *universal geothermal* technology, which is simply to drill two holes at least 10 kilometers down into hard rock and fracture the rock between them. Then water is pumped down one hole and harvested as steam when it comes back up the other, which in turn is used to power a turbine. Such facilities could be built almost anywhere in the world, since the heat is available at those depths worldwide.[4]

And on the extreme technology end of the geothermal energy spectrum, a consortium of utility companies in Iceland hopes to drill more than four kilometers (2.5 miles) into the earth's crust. They hope to tap much hotter steam, heated by magma to temperatures as high as 870° Fahrenheit—harder to handle, but far richer in energy.[5]

Even better, at a cost of about 5 cents per kWh,[6] it typically costs about half as much as grid utility power. What's more, the average geothermal power plant produces electricity 90 percent of the time, compared with 65 percent to 75 percent for coal- and nuclear-powered plants.

WHAT IS GEOTHERMAL POWER?

Geothermal power literally uses the heat inside the earth to generate electricity or heat facilities. So-called geothermal heat pumps, such as are commonly used in residential or commercial buildings, use similar principles but at a much smaller and shallower scale.

Although geothermal energy is experiencing a relatively recent resurgence, it's hardly new. It has been powering the United States since 1922,[7] and currently produces 65 percent more power there than solar and wind *combined*.[8] Yet despite its commercial success since 1960,[9] geothermal's full potential is just starting to be tapped by a few visionary companies.

The reservoirs of steam and hot water that make large-scale geothermal generation possible are primarily located in the western states, Alaska, Hawaii, and other parts of the Pacific Rim's "Ring of Fire."[10] But geothermal heat pumps and direct-use applications can tap earth energy almost anywhere.

In a traditional geothermal plant, steam or superheated water from deep inside the earth is used to drive a turbine and generate electricity.

The designs typically come in two flavors: steam plants and binary plants.

- *Steam*—Steam plants use steam and hot water resources (generally, hotter than 300 degrees Fahrenheit). Either the steam comes directly from the source or extremely hot, high-pressure water is depressurized (flashed) to produce steam. The steam then turns the turbines, which drive generators that produce electricity. Currently, energy produced this way costs about 4 to 6 cents per kWh and produces nearly 50 times less carbon dioxide, nitric oxide, and sulfur emissions than traditional fossil-fuel power plants.

- *Binary*—Binary plants use lower-temperature hot water resources (between 100 degrees Fahrenheit and 300 degrees Fahrenheit). The hot water is passed through a heat exchanger in conjunction with a secondary fluid with a lower boiling point (usually an organic fluid like Freon). The second fluid vaporizes, which turns the turbines that drive the generators. The secondary fluid is recycled through the heat exchanger.[11]

Let's take a look at these designs more closely in Figure 10.1.

With a traditional plant, a geothermal well is drilled, typically 5,000 to 10,000 feet deep, in order to access water that has trickled down through cracks in the earth's crust and collected in subterranean reservoirs, where it is heated by magma from the earth's core and becomes superheated steam (usually over 500 degrees Fahrenheit).

After the steam has spent its energy driving the turbines, it is reinjected into the geothermal reservoir to be reheated and used again.

With proper management of a geothermal resource, it can be made truly renewable.

But more modern binary cycle plants use a working fluid (usually an organic compound like Freon) to transfer the heat between the earth and the plant, as shown in Figure 10.2.

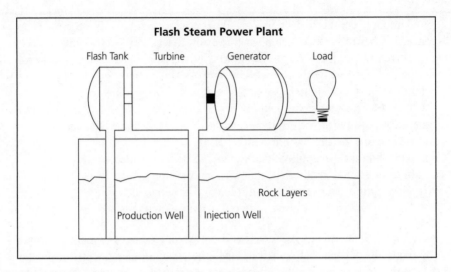

FIGURE 10.1   *Geothermal Flash Plant*

Source: U.S. Department of Energy, Energy Efficiency and Renewable Energy,
http://www.!eere.energy.gov/geothermal/powerplants.html#flashstream.

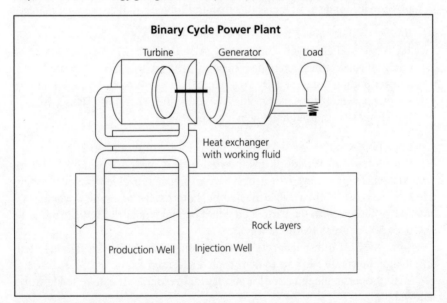

FIGURE 10.2   *Geothermal Binary Cycle Plant*

Source: U.S. Department of Energy, Energy Efficiency and Renewable Energy,
http://www.!eere.energy.gov/geothermal/powerplants.html#flashstream.

Binary cycle plants have the advantage of being able to harvest heat from a dry hole or from a lower-temperature source.

BENEFITS OF GEOTHERMAL POWER

Geothermal power holds several advantages over other forms of renewable energy, and many advantages over fossil fuels:

- Advanced geothermal generators have no emissions, not even steam. They make no smog, no toxic chemicals, and no waste. They're *clean.*

- They're tiny. The PureCycle® units made by United Technologies generate 225 kilowatts of power in an 11'×17' footprint—about one-tenth the footprint of solar photovoltaic (PV) for the same power output.

- They have minimal aesthetic impact. Units that harvest heat from hot underground water sources and reinject it back into the ground can be very low-profile.

- They use no fuel, because they provide all their own power.

- They run at 95 to 99 percent uptime, making them perfect for base-load utility generation, or power generation that's on all the time. That's the kind of generation that is normally provided by coal-fired and nuclear plants, because they're so hard to start up and shut down.

- The supply of geothermal energy is virtually inexhaustible.

In addition to the benefits, however, geothermal power also has some risks. The up-front investment required to start up a geothermal facility is very high, and the risk of the system's underproducing is nontrivial, so rounding up financing and power purchase agreements (PPAs) and mitigating the investment risk are key issues for geothermal developers. There are also some concerns that geothermal projects may be responsible for stimulating small earthquakes. However, on the whole, we believe that as the technology improves, and the industry gains a broader base of experience, these issues will be worked out.

EXPLOSIVE GROWTH

Utilities and independent developers have been researching and testing methods of producing electricity from geothermal energy for more than four decades at dozens of unique geothermal sites in California, Utah, and Nevada, but it has never been a big-money business. Now, after languishing for decades, geothermal power is once again catching fire, thanks to the twin challenges of peak oil and global warming.

In fact, according to a May 2007 survey by the Geothermal Energy Association (GEA), the installed capacity of geothermal power in the United States is set to nearly double. In addition to the 2,851 megawatts of geothermal capacity we have today, another 2,500 to 2,900 megawatts of capacity is currently under consideration or development in 12 states: Alaska, Arizona, California, Hawaii, Idaho, Nevada, New Mexico, Oregon, Texas, Utah, Washington, and Wyoming. That would be enough to supply the needs of 6 million households.[12]

"New federal and state initiatives to promote geothermal energy are paying off," commented Karl Gawell, GEA's executive director. "State renewable standards coupled with the federal production tax credit are creating a renaissance in U.S. geothermal power production," he added.

The United States is already the world's largest producer of geothermal energy, with 209 plants currently in operation and more coming online soon. But the industry is only just getting started. Currently production is limited to just five states—Alaska, California, Hawaii, Nevada, and Utah—and supplies only 0.37 percent of the nation's electricity.[13]

The main driver of geothermal energy's new life is renewed federal support. The Energy Policy Act of 2005 provided a full production tax credit, and increased funding and support from federal agencies such as the Department of Energy (DOE) and the Bureau of Land Management (BLM) have been instrumental in clearing the way for new geothermal projects.

The big money has smelled the opportunity, and now they're jumping in.

In May 2007, Merrill Lynch announced that it had made a $35 million investment in Vulcan Power Co., a private company and one of the largest geothermal property holders in the United States. "We believe that an investment in Vulcan is critical to accelerate development of geothermal resources that benefit the environment," said Rob Jones, the head of the Merrill global energy and power group.

But that's just the first round. In total, Vulcan intends to raise $150 million to develop some 900 megawatts' worth of geothermal energy from its portfolio. It hasn't even broken ground, and it already has buyers for the power. The company has announced 20-year power purchase agreements with Nevada Power Co., Pacific Gas & Electric Co., and Southern California Edison Co. for the project.

But the geothermal renaissance isn't limited to the United States. Geothermal power plants are springing up all across the globe.

Italy, Japan, Mexico, New Zealand, Indonesia, Nicaragua, and Russia are now using geothermal power to produce electricity and are aggressively increasing their capacity—by as much as 10 percent in the past five years alone. Iceland and the Philippines have gone even further, using it to satisfy a whopping 20 percent of their national power needs, with plans to bring much more online. China and India are devoting significant support to the technology as well, recognizing the limits of their other options.

INVESTMENT OPPORTUNITIES

There are currently only a small handful of publicly traded companies that are primarily focused on geothermal power—but they're hot!

Ormat

One of the best plays on the U.S. geothermal industry is Nevada-based Ormat Technologies (NYSE: ORA), which generates about 360 megawatts between six U.S. plants and four foreign plants.[14]

Ormat has more than doubled in value since its IPO in November 2004, skyrocketing 143 percent in just two years.[15]

Geothermal deals in the United States, Guatemala, Nicaragua, and the Philippines have also boosted Ormat's parent company, Ormat Industries Inc., which is listed in Tel Aviv. In the past 12 months, shares of Ormat Industries gained about 48 percent (in the same period, the Tel Aviv Stock Exchange's benchmark TA-25 index gained only 14 percent).[16]

Ormat added 51 megawatts of new capacity in 2006,[17] and expected to add up to 80 megawatts of U.S. capacity in 2007. Starting in 2008, that number will increase to 100 megawatts of capacity per year as regulations in more than 25 states require U.S. utilities to buy more power from renewable sources.[18] The company currently has 250 megawatts of new production under construction and development.[19]

In addition, Ormat recently won a bid to build the world's largest geothermal plant in Indonesia, a $600 million plant capable of generating 340 megawatts that will come online in about five years.[20]

Ormat has even adapted its geothermal technologies to capture waste heat from manufacturing plants and other facilities. Sales in this new recovered energy power generation (REG) market totaled $9.2 million in the first half of 2006, up from $600,000 the year before.[21]

Raser Technologies

Some of the most exciting developments in the geothermal industry are coming from Raser Technologies (NYSE: RZ), a $618 million company that is revitalizing the industry.

Raser's is a twofold "wells to wheels" strategy.

One side of the business focuses on components to power cars. The Symetron™ electromagnetic motor system, designed for use in hybrid cars, got the Frost & Sullivan 2006 Technology Innovation of the Year Award.

The Symetron system is an AC induction motor that can function as both the alternator and the starter. It's only four inches long, weighs a lightweight 66 pounds, and can deliver 64 horsepower with a 170 lb/ft torque to move the car—a lot of punch in a small package.

When functioning as a generator, it delivers a whopping 20 kilowatts of power, enough to recharge the car's lithium-ion batteries and still run all the accessories.

The company believes that the increased power, lower cost per kilowatt, high torque, and high reliability of the Symetron motor can help make plug-in hybrids an economical reality for millions of drivers. That makes it what the Frost & Sullivan analysts called a "disruptive technology," something that can really change the paradigm of transportation. Raser has been hard at work getting the system ready for mass production and striking partnerships with key players to manufacture it.

The other side of the business generates the power to run those cars most of the time from geothermal power. Using a variety of licensed technologies and binary cycle generator units made by United Technologies Corporation (NYSE: UTX), Raser is in hot pursuit of the geothermal potential of the West.

The unique advantage of United Technologies' geothermal generators is that they can harvest some usable heat from relatively low-temperature heat sources—as low as 165 degrees, depending on the site. This temperature range was previously unusable for the geothermal generators of the past, which needed a heat source of at least 500 degrees.

Such generators can even use waste heat from other industrial processes as their heat source, or use tapped-out oil and gas wells to access the heat below. Deploying units in such locations can be immensely profitable due to the very low start-up cost.

These generators are basically overgrown refrigerators running in reverse. "The organic Rankine cycle-based power system is an advanced binary cycle system that is driven by a simple evaporation process and is entirely enclosed, which means it produces no emissions," according to a Raser press release.

Essentially, they take about 30 to 40 degrees from the hot side (such as a hot hole in the ground) and dissipate it to the cool side (using an air-cooled heat exchanger on the surface), turning a turbine as they do so. The turbine spins as the refrigerant fluid cycles through the system and is heated and cooled. It's the temperature differential between the two sides that makes the system work. So even if you have to dissipate the heat with an air-cooled system in the hot desert sun, as long as the temperature of the heat source is at least 140 degrees hotter, you're good to go.

At night, when it's cold outside but still toasty underground, these generators really perform, pumping out their best power precisely when solar panels are nonfunctional.

Put one of these units next to another industrial operation—say, a smelter or a paper mill—where you've got a lot of waste heat being generated, and dissipate it to, for example, a shallow, cold underground aquifer, and you're basically harvesting free energy. You're making use of otherwise wasted Btus while doing no harm to the environment.

Raser's growth potential is enormous. Its goal is to build geothermal generating capacity at the rate of 100 megawatts per year for the next three years. That's equivalent to about 4 percent of the entire current U.S. geothermal generating capacity, every year, just by one company. Raser has been buying up leases left and right for the past few years, and now holds leases on 34,000 acres in Utah and additional acreage in Nevada. A report Raser did in March 2007 showed that just one of the leased properties in Nevada could potentially support 300 to 500 megawatts of power generation—again, in a relatively tiny footprint.

U.S. Geothermal Inc.

An aggressive, development-stage geothermal company, U.S. Geothermal (OTC: UGTH) is buying up geothermal leases voraciously in the American West. With $12 million in cash, $22 million in total assets, and no debt,[22] the company is poised to become a major player in the geothermal boom. The stock has tripled in price over the past year, but it's still very much under the radar.

U.S. Geothermal has been acquiring not only potential geothermal resources, but also existing developed but long-forgotten sites that are much more usable with today's technology. The company has contracts to sell 10 megawatts of its clean, green electricity, and is negotiating the sale of an additional 26 megawatts. But this is just the beginning. According to the Department of Energy, the projected capacity from just one of the sites is as high as 1,000 megawatts.

United Technologies Corporation

United Technologies Corporation (NYSE: UTX) makes the high-efficiency binary cycle turbines that Raser uses, so it is, technically speaking, a way to invest in energy. However, the company is a giant industrial conglomerate (including such recognizable names as Otis, Carrier, Pratt & Whitney, and Hamilton Sundstrand), whose business is far more weighted to aerospace and the building industry than it is to geothermal energy.

CHAPTER

NUCLEAR'S SECOND ACT

The ease with which we all lived in the last 50 years, with cheap energy, is coming to a close. The next 50 years cannot be like the last 50 years. . . . The oil demand-and-supply equation now constantly flirts with crisis. Americans need to develop a sense of privilege rather than entitlement when it comes to energy use.

—John Hofmeister

At the dawn of the nuclear age, industry proponents claimed that nuclear power would solve all of humanity's energy problems forever, by making power that was "too cheap to meter."

Unfortunately, it hasn't quite worked out that way.

But to understand why, we must understand something about the nature of uranium itself.

Uranium is a very common element, found in about the same abundance as tin worldwide, in everything from granite to seawater. Almost all—99.3 percent—of the uranium found on Earth is uranium-238, an isotope of uranium containing

238 protons per atom. The remaining uranium—0.7 percent—is uranium-235, and that's what is used as fuel for our "light water" nuclear reactors.[1]

In a light water reactor, a chain reaction causes the fission (breaking apart) of the nuclei of the uranium-235 atoms, which generates an enormous amount of heat. (Some of the uranium-238 atoms also contribute, by converting to plutonium-239, of which about half is consumed in the process.) The heat is used to turn water into steam, which is then used to turn a turbine and generate electricity. Water is used as a moderator that slows down the neutrons in the nucleus sufficiently to support the chain reaction.

The most common type of nuclear plant today, and the ones currently being planned, are pressurized water reactors, which use pressurized water as a coolant and neutron moderator. This type of reactor is generally considered to be the safest and most reliable.

In the early days of nuclear energy, it was assumed that the industry would quickly move beyond simple water reactors and develop *breeder* reactors, which can use the far more abundant uranium-238. Breeder reactors are so called because they generate more fuel than they consume, by neutron irradiation of uranium-238 and thorium-232. With breeder reactors, the initial fuel charge is gradually consumed and then the reactor runs on the fuel it has generated itself. Breeder reactors are cooled by liquid metal (such as sodium or lead) and have the advantage of being able to use depleted uranium-238 and uranium formerly used in weapons as fuel.[2]

After it is used, the fuel must be taken out of a breeder reactor and reprocessed in order to be reused. In this step, it is conceivable that some plutonium could be diverted from the reprocessing and fall into the hands of illicit weapons builders, which is why breeder reactors have aroused fresh fears of terrorists armed with nukes.

Although reprocessing spent fuel is the foundation of France's robust nuclear energy program, concerns about safety, nuclear weapons proliferation, and economics have halted nuclear fuel reprocessing in the United States for over 30 years.[3]

There are actually dozens of different types of nuclear reactors, each with its own fuel needs, pros and cons. But all commercial nuclear reactors in use today are either water reactors or some type of fast breeder reactor.[4]

NUCLEAR POTENTIAL

The first commercial nuclear power stations started operation in the 1950s. Today, there are 435 commercial nuclear reactors operating in 30 countries, providing 370,000 megawatts of capacity—that's 6.2 percent of the total energy produced worldwide, or about 16 percent of the world's base-load electricity.[5]

Sixteen countries derive at least one-quarter of their electricity from nuclear power. France and Lithuania are the most dependent on it, deriving around three-quarters of their power from nuclear energy.[6]

The United States supplies more commercial nuclear power than any other nation in the world, and currently has 104 commercial nuclear generating units licensed to operate,[7] which constitute 11.5 percent of the nation's energy needs.[8]

Because nuclear power offers the tantalizing potential of generating a great deal of energy from a relatively small amount of material without creating greenhouse gases (if one ignores the emissions that went into plant construction and mining the ores), an unlikely alliance of everyone from energy industry players to green hawks to environmentalists have recently come out in support of nuclear energy. By rapidly scaling up our usage of nuclear power, they argue, we could significantly reduce our use of coal and natural gas. For example, it has been suggested that 100 new nuclear plants could drive a hydrogen transportation infrastructure for the UK.[9]

There is no question that the demand outlook is challenging. According to the Energy Information Administration (EIA)'s *International Energy Outlook 2007*, world electricity generation will need to nearly double from 2004 to 2030.[10] Can nuclear energy meet that massively surging demand?

CHINA AND NUCLEAR POWER

China is building nuclear plants at a breakneck pace—in part, to reduce its carbon footprint.

China's leaders have long been aware of the environmental damage caused by its rapid industrialization, and have debated how to deal with the issue for years. But nuclear power has emerged with consensus support.

"Our irrational energy structure is causing serious pollution and greenhouse problems," says Gu Zhongmao, a professor at the China Institute of Atomic Energy, a government-affiliated research center. For China, he adds, "nuclear power is regarded as a clean energy."

Accordingly, China has announced plans to spend $50 billion to build 32 nuclear plants by 2020. But experts from China's leading technical university, Tsinghua University, say they could build as many as 300 more by the middle of the century—about the same as the total nuclear generating capacity in the world today.

To secure fuel for all those new reactors, Chinese Premier Wen Jiabao has recently struck supply deals with Australia and Niger. This has contributed to a rapidly escalating worldwide demand for uranium, helping to drive the price of processed uranium ore from $10 a pound in 2003 to $120 in 2007.[11]

LIMITS TO NUCLEAR POWER

How realistic would such an expansion of nuclear power be?

According to the EIA's *International Energy Outlook 2007*, nuclear power will remain a bit player. Figure 11.1 illustrates the EIA's projection.

The long lead times for nuclear plants, plus their high cost of construction and fuel production, necessarily limit their future. Coal and natural gas, despite their environmental consequences, are far easier, faster, and cheaper to build, so the EIA is probably correct in this forecast.

An April 2007 study by Charles D. Ferguson of the Council on Foreign Relations, "Nuclear Energy: Balancing Benefits and Risks," sees some inherent limits to the industry for the usual litany of reasons:

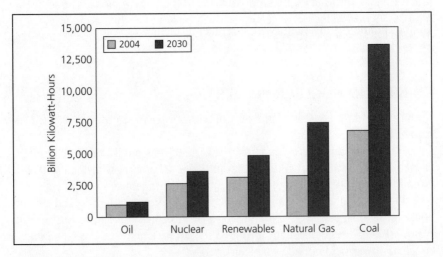

FIGURE 11.1   *World Electricity Generation by Fuel, 2004 and 2030*

Sources: www.eia.doe.gov/oiaf/ieo/pdf/electricity.pdf. 2004: Derived from Energy Information Administration (EIA), *International Energy Annual 2004* (May–July 2006), www.eia.doe.gov/iea. 2030: EIA, *System for the Analysis of Global Energy Markets* (2007).

Nuclear energy is not a major part of the solution to further countering global warming or energy insecurity. Expanding nuclear energy use to make a relatively modest contribution to combating climate change would require constructing nuclear power plants at a rate so rapid as to create shortages in building materials, trained personnel, and safety controls.[12]

Shortages in building materials and skilled labor—the same limits that face the oil and gas industries.

Of course, the most prominent limit to the nuclear power industry is NIMBYism. It's nearly impossible, at least in the United States, to find any community willing to host a new nuclear plant or a nuclear waste storage site.

The last reactor built in the United States was ordered nearly four decades ago, took three decades to approve and build, and became operational in 1996. That's a very long lead time. Even if the political will can be mustered to grease the skids for new plants, it's hard to imagine that lead time being shortened by much, if at all, as environmental review requirements and community resistance are greater now than they were then.

Then there is the problem of just maintaining our current nuclear capacity. Of the 104 reactors currently operating in the United States, many are approaching the end of their intended life spans. Even with 20-year extensions of their planned life spans, all existing reactors will be decommissioned by the middle of this century. Just replacing them will require building two reactors a year for the next 50 years—in itself a dubious prospect.[13]

There are serious questions about how much we can expand global nuclear capacity as well. A 2007 paper by leading researchers the Oxford Research Group estimates that over the next 25 years, capacity is actually set to decrease. As in the United States, many of the world's 429 currently operational reactors are nearing the end of their lives and must be replaced just to maintain current capacity. (But the nuclear share of the total energy mix would actually decrease, because electricity demand is expected to rise 50 percent.) However, the replacement reactors aren't forthcoming: There are only 25 new nuclear reactors currently being built, with 76 more planned and another 162 proposed but hardly certain. Even if all of them materialized in the next 25 years, we'd still be nearly 40 percent shy of just replacing all of today's reactors.[14]

Peak Uranium?

From a practical standpoint, we may be past the global peak of uranium production as well.

Gerald Grandey, the president and CEO of Cameco Corporation, the largest uranium producer in the United States, believes that demand for uranium will exceed supply for the next eight or nine years, forcing utilities to depend on inventories for fissionable fuel rather than new production. In a June 2007 press conference, he indicated that he expects demand to grow at 3 percent annually for the next decade, but doesn't see uranium mining being able to keep pace with demand. Nor does he see much in the way of opportunity to acquire smaller producers in order to increase his company's output: "There isn't a whole lot out there to acquire that's meaningful," he said.[15]

This is a complex topic, but essentially, like coal, uranium comes down to a question of energetics. Only the highest-quality ores are net energy positive when used in a typical fission reactor.

According to independent nuclear analyst Jan Willem Storm van Leeuwen, when the Uranium-235 content of the ore is under 0.02 percent, more energy is required to mine and refine the uranium than can be captured from it in a nuclear reactor, so it's not worth doing.

In a 2002 paper by van Leeuwen and Philip Smith, "Can Nuclear Power Provide Energy for the Future; Would It Solve the CO_2-Emission Problem?" the authors predict that the diminishing availability of high-grade uranium ores will pose a hard limit to the future growth of nuclear energy: "Another way of putting it is to say that if all of the electrical energy used today were to be obtained from nuclear power, all known useful reserves of uranium would be exhausted in less than three years."[16]

Naturally, as they are consumed, the world's reserves of high-grade ore are dropping. The vast majority of the remaining uranium, and the largest deposits of it, have ore grades lower than 0.1 percent. That is 100 to 1,000 times poorer a fuel than the ore used today, making it uneconomical to mine.[17] (See Figure 11.2.)

As the chart shows, van Leeuwen estimates that at current rates of consumption—again, not accounting for the expected massive upscaling of nuclear energy usage—high-grade uranium ore will last only to about 2034, and nuclear energy will become a net energy loser by 2070.[18]

The remaining sources of uranium, from lower-quality ores to seawater, are ultimately net energy losers because it takes so much energy from fossil fuels to mine and produce the fissionable material that it would be pointless to use those fuels for mining and processing uranium to drive a reactor. It would be far better just to burn them.

The Oxford Research Group paper supports the conclusion that there are adequate reserves of high-grade uranium ores for only about another 25 years of operation, and that any increases beyond that point will have to come from breeder reactors, which primarily use the much more abundant plutonium for fuel.[19]

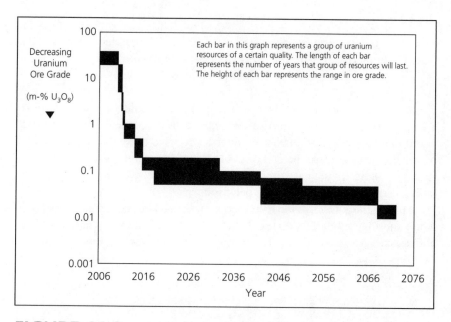

FIGURE 11.2   *Uranium Ore Grade, 2006–2076*

Source: Energy Watch Group, "Uranium Resources and Nuclear Energy," December 2006.

A 2006 study by the Energy Watch Group (EWG) of Germany (the same group that did the coal report), "Uranium Resources and Nuclear Energy," indicates that even under the best-case estimates of uranium resources, production will peak before 2050, and that's assuming today's relatively minuscule rate of use.[20] Increase the rate of use, or use a less optimistic reserve number, and that date comes in quickly.

The EWG study's conclusion was sobering:

> *The analysis of data on uranium resources leads to the assessment that discovered reserves are not sufficient to guarantee the uranium supply for more than thirty years.*

> *Eleven countries have already exhausted their uranium reserves. In total, about 2.3 Mt of uranium have already been produced. At present only one country (Canada) is left having uranium deposits containing uranium with an ore grade of more than 1%, most of the remaining reserves in other countries have ore grades below 0.1%, and two-thirds of reserves have ore grades below 0.06%.[21]*

The Energy Watch Group estimates that the uranium peak would be around 2025 for "probable reserves" and 2030 for "possible reserves,"[22] the latter being more or less in line with van Leeuwen's estimate.

Figure 11.3 is their chart of possible reserves—in other words, their best-case scenario.

As shocking as this projection is, the reality could be worse. EWG's assumptions about the rate of use were based on the nuclear plants and uranium mining operations currently in existence, plus those that were planned or under construction at the end of 2006. But if the ambitions of government leaders to radically increase nuclear-generating capacity are realized, then the rate of use will be higher, and the peak sooner.

Finally, the authors of the EWG report note that alternative reactor designs won't substantively affect their calculation, saying, "At least within this time horizon, neither nuclear breeding reactors nor thorium reactors will play a

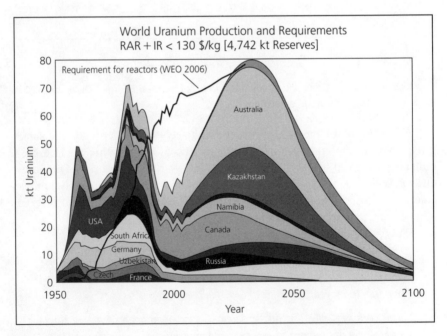

FIGURE 11.3 *Future Production Profile of Uranium—All "Possible Reserves"*

Source: Energy Watch Group, "Uranium Resources and Nuclear Energy," December 2006. EWG Series No. 1/2006. www.lbst.de/publications/studies__e/2006/EWG-paper_ 1-06_Uranium-Resources-Nuclear-Energy_03DEC2006.pdf.

significant role because of the long lead times for their development and market penetration."[23]

Nuclear energy has other challenges, too, besides the availability of uranium. The true cost of building nuke plants, from planning all the way through decommissioning, is never accounted for, nor paid, by the operators of the plants. The decommissioning costs are invariably externalized, or foisted onto the public. And we have yet to deal with the past 60 years' worth of toxic spent fuel, some quarter of a million tons of it, now scattered around the globe. Once all of those costs are taken into account, nuclear energy may in fact be a net energy loser.

Security Risks of Breeder Reactors

Due to the depletion of high-grade uranium ores, the nuclear industry plans to use a combination of uranium from spent uranium fuel and plutonium dioxide (MOX fuel) to power future nuclear reactors.

Newer designs for nuke plants, such as breeder reactors and thorium cycle reactors, offer some hope for reusing spent fuel from fission reactors and military applications. However, they are also questionable from a net cost standpoint, and in any case large-scale commercial deployment of those technologies is, as EWG noted, unlikely or at least far off in the future.

However, this raises the concern of security risks, because MOX fuel can be used to create nuclear weapons.[24]

The Oxford Research Group also warned that the proliferation of breeder reactors will drastically increase the global production of weapons-grade plutonium, and possibly set the stage for a dangerous new proliferation of nuclear weapons, including small nuclear weapons suitable for terrorist purposes.

> *According to the UN's International Atomic Energy Agency, within 30–40 years at least 30 countries are likely to have access to fissile materials from their civil nuclear power programmes that can be used for nuclear weapons and competent nuclear physicists and engineers who could design and fabricate them. . . . The question is whether in the 21st century the security risks associated with civil nuclear power can be managed, or not? Society has to decide whether or not the risks of proliferation and nuclear terrorism in a world with many nuclear power reactors are acceptable.*[25]

INVESTMENT OPPORTUNITIES

According to uranium analyst Keith Kohl of the Energy and Capital newsletter, uranium mines are currently producing only 62 percent of the global demand, with the rest coming from sources such as government stockpiles, used reactor fuel that has been reprocessed, and uranium from nuclear weapons and depleted uranium stockpiles.

However, within a few years we'll have worked our way through the stockpile of uranium from old nukes, and new uranium production will have to make up the difference. Since new uranium production can't meet our current demand, Kohl anticipates much higher prices for uranium in the next few years—possibly as high as $500 a pound, up from the current $135. He believes it will break $255 a pound by 2008.[26]

Uranium prices are now just off their historic high, having pulled back from a recent meteoric charge for the stars. Figure 11.4 is a price chart from 1987 to the present.

How to capitalize on this spike in prices?

Unlike oil, gas, and most other commodities, uranium does not trade on an open market. Instead, buyers and sellers negotiate contracts privately, and prices are tracked by independent market consultants such as Ux Consulting.

Fortunately, there are several equities that make fine candidates:

Cameco Corporation (NYSE: CCJ) is the world's largest uranium producer, accounting for 20 percent of world production from its mines in Canada and the United States. The company claims 500 million pounds of proven and probable reserves, extensive resources, and premier positions in the world's most promising areas for uranium exploration in Canada and Australia. Cameco

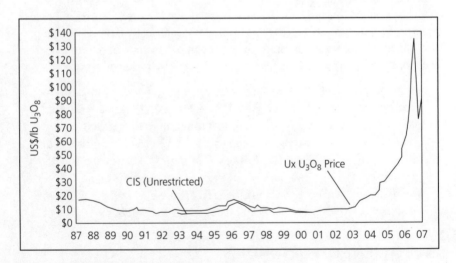

FIGURE 11.4 *Ux U_3O_8 vs. CIS Prices*

Source: The Ux Consulting Company, LLC, www.uxc.com/review/uxc_g_hist-price.html.

also processes fuel for nuclear power plants. Although the flooding of its Cigar Lake project in Saskatchewan in October 2006 caused a major sell-off in its stock, it still maintains a commanding position in the uranium market.

USEC Inc. (NYSE: USU) is a global energy company that supplies low enriched uranium (LEU) to about 150 nuclear power plants worldwide. It is also a provider of nuclear energy solutions and services, specializing in design, fabrication, and implementation of spent nuclear fuel technologies; nuclear materials transportation; and nuclear fuel cycle consulting services. USEC also does nuclear nonproliferation work for the U.S. government and contract work for the U.S. Department of Energy.[27]

Uranerz Energy Corp. (AMEX: URZ) is a micro-cap exploration-stage company engaged in the acquisition, exploration, and development of uranium properties. It owns interests in properties in the prolific Power River Basin area of Wyoming, as well as properties in Saskatchewan and Mongolia.

CHAPTER

12

WHAT'S NEEDED: A MANHATTAN PROJECT FOR ENERGY

We need an energy bill that encourages consumption.

—President George W. Bush

Conservation may be a sign of personal virtue but it is not a sufficient basis for a sound, comprehensive energy policy.

—Vice President Dick Cheney

According to the International Energy Agency (IEA), the world will need to make an estimated $16 trillion worth of investment in the energy sector for 2003–2030 in order to keep pace with anticipated demand and the decline of existing energy sources. In Europe alone, some €500 billion worth of investment will be needed to upgrade the electricity transmission and distribution infrastructure.[1]

Some have referred to the need for a comprehensive plan in response to peak oil as a Manhattan Project times the Apollo Project times 10. And that's an apt metaphor. While both projects were famous for unprecedented technical achievements—the Manhattan Project cracked the secret of the atomic bomb, and the Apollo Project put a man on the moon—we need to do more than come up with new technology to solve the problems we now face. We also need to rethink and remake our entire infrastructure, our economics, and even our culture. This isn't just a project for a crack team of scientists. This one is going to need the help of every one of us.

We will need to attack the problem from both ends: by reducing demand and by increasing supply (from renewables) simultaneously.

The Council on Foreign Relations put it bluntly: "No energy security policy can be considered comprehensive without a significant emphasis on reducing the consumption of oil and oil products. The United States daily consumes some 21 million barrels of oil and oil products. The policy question is how best to slow or better yet reverse this growth."[2]

THE IMPORTANCE OF TIMELY RESPONSE

One of the most well-respected studies on mitigation strategies for peak oil was published in February 2005 by Robert L. Hirsch (project leader), Roger Bezdek, and Robert Wendling, in a report titled "Peaking of World Oil Production: Impacts, Mitigation, & Risk Management"[3] that they did for the Department of Energy, which has come to be known as simply the "Hirsch Report."

The point of the study was to determine when we need to take action to deal with the peak oil challenge in order to avoid a painful adjustment.

Their approach was elegantly simple: First, they determined how much oil could be offset by various mitigation strategies. They made some reasonable assumptions about the future potential of all exploitable sources of energy and about the amount of savings that might be achieved through conservation and higher efficiency, and charted each as a wedge on an aggregate chart. (See Figure 12.1.)

And then they charted that against what they considered to be a reasonable forecast of world oil production under three different scenarios:

Scenario I: Mitigation begins at the time of peaking.

Scenario II: Mitigation starts 10 years before peaking.

Scenario III: Mitigation starts 20 years before peaking.

Their findings are shown in Figure 12.2.

Scenario I shows us that if we wait until we're at the peak before we begin intensive mitigation efforts, we wind up with about a 20-year shortfall in supply, simply because it takes that long to replace infrastructure and make

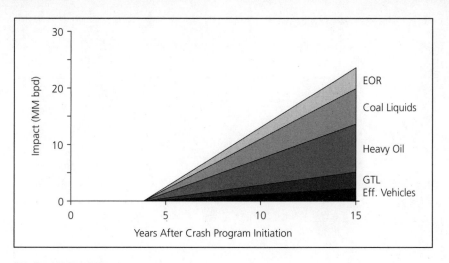

FIGURE 12.1 *Hirsch Report's "Assumed Wedges"*

Source: Robert Hirsch and Roger Bezdek, "Peaking of World Oil Production: Impacts, Mitigation, & Risk Management," February 2005, www.netl.doe.gov/publications/others/pdf/Oil_Peaking_NETL.pdf.

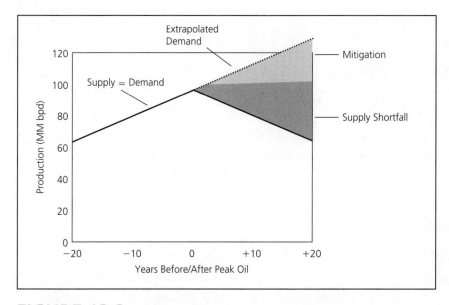

FIGURE 12.2 *Hirsch Report Scenario I—Mitigation Begins at the Time of Peaking*

Source: Robert Hirsch and Roger Bezdek, "Peaking of World Oil Production: Impacts, Mitigation, & Risk Management," February 2005, www.netl.doe.gov/publications/others/pdf/Oil_Peaking_NETL.pdf.

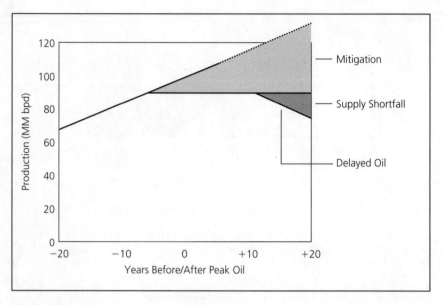

FIGURE 12.3 *Hirsch Report Scenario II—Mitigation Starts 10 Years before Peaking*

Source: Robert Hirsch and Roger Bezdek, "Peaking of World Oil Production: Impacts, Mitigation, & Risk Management," February 2005, www.netl.doe.gov/publications/others/pdf/Oil_Peaking_NETL.pdf.

other necessary adjustments to live within a reducing, rather than expanding, energy budget. This is the scenario we want to avoid.

Next, they considered what would happen if we begin mitigation efforts 10 years before the peak. (See Figure 12.3.)

Under this scenario, we still wind up with about a 10-year shortfall in oil supply.

Only if we commence our efforts a full 20 years before the peak can we manage a smooth transition. (See Figure 12.4.)

Their conclusion was blunt:

The peaking of world oil production presents the U.S. and the world with an unprecedented risk management problem. As peaking is approached, liquid fuel prices and price volatility will increase dramatically, and, without timely mitigation, the economic, social, and political costs will be unprecedented. Viable mitigation options exist on both the supply and demand sides, but to have substantial impact, they must be initiated more than a decade in advance of peaking. . . .

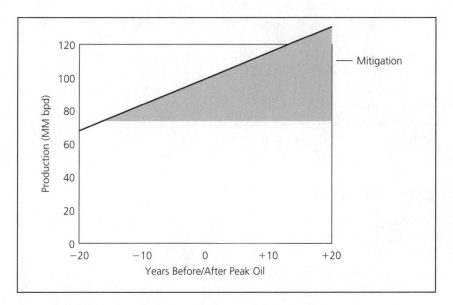

FIGURE 12.4 *Hirsch Report Scenario III—Mitigation Starts 20 Years before Peaking*

Source: Robert Hirsch and Roger Bezdek, "Peaking of World Oil Production: Impacts, Mitigation, & Risk Management," February 2005, www.netl.doe.gov/publications/others/pdf/Oil_Peaking_NETL.pdf.

> *If mitigation were to be too little, too late, world supply/demand balance will be achieved through massive demand destruction (shortages), which would translate to significant economic hardship. . . . The world has never faced a problem like this. Without massive mitigation more than a decade before the fact, the problem will be pervasive and will not be temporary. Previous energy transitions (wood to coal and coal to oil) were gradual and evolutionary; oil peaking will be abrupt and revolutionary.*

As we have seen, however, much turns on the question of when world production peaks. Unfortunately, the Hirsch report selected as its "most meaningful EIA oil peaking case" the United States Geological Survey's (USGS) 3 trillion barrel number for the estimated ultimately recoverable (EUR) amount, and used 2 percent for the rate of annual world oil demand escalation. As we have seen in the foregoing chapters, the world EUR is likely closer to 2.5 trillion barrels (the ASPO case) or even as little as 1.8 trillion (after adjusting for bogus OPEC reserves statements) and the decline rate is 2.5 percent or higher.[4]

In other words, the situation is even worse—maybe by 50 percent—than the Hirsch model projects.

Since it was published, the study has received an enormous amount of attention in the energy world, and no one has raised any serious objections to it. If the conclusions speak for themselves, and we accept that we have indeed waited until the peak to begin serious mitigation efforts, then we should be scrambling right now to take action, unreservedly, with all hands on deck, instead of wasting precious time arguing about how much oil is left.

APOLLO ALLIANCE

One group that has taken up the challenge directly is the Apollo Alliance, a nonprofit group that aims to emulate President John F. Kennedy's leadership by offering "a message of optimism and hope, framed around rejuvenating our nation's economy by creating the next generation of American industrial jobs and treating clean energy as an economic and security mandate to rebuild America."[5]

In addition to lobbying, partnering with local groups interested in sustainability and the environment, and so on, the Apollo Alliance has issued a "Ten-Point Plan for Good Jobs and Energy Independence."[6]

1. *Promote advanced technology and hybrid cars.* The Apollo Alliance calls for the American auto industry to switch over to making highly efficient cars.

2. *Invest in more efficient factories.* Essentially tweaking tax and other incentives to persuade manufacturers to use the best-of-breed technologies to lower their energy footprints.

3. *Encourage high-performance building.* Investing in and providing incentives for so-called green buildings and energy-efficient homes and offices.

4. *Increase use of energy-efficient appliances.* Calling for Americans to buy more energy-efficient appliances, and for incentives for manufacturers to produce them.

5. *Modernize electrical infrastructure.* Involving everything from "clean coal" technology to smart grids and distributed generation from renewables.

6. *Expand renewable energy development.* Calling for a comprehensive program for increasing renewable energy generation.

7. *Improve transportation options.* "Investing in effective multimodal networks including bicycle, local bus and rail transit, regional high-speed rail and magnetic levitation rail projects."

8. *Reinvest in smart urban growth.* Rebuilding our urban centers to attract residents with improved infrastructures and walkable communities.

9. *Plan for a hydrogen future.* Investing in long-term R&D for the hydrogen economy.

10. *Preserve regulatory protections.* Regulating energy production better to protect the environment and to give new energy technologies a fighting chance. Encouraging balanced growth and investment through regulation that ensures energy diversity and system reliability, that protects workers and the environment, that rewards consumers, and that establishes a fair framework for emerging technologies.

Aside from supporting the hydrogen economy (we'll see what's wrong with that later in this chapter), the Apollo Alliance's plan makes a great deal of sense. It remains to be seen, however, if it can get traction where it counts: in the halls of government.

CARBON TAXES AND CAP-AND-TRADE SYSTEMS

Two proposals for combating global warming would also help to reduce our use of fossil fuel: carbon taxes and cap-and-trade strategy.

Carbon taxes are probably the simplest, most effective, and least economically damaging option, because they let the market decide what the best solutions are.

The idea is simple: Tax the burning of all fossil fuels in proportion to their carbon content. The tax would be easily implemented with a minimum of administrative overhead, and would have the desired effect: offering incentives for using low-carbon or carbon-free fuels, while discouraging the use of carbon fuels. In this way we can assign a real cost to (i.e., internalize) the emissions that are currently externalized onto the public and the environment.

This type of approach would provide an immediate incentive to reduce carbon emissions, unlike voluntary approaches, which may not achieve enough of a reduction in time to reverse the current global warming trend. It would also provide a solid basis for future investment decisions by utilities and municipalities.

But most importantly, by internalizing what is now externalized, the market will finally be able to make intelligent decisions based in reality. Under a carbon tax regime, coal would no longer be the cheap alternative that it appears to be today.

In order to reduce the burden on low-income consumers, carbon taxes could be offset elsewhere, for example by lower payroll taxes.

Yet carbon taxes are a difficult thing to sell to the public, because voters already struggling with today's high energy costs are going to take a very jaundiced view of additional taxes. Only if the public truly understands the situation, and has strong leadership to explain the necessity and the benefits of carbon taxes, could the idea really succeed.

Cap-and-Trade

An alternate approach is emissions trading, otherwise known as "cap-and-trade." Under this scheme, a central authority (like a government agency) sets a cap on the amount of emissions that can be generated. Allowances are granted to polluters to emit a certain amount of carbon dioxide, to keep the sum of pollutants within the established cap.

At the same time, those who reduce their emissions below their allowance can sell "carbon credits." For example, a utility that runs coal-burning plants would be allowed to exceed its allowance by buying carbon credits from its customers who generate solar power. The exchange is called a trade, and essentially could financially reward carbon dioxide reduction and penalize production.

Another flavor of carbon credits is renewable energy certificates (RECs), otherwise known as green tags. A green tag represents 1,000 kWh of clean, renewable energy, and can be sold by the producer of that energy on the open market. Once a green tag is purchased, it is retired in recognition of the carbon trade.

As time goes on, the overall cap can be lowered to achieve a net reduction in emissions. An open market in carbon credits can allow the scheme to work without a great deal of administrative interference, although the caps must be established administratively.

Carbon trading markets are planned or already in operation in the United States, the European Union, and Australia.[7]

Because cap-and-trade systems are generally voluntary, however, only motivated parties tend to participate in them. For example, a utility may be required by a local renewable portfolio standard to buy a certain percentage of its power from renewable sources, which it might satisfy by buying green tags. But after its requirement is met, it tends to stop purchasing them, and those polluters who are under no such requirements tend not to buy them at all.

Advantages of a Carbon Tax

According to the Carbon Tax Center, carbon taxation is the preferable approach for these reasons: predictability, transparency, immediacy, universality, and equity. As the *Los Angeles Times* put it, "While cap-and-trade creates opportunities for cheating, leads to unpredictable fluctuations in energy prices, and does nothing to offset high power costs for consumers, carbon taxes can be structured to sidestep all those problems while providing a more reliable market incentive to produce clean-energy technology."

The Carbon Tax Center identifies six fundamental advantages[8] of a carbon tax:

1. Carbon taxes make energy prices more predictable, whereas cap-and-trade systems make them more volatile. Carbon taxes incentivize carbon reduction better than cap-and-trade systems do.

2. Thanks to their simplicity, carbon taxes can be implemented faster and more easily than complex cap-and-trade systems.

3. Carbon taxes are simpler, more easily understood, and more easily audited.

4. Carbon taxes are straightforward and less vulnerable to manipulation and subversion.

5. Carbon taxes can reduce emissions across the board, not just in the utility sector, at which cap-and-trade schemes are primarily targeted.

6. Carbon taxes can be transparent and progressive, but cap-and-trade systems tend to function as a hidden tax on the entire system, with many of its benefits accruing to lawyers and other consultants.

We believe that carbon taxes are the most sensible, direct, economic, and effective approach to reducing greenhouse gases, by steering the economy toward renewable and sustainable sources and away from fossil fuels.

At a July 2007 business conference, Glenn Hubbard, the dean of Columbia University Business School and an economic adviser under President George W. Bush, argued in favor of "some sort of a cap-and-trade system with a safety valve, which amounts to a tax." He said, "I believe that technology is the vital solution to fixing the problems of climate change. But businesspeople don't innovate because it feels good; they innovate because there's a return to that innovation. If you want a return to that innovation, you will have to price it—you will need to put a price on carbon, which means having, either through a cap-and-trade system or through an explicit tax, some incentive to innovate carbon-saving technology."[9]

Investment Opportunities

Aside from the obvious angle of investing in renewable energy production, such as buying a solar system and selling green tags on its production, there are other ways to invest in emissions trading.

For a stock market pick, consider Peerless Mfg. Co. (NASDAQ: PMFG), a company that specializes in air pollution abatement. One business segment makes catalytic reduction systems that can clean up the exhaust from coal, gasoline, natural gas, and oil, converting the nitrogen oxide (NOx) emissions into harmless nitrogen and water. The other business segment makes specialized filters for removing contaminants from natural gas and air piping systems.[10]

For sophisticated traders, there are new markets in greenhouse gas emissions being created, with structures similar to those of options and futures markets. This is an emerging area and the rules are not yet fixed, but it is an exciting and rapidly evolving area of finance. More information on these markets is available on the web site of the International Emissions Trading Association at www.ieta.org.

According to a July 2007 article in the *New York Times*, carbon trading is now one of the "fastest-growing specialties in financial services,"[11] with companies scrambling to take "a slice of a market now worth about $30 billion and that could grow to $1 trillion within a decade." It has spawned a whole new army of financial experts in carbon trading.

In fact, the article claims, "Carbon will be the world's biggest commodity market, and it could become the world's biggest market overall." The head of emissions trading at Merrill Lynch agrees, calling it "one of the fastest-growing markets ever, with volumes comparable to credit derivatives inside of a decade."

The world's biggest market overall? Isn't that just a bit hyperbolic?

Not really. Take a look at a chart of the price of carbon on the Chicago Climate Exchange (CCX) (Figure 12.5).

At its price of about $3.50 per ton, the potential carbon market stands at roughly $133 billion (38 billion × $3.50).

But only a tiny fraction of emissions are regulated. As more and more governments start to regulate their countries' emissions, and as more companies start to voluntarily limit their emissions, the demand for available carbon credits will skyrocket—particularly because renewable energy is still very much a fledgling market, so the pool of carbon credits is limited.

Other companies profit from carbon by finding ways to reduce emissions, earning a portion of the carbon credits along with their consulting fees as part of

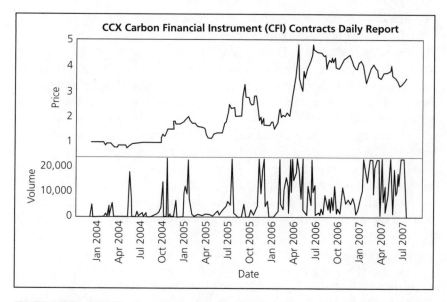

FIGURE 12.5   *Chicago Climate Exchange (CCX) Carbon Financial Instrument (CFI) Contracts Daily Report*

Source: Chicago Climate Exchange, CCX Carbon Financial Instrument (CFI) Contracts Daily Report, June 2007.

their compensation. One such company is Ecology & Environment Inc. (AMEX: EEI), which offers a range of environmental consulting services, including environmental planning, management, and regulatory compliance support. In one year, it was up 34 percent—six percentage points more than the record-breaking Dow—and has increased its annual net income by over 62 percent.

Inasmuch as the world seems to prefer market-based approaches to controlling carbon emissions, there is no doubt that the carbon trading market is going to experience a huge boom, whether it is the "biggest market overall" or not.

GASOLINE TAXES

Most observers agree that the best, and possibly the only, way to achieve a reduction in the amount of oil used in this country is through the price mechanism, particularly in transportation fuels. It seems to require a pinch in the pocketbook to make consumers drive less.

The obvious and shortest path, then, is to levy higher taxes on fuel, and then use that tax revenue to invest in alternatives, such as rail. This approach has been quite effective in Europe, in particular. In the United States, federal taxes on gasoline are among the lowest of all industrialized nations, at just 18.4 cents a gallon. In order to keep the taxes from becoming an onerous burden and a regressive tax on consumers, they could be offset by reductions or rebates on other taxes.

However, it's nearly axiomatic that Americans will resist all forms of gasoline taxes for any reason. Until regular citizens come to clearly comprehend the energy situation they are in, it will remain political suicide to back new gasoline taxes, even though most analysts agree that it is the smartest and shortest path to reducing demand, and even though it has succeeded nicely in helping Europe to reduce its petroleum use and build mass transportation.

NEGAWATTS

As anybody in the energy field can tell you, the cheapest watts are "*negawatts*"— energy you don't have to generate in the first place—because efficiency is, by far, the low-hanging fruit in responding to the challenge of declining energy supplies.

For example: One oft-cited metric is that for every dollar one spends to improve the efficiency of appliances and buildings, one would have to spend five to nine dollars on solar power to achieve the same thing.

According to a May 2007 report by the American Council for an Energy-Efficient Economy (ACEEE) and the American Council on Renewable Energy (ACORE), the "twin pillars of sustainable energy" are efficiency and renewable energy. They estimate that the United States could cut its conventional electricity generation and carbon emissions almost in half within 20 years, using realistic technology, given the current level of interest and policy commitments being made by Congress and many states.[12]

One company has capitalized on negawatts by offering demand-response systems. EnerNOC, Inc. (NASDAQ: ENOC) launched a $99 million IPO in May 2007 amid a flurry of deals with utilities and other commercial customers. EnerNOC's systems can control demand loads on the grid using state-of-the-art hardware and software systems, effectively squeezing the most capacity out of the grid. When grid demand is peaking, EnerNOC can alert and curtail power to thousands of large energy consumers in real time, under prearranged agreements with those users. By doing so, the company claims it avoids the need for a new "peaker" plant every quarter.[13]

Perhaps the biggest negawatt opportunity is in capturing waste heat. Over half the energy we generate is ultimately wasted as heat, as shown in Figure 12.6.

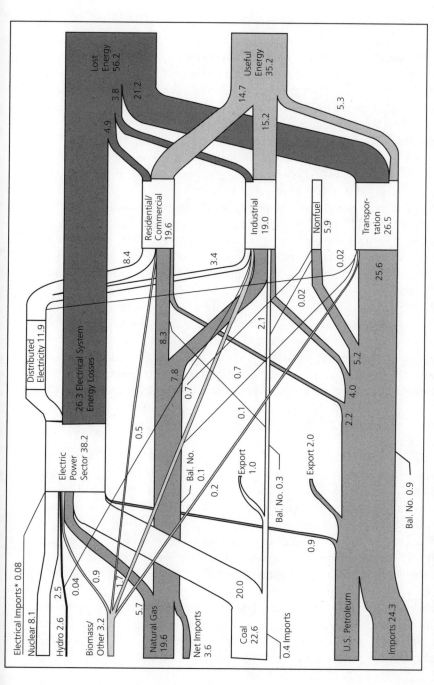

FIGURE 12.6 *U.S. Energy Generation and Use, All Sources (Quads)*

Source: Lawrence Livermore National Laboratory, "U.S. Energy Flow Trends—2002," http://eed.llnl.gov/flow/02flow.php.

Banning the Bulb

The "ban the bulb" movement is catching on worldwide to replace inefficient regular incandescent lightbulbs, which waste much of the power they consume as heat, with compact fluorescent (CFL) bulbs. CFL bulbs fit the same sockets as regular incandescent bulbs, but produce the same amount of light for only about 20 percent of the electricity. They've been available for several years now, but were regarded as being too expensive.

No more. CFLs last much longer, between 8,000 and 15,000 hours versus only 1,000 hours for their incandescent counterparts, and they reach their payback point in around 500 hours, resulting in about one-third the total cost over three years. That makes good sense all around.

Consequently, a trade group of European lighting manufacturers has agreed to a pact to phase out the incandescent bulb. In Australia, officials have announced their own phaseout by 2009—in only two years! And in California, the energy commission is discussing a 10-year phaseout, with the full support of bulb manufacturers. (Now, how often do you see manufacturers supporting moves away from their products?) A California legislator has gone further, introducing a bill that would ban the sale of incandescent bulbs by 2012. The New Jersey legislature is also poised to require that compact fluorescents replace all incandescent bulbs in state government buildings by 2010.

According to the Department of Energy, incandescent bulbs use about 10 percent of the nation's electricity. So swapping out those three to four billion bulbs is a very easy, inexpensive, and quickly implemented part of the solution to reducing our energy needs—enough to eliminate the need for dozens of coal-fired electricity plants, according to the National Resource Defense Council.

Lester Brown, president of the Earth Policy Institute and author of *Plan B 2.0: Rescuing a Planet under Stress and a Civilization in Trouble* (W. W. Norton, rev. ed., 2006), estimates that if the world shifted to compact fluorescent bulbs from incandescents, enough energy could be saved to close 270 coal-fired power plants, a reduction of more than 3 percent in world electricity consumption.[14]

The 18seconds.org web site, so named for the time it takes to change a lightbulb, tracks the number of compact fluorescents sold in the United States since the beginning of 2007. (As of November 7, 2007, it was nearly 106 million, for a savings of $3.1 billion!)

Philips Electronics, the largest lighting manufacturer in the world, has announced that it will stop selling incandescents in Europe and the United States by 2016. And Britain's largest electrical retail chain, Currys, has announced that it will discontinue selling incandescent lightbulbs as well.

In the European Union, the European Lamp Companies Federation (a trade association for bulb manufacturers) supports a phaseout of incandescent bulbs.

OIL DEPLETION PROTOCOL

Probably the most sensible (and therefore doomed) proposal for peak oil mitigation is the Oil Depletion Protocol. Originally proposed by Association for the Study of Peak Oil and Gas (ASPO) founder Colin Campbell, and elaborated upon in a book by Richard Heinberg of the same name, the concept is simple: "Importers would reduce their imports by the world oil depletion rate, while producing countries would reduce their rate of production by their national depletion rate."[15]

Let's look at some examples of how this might work.

Calculating the depletion rate depends on knowing how much oil remains to be produced, from both known and yet-to-be-discovered fields. Given our knowledge that many oil producers fudge their numbers, this could be a politically tricky task, but geologists at ASPO and other observers are confident that they can state the reserves numbers within a reasonably small margin of error, given the historical production of fields and the discovery curves for oil provinces.

Once we estimate the amount of remaining oil to be produced, calculating the depletion rate is straightforward: It is the total remaining oil divided into the yearly production. To use Heinberg's example, suppose we have a hypothetical country with a billion barrels of oil in reserves, which starts producing its oil at the rate of 30 million barrels per year. Dividing 30 million by one billion gives us a depletion rate of 3 percent. In the second year of its production, the country would have 970 million barrels yet to produce, so to reduce its production by 3 percent, it could only produce 29.1 million barrels. And so on.

Likewise, net importers would have to reduce their imports by the global depletion rate, which Dr. Campbell calculates at 2.6 percent per year. Let's take the United States as an example. We currently import 10.1 million barrels per day of crude. If we began implementing the protocol next year and reduced this amount by 2.6 percent, we could only import 9.8 mbpd next year, 9.6 mbpd the year after that, 9.3 mbpd the year after that, and so on.

The beauty of the protocol is that it would allow both net producers and net importers to gradually and smoothly adjust their ways, and thus avoid jarring and catastrophic changes. Under this regime, the United States theoretically could still import some 53,000 bpd after 200 years! It would also deliver a reduction in carbon emissions, which continues to be resisted by the United States, China, and Australia.

But Campbell and Heinberg are quick to point out that, unlike the Kyoto Protocol, it doesn't require full participation by all countries to make the protocol work. Those countries who voluntarily reduce their production will save a little more oil for the future, when it will no doubt be worth more than it is today, making the reduction in production effectively a wise investment. And net importers would benefit, in that they would wean themselves off of oil earlier, thus realizing a substantial cost savings and an earlier reduction in their geopolitical exposure to risks. As the old Billie Holiday song goes, "God bless the child who's got his own."

The protocol can be looked at as an exercise in simple budgeting, not unlike making a budget for a household or a company. Just as no sensible person would expect to live or do business without making sure that they earn more than they spend, it is madness for us to use energy so profligately without stopping to consider that we're depleting our bank account of natural capital as if it were bottomless—because it surely is not.

Heinberg has further suggested that we plan to deliberately "power down" our economies to adapt to our shrinking energy budgets. This would be an all-out effort to "reduce per-capita resource usage in wealthy countries, develop alternative energy sources, distribute resources more equitably, and reduce the human population humanely but systematically over time."[16] It is an eminently sane and sensible response to oil peaking, but, recognizing that it's still a difficult task to convince policy makers that peak oil is a real and urgent problem, such deliberate responses still seem uncomfortably far off in the future.

REPLACING THE FLEET

As we have seen, peak oil is primarily a liquid fuels problem. Transportation is the biggest user of energy, accounting for 29 percent of all energy consumed in the United States, and 96 percent of the energy used for transportation comes from petroleum.[17] So mitigating the effects of peak oil must begin with reducing transportation demand for fuel. Switching to hybrids, all-electric vehicles, high-efficiency diesels, and vehicles that can burn E85 could significantly reduce our need for petroleum-based fuels.

But how long would it take, for example, to replace the United States' 210 million privately owned vehicles with something else? The average life span of today's vehicles is 16.8 years, and the average age of our fleet is

8.5 years. If the past replacement rate holds for the future, then we will need to continue running vehicles on conventional fuels for at least another 10, possibly 20 years, even if every vehicle produced from now on could run on an alternative fuel.[18]

This is why we must plan to remain at least somewhat dependent on liquid fuels for the next decade or two, even if we're switching to an all-electric infrastructure as we'll discuss in the next chapter.

COMBINED HEAT AND POWER

Although they are hardly new, combined heat and power (CHP) systems offer a huge opportunity—where applicable—to save an enormous amount of energy.

These systems usually burn natural gas or liquid fuel to generate electricity, while also capturing the heat from the generation process and using it rather than wasting it. Typically one-half to three-quarters of the primary energy used in power generation is wasted—just vented into the environment.[19]

Typical CHP applications are for large commercial buildings, which use the waste heat to heat the building or its hot water. CHP systems currently provide about 9 percent of the electricity generated in the United States. But other, larger-scale applications are feasible, such as using the waste heat from a large utility power plant, or a smelter, to provide area heating to an entire district of a city. Such large-scale designs are being evaluated for feasibility in many parts of Europe, and the UK has a target to deploy an additional 5,000 MWe (megawatts-equivalent).[20]

Similarly, progressive city planners and businesspeople everywhere are exploring unique combinations of physical plants that can work together, so that, for example, the waste heat from one factory can be used as an input to another, right next door. Other similar cooperative strategies are being considered to reuse and recycle various materials on site.

Because less energy is wasted, CHP plants also help reduce CO_2 emissions—by as much as 27 percent for a citywide CHP system.[21]

SMART GRIDS

As we have seen, the future of energy will be largely electric. As liquid fuels from oil continue their relentless decline, and as we find the firm limits of biofuel expansion in the form of competition for arable land and water, fertilizer, and so on, electricity seems to be the final frontier of energy.

But before we can realize the vision of a new fleet of electric cars and electric trains powered by clean, green, renewable energy, we will have to substantially upgrade the grid. In most localities, it is already stretched to capacity, which makes it vulnerable to widespread blackouts that begin with a relatively small glitch somewhere.

Consider the Northeast blackout of 2003, which plunged parts of the Northeastern and Midwestern United States, and Ontario, Canada, into blackness within two hours on Thursday, August 14, 2003. It was the largest blackout in North American history, affecting some 10 million people in Ontario (about one-third of the population of Canada) and 40 million people in eight U.S. states (about one-seventh of the population of the United States).

And why did the blackout happen? Because a high-power transmission line came in contact with a tree in Cleveland, Ohio. This small event led to a cascading series of failures, ultimately forcing more than 508 generating units at 265 power plants to be shut down, including 22 nuclear power plants. The cost of the blackout has been estimated at $6 billion.[22]

The subsequent investigations turned up a whole host of issues, including failure to trim trees near high-capacity transmission lines, failure to maintain the electrical infrastructure, insufficient headroom on the grid, failure to upgrade to "smart cables," failure of shunting and rerouting mechanisms, problems with AC versus DC intersystem ties, and other problems.

In response, many experts have called for the development of "smart grids" or "distributed energy grids," in which power is generated by microplants everywhere and stored everywhere, in a distributed fashion.

This would enable more widespread deployment of residential and commercially sized solar PV systems, wind turbines, micro-hydro systems, CHP systems, and other small-scale power generators, because generation capacity wouldn't need to be limited to the needs of the property on which the generator is installed—indeed, overgeneration would be welcomed, instead of prohibited as it is today.

Likewise, power storage could be localized, using large arrays of batteries in households and commercial buildings, or other storage systems including: pumping water uphill to a storage tank and then recapturing the energy with a micro-hydro system as it comes back downhill; futuristic hydrogen generators and fuel cells; and flywheel units that store kinetic energy and spin an electromagnetic motor to turn it back into usable electricity.

With the smart grid concept, each locality deploys its own unique mix of generation and storage technologies appropriate to its own geography and resources. Together, these distributed energy generation and storage systems are more stable, less vulnerable to failure or malicious attack, and more easily self-managed than the hub-and-spoke architecture of the current grid.

Some key elements to making the smart grid concept work include upgrading the grid management systems to incorporate smarter software, better and more redundant sensing and switching, and more efficient power distribution.

For example, instead of having one large power plant sending its power down hundreds or even thousands of miles of transmission lines, losing some 7.2 percent[23] of the original power due to line loss along the way, we could have thousands of microgenerators sending their power to a central local switch, with negligible line loss and far greater stability on the local grid, and local storage of any excess power.

Smart grids could also enable greater use of widely dispersed and under-utilized energy sources such as wind generators, which are often most productive far from where the users are located. For example, the best wind resource in the United States is located in North Dakota, far from any sizeable population centers.

Grid transmission capacity in such relatively remote areas is weak, and the distribution networks are constrained by the minimum and maximum voltages they must maintain. Due to the intermittent production of wind, large wind farms tend to destabilize their local grids, and require overbuilt transmission capacity to accommodate their peak outputs; for example, a 10 megawatt wind farm grid connection would use only about 3.5 to 4 megawatts of that capacity on average.[24] Smart grids could help change all that by tempering the irregular production with storage and by controlling and directing the generation.

Microgrids

Taking the smart grid concept a step further, the concept of microgrids offers even greater benefits.

The way the grid works today, any grid-connected power source—such as a solar PV system or a wind turbine—must shut down when the grid goes down, for the protection of utility workers. That power source will reconnect to the grid only when the grid is functioning normally and within the required range of voltages.

With microgrids, small (say, small town-sized) groups of distributed power sources could coordinate their power production electronically, present themselves to the grid for interconnection when the grid is up, and then disconnect (or "island") themselves elegantly from the grid when it goes down. While the main grid is down, they can maintain their own local power using their local production and storage.

Microgrids offer a way to exploit energy production and storage opportunities nearly everywhere that just aren't feasible today for one reason or another. In your author's northern California town of Mill Valley, for example, we could harvest quite a bit of local energy that we don't even use today, by using micro-hydro to capture the falling energy of water as it descends down the local mountain watershed into our freshwater capture system, not to mention deploying small wind turbines and even tidal energy from the coast right nearby. We could store that energy by pumping water back up the mountain. And we have a decent solar resource as well, even near the coast. This little valley town could probably keep itself going quite nicely, thank you very much, if we could island from the main grid. Similarly, it should be possible, with the right mix of energy generation and storage technologies, for almost any location to support its basic needs as a microgrid.

Deploying microgrids will require new hardware and software systems for controlling microsource generators, coordinating the operation and balancing the load of the microgrid, maintaining proper grid frequency and voltages, handling network communications, and the switching gear and separation devices needed to disconnect and reconnect sources within the microgrid, and externally with the main grid.

Microgrids will also require the enthusiastic support of local communities in order to establish the required political, regulatory, technical, and market frameworks to make them possible. Some communities are already beginning that effort.

Microgrids, in combination with smart grid technologies and expanded use of CHP systems, could radically remake the grid system by decentralizing it and, in the process, reduce the burden on long-distance transmission and high-capacity wires. In so doing, it could also transform the electricity business, leveling the playing field significantly. What town would choose to pay for grid power from some coal-fired plant a few hundred miles away when instead it could buy the power at close to the same price locally from renewable generation, keep that money in the local community, and not create any greenhouse gases in the process?

Smart Meters

A related concept, or a component, of smart grids could be new smart meters.

These are the next generation of the standard electric meter. But unlike the old meters, which are simple analog devices that have to be checked by a meter reader so that the utility can know how much to charge for power consumed, smart meters are sophisticated electronic devices that can report usage to a utility automatically. Some communicate with the utility using the existing power lines as data lines, and others report their data wirelessly over a short range, so that it can be picked up by a utility employee simply driving a truck equipped with a receiver up and down the street.

Smart meters can also give useful feedback to the customers, so that they can moderate their usage in order to save money voluntarily and reduce demand at peak times when given an alert by the utility.

This enables a *demand response* strategy, where instead of the utility having to build new "peaker plants" for extra generation during times of peak demand, it can simply request that customers scale back their usage when demand is high, or even cut back on electricity supply to large commercial customers who have agreed in advance to such involuntary curtailments in exchange for lower rates overall. In this way, blackouts can be prevented painlessly.

Combined with tiered pricing plans, which charge more for power consumed during peak demand than off-peak demand, smart meters could give utilities a way to adjust energy prices in real time, which the meters could reflect immediately, thus encouraging customers to reduce demand when it matters most, saving money for themselves and for the utility.

A wise deployment of smart meters could make it possible to maximize the capacity of the grid, and of our existing power plants, while simultaneously developing power consumers' awareness, all at a very marginal cost.

And in combination with on-site power generation facilities such as wind turbines, solar power systems, and other microgenerators, smart meters could provide an important component of a distributed energy infrastructure. For example, instead of the burdensome requirements now put upon solar customers and contractors to evaluate customers' energy requirements and establish their eligibility for rebates on solar energy systems, customers could simply install whatever they like, wherever and however they like, and be reimbursed by the utility for their net contributions to the grid—a far simpler approach, and one that would encourage a much more rapid deployment of distributed renewable energy.

Investment Opportunities

There are many investment opportunities in the smart grid and microgrid areas.

Companies such as Distributed Energy Systems Corporation (NASDAQ: DESC) make a variety of energy storage and energy generation devices, as well as advanced architectures for power networks that make the most of the available power.

Beacon Technologies (NASDAQ: BCON) makes products and services to support reliable electricity grid operation, including flywheel-based energy storage technologies that are currently used for large-scale uninterruptible power supply applications (like backing up a telephone switching station or moderating the voltage of the grid) but could potentially be adapted to home- or commercial-sized applications.

Although it is a much larger business than just demand-response systems and smart meters, General Electric (NYSE: GE) is another way to play this sector.

General Electric (GE) makes a variety of products for the generation, transmission, distribution, control, and utilization of electricity, and it has a whole raft of products that will be useful to a future of smart grids. Their "Ecomagination" campaign, now three years old, has quickly taken off to become GE's fastest-growing business segment, doubling in two years while the rest of GE's business grew only 20 percent.

The growth of GE's green business segment is due to the staunch commitment of its CEO, Jeffrey Immelt, who has been inspired by the concepts of the green revolution such as those discussed in Paul Hawken's *Natural Capitalism*. He knows that the triple bottom line—profit, people, and planet—is the name of the game going forward.

Sales of GE's environmentally friendly products, such as wind turbines, water-purification systems, and energy-efficient appliances, rose from $6 billion in 2004 to $10 billion in 2005, and to $12 billion in 2006. The company currently is set to meet its target of $20 billion in green sales by 2010.

Plus, the green energy group already has $50 billion worth of new environmentally friendly projects in the pipeline—that's equivalent to nearly a third of GE's total sales from all parts of the business.[25]

Comverge Inc. (NASDAQ: COMV) and EnerNOC (NASDAQ: ENOC) are two companies that provide energy reduction solutions for utilities. Both went public in 2007, and both offer hardware and software solutions that enable utilities to increase available electric capacity during periods of peak demand, while enhancing grid reliability. Such demand management solutions produce no harmful emissions and are as much as 40 percent less expensive than building and operating a new natural gas–fired power plant, without requiring any additional investment in transmission and distribution assets. Essentially, both offer ways to encourage customers to reduce demand from nonessential loads such as pool pumps and heating, ventilating, and air-conditioning (HVAC) systems during peak times.

Itron (NASDAQ: ITRI) is the clear-cut pure-play leader in smart metering of both electric and water meters, and has a 55 percent market share in North America. Based in the state of Washington, Itron makes smart meters and associated power grid forecasting and management software. Now that it has acquired a European competitor, Actaris, the company claims it will be "the No. 1 electric meter supplier, No. 2 gas meter supplier, and No. 4 water meter supplier in the world."

Echelon (NASDAQ: ELON) is another demand-response company that specializes in automation technologies for businesses. Its systems reduce demand by fine-tuning the use of lighting, HVAC systems, and other energy loads in commercial buildings. "Because we have this whole two-way idea of communicating devices, we are able to do things that makers of vertical systems can't do," says chief operating officer Bea Yormark. "For example, in a building we can link the lights and HVAC system on the same network." Echelon's systems are now being evaluated by McDonald's restaurants, utilities in Europe, Asian businesses, and the Chinese government.

WIND ENERGY

Wind energy is a major renewable energy resource. After decades of languishing investment, the wind power industry got a jump start in recent years by providing a source of clean, green power that utilities could buy in order to meet renewable portfolio standards that are cropping up across the country.

But wind power itself dates back to at least 5000 B.C.E., when it was used to propel boats along the Nile river. By 200 B.C.E., simple windmills were pumping water in China and grinding grain in the Middle East.

Windmills designed to generate electricity, known as turbines, first appeared in Denmark around 1890. They operate on a simple principle: two or three propeller-like blades are attached to a rotor, which is in turn connected to an electrical generator. When the wind blows, the propeller turns the rotor, spinning the generator and creating electrical current. The propeller is typically mounted 75 feet or more off the ground, to take advantage of faster, less turbulent winds.

The newest turbines are larger and more efficient, capable of producing electricity for as little as four to six cents per kilowatt-hour, about the same as burning coal. That has driven a major expansion of wind power in the United States in the past five years. Most recently, total generating capacity surged 36 percent to 9,100 megawatts in 2005.

An Exploding Industry

Europe has built a flourishing wind industry overseas in the last decade, but the same explosive growth is just getting started here in the United States.

Of all renewable power sources, wind is adding more generating capacity than anything else, and is growing at the rate of about 29 percent per year worldwide.[26] The current worldwide wind generating capacity is about 74 gigawatts (GW).[27]

Between 1994 and 2005 the wind power in the European Union skyrocketed from 1,700 to 40,000 megawatts. Germany has been particularly aggressive, and now boasts more than 18,000 megawatts of capacity.

Although wind currently provides less than 1 percent of all electric power in the United States, our potential resources are much greater, especially in the Great Plains states. In fact, Germany's success could easily be topped by the state of North Dakota alone.

According to Xavier Viteri, the head of Spanish utility Iberdrola's renewable-energy business, "There's a lot of room for development there, and there is a lot of expertise here." Wind energy in the United States, he says, "is like Europe was years ago."

In the United States, wind power increased by 27 percent and accounted for 16 percent of new worldwide generating capacity in 2006,[28] making it the fastest-growing wind power market in the world in 2005 and 2006. The United States installed 2,454 megawatts of wind power capacity in 2006—more than the power equivalent of two nuclear reactors—accounting for 16 percent of the worldwide capacity installed that year. Texas, Washington, and California installed most of that capacity.

The Horse Hollow Wind Energy Center is the latest in a series of wind initiatives that are taking off in Texas. At 47,000 acres and 735 megawatts, it's the largest of its kind in the world. The operator, FPL Energy, is the largest owner and operator of wind turbines in the world, and generates more than 1,600 megawatts of wind power in Texas alone. The company's total U.S. wind portfolio has 4,100 megawatts of capacity, enough to power more than a million homes. FPL Energy dropped $1 billion on wind power in Texas in 2006 alone, and it has grand plans for expansion.

Residents of windy states with at least half an acre (and friendly neighbors) spent more than $17 million on small wind-power systems in 2005, up 62 percent from 2004. Some report a savings of 35 percent or more and enjoy watching their electric meters spin backward on blustery days.

Part of the reason wind energy is growing so quickly is that it just makes good economic sense. In May 2007, the U.S. Department of Energy released its first annual report on the U.S. wind power market, entitled "Annual Report on U.S. Wind Power Installation, Cost, and Performance Trends: 2006." It analyzed project costs, turbine sizes, and developer consolidation, and concluded that wind power is already competitive with grid power produced by fossil-fueled or nuclear power plants. It also found that the performance of wind projects has been increasing due to improved placement and technological advances in the turbines.[29]

The recent surge in Texas wind power has nothing to do with environmental issues or a sudden outbreak of green feeling. It's simply a profitable business, especially in the coast and panhandle regions, where the wind blows reliably year-round.

By the end of 2005 Texas was second only to California in wind power, but locals are aggressively gunning to be number one, if they aren't already. The state legislature set a goal of 2,000 megawatts by 2010, but Russel E. Smith, executive director of the trade group Texas Renewable Industries Association, is much more bullish: "At this point, we think 10,000-plus megawatts in the next five to eight years is doable," he says.

State governments are encouraging the trend. Incentives to install small wind systems are available in California, Massachusetts, New Jersey, New York, Pennsylvania, Ohio, and Wisconsin, and the list is growing rapidly.

Forecast: Windy and Profitable

In the United States, according to the American Wind Energy Association, wind power generation grew 27 percent in 2005, 26 percent in 2006 (surpassed only by new natural gas plants!), and 45 percent in 2007, amounting to $49 billion in investment for the year.[30]

In reality, we believe that in 2007 and the coming years, the growth of the industry will knock all previous estimates out of the park. We're going to continue to see 25 percent growth rates for some years in the future, and more than $4 billion in new wind projects annually, until the resource is more fully exploited.

As part of the Energy Policy Act of 2005, the production tax credit for wind was extended through December 2008, ensuring that wind energy will continue to grow apace for another year. But even without federal tax credits (1.9 cents per kilowatt-hour in 2006, and adjusted for inflation each year), wind power is now the cheapest form of electricity generation in many parts of the country.

A report from the Energy Research Centre in the Netherlands that was leaked in July 2007 concludes that wind will overtake nuclear worldwide as the cheap alternative to fossil fuels. The group claims that wind has already achieved cost parity with nuclear at 6.6 euro-cents per kilowatt hour, and that technological advances in the coming years will further improve the economics of wind even as security costs make nuclear energy less financially attractive.[31]

Wind energy is superior to nuclear energy in every way except one: the need for storage. Wind energy is inconstant, and nuclear energy is extremely steady, which is what makes it desirable for "baseload" supply.

However, we believe that the development of storage systems both large and small, as well as the reforming of the grids to be more distributed and smarter, will provide the storage solution that wind energy needs to become a vital and significant part of the future's energy supply.

Investment Opportunities

Some of the best investing opportunities in renewable energy are in the wind sector.

The worldwide boom in wind development has led to a shortage of wind turbine equipment, because it takes years to ramp up turbine manufacturing due to the dispersed, worldwide supply chain of the some 8,000 parts needed to make up a turbine.

Other than GE, most turbine and parts manufacturers are outside the United States, but new initiatives are under way. Texans, in particular, are tired of buying turbines from Europe, and are already courting port towns along the Gulf that might be willing to set up local manufacturing.

General Electric (NYSE: GE) is probably the blue-chip U.S. play on wind energy. Even though it is an enormous diversified industrial conglomerate, ranking 11th on the *Fortune* Global 500 list, it also happens to be the largest producer of wind turbines in the United States, along with a variety of other environmentally friendly products such as water-purification systems and energy-efficient appliances.

General Electric has seen orders for wind turbines skyrocket since the end of 2005. GE has now shipped more than 6,000 of its popular 1.5-megawatt wind turbines worldwide,[32] but GE anticipates that it could have twice that many operating worldwide by the end of 2008.

Gamesa SA of Spain (GAM.MC) is another excellent choice. Not only is it the world's second-largest wind turbine manufacturer, it also makes and markets solar PV and solar thermal equipment. With worldwide operations and a $10 billion market capitalization, it's as blue-chip a play as you'll find in the sector, but the stock has still delivered impressive growth over the past three years. Anticipating the backlog in turbines, Spanish utility Iberdrola has cut a $4 billion deal to buy most of Gamesa's production through 2009, as well as taking a 24 percent equity stake in Gamesa.[33]

Iberdrola (MCE: IBE.MC) is itself an excellent choice, with a stock that grew 60 percent over 2006 and 2007. But Iberdrola isn't resting on its laurels;

in the past year, it has bought four small wind developers and utilities in the United States that lacked the funding and turbines to build their wind businesses, paying anywhere from $40 million to $4 billion for the properties.[34] Iberdrola seems bent on becoming a major player in the U.S. wind business.

Zoltek Companies, Inc. (NASDAQ: ZOLT) is a U.S.-based maker of carbon fibers, a key component of modern wind turbines. With manufacturing plants in Hungary, Texas, and Missouri, Zoltek supplies carbon fibers to turbine manufacturers such as Vestas Wind Systems. The company posted $92 million in sales in 2006.[35]

Vestas Wind Systems (CPH: VWS), based in Denmark, is the world's largest producer of wind turbine generators,[36] as well as being a producer of some of the world's largest turbines, capable of generating 850 kilowatts to 3 megawatts each. Vestas operates more than 35,000 wind turbines in 63 countries on five continents.[37]

Acciona Windpower, a subsidiary of the Spanish company Acciona Group (MCE: ANA), is building an assembly plant in West Branch, Iowa, that will produce 250 1.5-megawatt wind turbines per year starting in 2008[38] (375 megawatts annually).

Mitsubishi Heavy Industries (TYO: 7011) is a Japanese heavy manufacturing company that makes a huge assortment of big machines, from boilers to bridges and from tankers to torpedoes. It announced in June 2007 that it has orders for 788 wind turbines from the U.S. market, with a collective capacity of 1,363.4 megawatts.[39]

Suzlon Energy Ltd (BOM: 532667), an Indian integrated wind power company, makes wind turbine generators with capacities ranging from 0.35 megawatts to 2.1 megawatts in size. It is currently delivering 400 megawatts of wind turbines to PPM Energy.[40]

Clipper Windpower, Inc. (SEA: CWP) is a UK wind energy technology company that manufactures a 2.5-megawatt Liberty turbine in Cedar Rapids, Iowa. Eight of the turbines are already in operation in Buffalo, New York, and the company has announced firm and contingent orders for 2,240 more of the units over the next five years.[41]

WAVE AND TIDAL ENERGY

One of the largest sources of energy on the planet is ocean energy: harvesting the motion of waves and tides. Both sources of energy are inexhaustible: Waves are caused by winds and the heating of water, which in turn are caused by the sun; tides are caused by the gravitational attraction between the earth, sun, and moon.

Next to solar and geothermal energy, ocean power is arguably our largest untapped energy source, spending enough wave energy in a single day (72 trillion watt-hours) to power more than half of all American households for an entire year. Just 1 to 2 percent of global wave power could meet 13 percent of the world's electricity needs.[42]

A recent study by the nonprofit Electric Power Research Institute found that marine energy could easily outperform hydroelectric power, which is currently our primary source of renewable energy. And that's assuming that we use just 20 percent of the commercially viable offshore wave resources at only 50 percent efficiency!

Ocean energy offers clean, green, extremely consistent power, at a relatively low cost, with negligible environmental impact, being pollution free and very quiet. And since the "fuel" of ocean generators—the movement of waves and tides—costs nothing, marine energy holds the promise of being able to generate electricity at highly competitive rates.

Types of Generators

Tidal energy generators similar to dams have been around for centuries. The oldest tidal mill in England has been operating for over 900 years.

Today, there are nearly two dozen very different designs for wave energy systems in development, employing a variety of technologies using pumps, pistons, turbines, and hydraulics: wave energy, tidal energy, ocean current energy, offshore wind, salinity gradient energy, and ocean thermal gradient energy. But wave and tidal designs are taking the lion's share of investment bucks. Let's take a closer look at them:

- The barrage type of tidal generator, such as the Rance tidal power in Bretagne, France, essentially creates a dam across a body of water such as a lagoon, which traps water when the tide is high and then uses it to power turbines by letting the water out when the tide is low.

- Wave generators are typically anchored to the ocean floor and use the motion of waves to make something on the surface drive hydraulic pistons as it bobs up and down. The Pelamis, developed by Ocean Power Delivery, is one such design, a snakelike machine the length of a freight train that bobs on the surface of the water, delivering energy to pistons.[43]

- Tidal stream or marine current generators are like underwater wind turbines, and are typically situated in a narrow strait such as the Golden Gate at the mouth of the San Francisco Bay, or an oceanic current, where a regular stream of water movement takes place. Tide farms, like those developed by Marine Current Turbines, resemble underwater windmills on steroids and are mounted on concrete pylons on the ocean floor.

Although tidal and wave energy generators have been considered for decades and many prototype systems have been designed and constructed, very few commercial-scale systems have been built. The problem has been that the source of energy, while immense, is too diffuse to harvest economically. It simply takes so many devices spread out over so large an area that the capital costs, technical challenges, and environmental review considerations become onerous. Most projects have ultimately failed to raise sufficient capital.

To be sure, this technology is in its infancy. In an interview with *Scientific American*, a leading ocean energy expert estimated that marine power is about 20 years behind wind power. "But it certainly isn't going to take 20 years to catch up," he added.[44]

A Wave of New Investment

However, with constrained oil supplies, governments the world over have been looking again at these potential generators, and generating a wave of investment capital for private-public research and demonstration projects. So while it is unlikely that wave and tidal energy will provide more than a fraction of the total energy supply any time soon, it is assured that technical advances and efficiency gains will be made.

We must therefore view it as an emerging and promising area of renewable energy, albeit one that is in a developmental phase and primarily appropriate for long-term investing. Investors who get in the water now have an opportunity to ride one of the biggest waves in energy investing.

The Energy Policy Act of 2005 requires the Department of Energy to consider ocean energy in its inventory of renewables, and makes it eligible for R&D monies. That's going to mean big research bucks for ocean power!

And as of this writing, the Federal Energy Regulatory Commission (FERC) is considering an expedited licensing process for pilot projects involving wave and tidal energy technologies. The change would promote the rapid deployment of pilot projects, as long as they are five megawatts or smaller in capacity, located in waters that have no sensitive designations, and removable or able to be shut down on relatively short notice.[45] Such expedited licensing should remove much of the regulatory risk that has so far inhibited investment.

New projects are starting up in several U.S. locations:

- In June 2007, New York began generating power from a tidal energy system on the bed of the East River. The project uses six 35-kilowatt tidal current turbines made by Verdant Power LLC, which are now generating

1,000 kWh per day for Roosevelt Island while a $1.5 million sonar system monitors effects on local fish populations.[46]

■ California's Pacific Gas and Electric Company (PG&E) is working with local agencies to explore tidal power options in San Francisco Bay. A recent article in the *San Francisco Chronicle* estimated that the city could supply 100 percent of its electricity demand with marine energy.[47]

■ In Washington State, the Snohomish County Public Utility District (PUD) is looking at potential tidal energy sites along the coast.[48]

■ Prototype projects are surfacing in Rhode Island as well.

At least nine other countries are considering tidal and wave energy projects, but again, most of them are in pilot or development stage.[49]

Global energy giants like General Electric, Norsk Hydro of Norway, and E.ON of Germany are betting that the ocean holds as much promise as the solar and wind industries. They've already poured more than $100 million of funding into tiny marine energy companies in 2006, and are pledging more for the future.[50]

The British government has already spent more than £25 million ($46.7 million) on research and development, plus another £50 million to make marine energy a commercial reality.[51] Marine plants are scheduled to come on line in Cornwall by 2008 and in Northern Devon by 2010.

If the plan works, Britain will be able to satisfy all of its obligations under the Kyoto Protocol using marine energy alone![52]

At least four companies are currently testing wave conversion devices worldwide.[53] The most ambitious of these projects is in Great Britain, where the government hopes to supply one-fifth of its power needs with marine energy.

The world's first commercial wave farm is now being built in Portugal.[54] The initial phase will consist of three Pelamis machines located off the north coast. The €8 million, 2.25-megawatt project will meet the electricity demand of more than 1,500 households.[55]

An even bigger installation has been proposed for a site in the sea 10 miles off Cornwall in southwest England. The potential 5-megawatt wave power project, called WestWave, would consist of seven Pelamis machines, enough to power the equivalent of 3,000 households.[56]

It seems a bit ironic that the Pelamis wave energy converters are made by a Scottish company but its initial commercial projects are elsewhere. Not to be outdone, Scotland's Enterprise Minister, Nicol Stephen, said in August 2006 that he wanted to see the technology operating in Scottish waters. "I am committed to supporting Scotland's huge wave and tidal energy resource. Scotland has a real opportunity to be a world leader in this field," he said.[57]

There is a tidal wave of investment money building around the world, just looking for viable marine energy projects. As long as these new projects deliver on their promises, we may expect the sector to increase exponentially. You can't get much cleaner or greener than ocean power, and the need and the supply are vast.

RELOCALIZATION

Although relocalization does not have many direct investment opportunities, this book would be incomplete without a mention of the incredible work that is under way across the world toward relocalization.

Relocalization is, just as it sounds, essentially the opposite of globalization. The more food, fuel, and other needs that can be produced locally to satisfy local markets, the less energy will be needed to transport stuff around, so the benefits in reduced fuel consumption are clear.

But relocalization also offers less tangible benefits. When consumers and producers are in close proximity, the quality of goods increases, and the market distortions that are so common in a globalized economy tend to disappear. Likewise, when consumers can see for themselves the full range of costs and benefits of a particular activity, they can make smart choices about how to spend their discretionary dollars, instead of, for example, having to wonder if that shirt they're buying was made with child labor a half a world away. In addition, money stays within the local economy, so that a community can build on its own success. Just as globalization leads to disconnected markets and suppliers and unsustainable market choices, relocalization leads toward cohesive, sustainable communities.

The first serious effort at devising a relocalization plan in the United States was done by the tiny northern Californian town of Willits. It began when Dr. Jason Bradford, a resident, starting showing the documentary film *The End of Suburbia* in October 2004 to interested residents in Willits, out of his concern about peak oil and his desire to organize a response. As he continued his efforts, interest grew, and eventually the community organized a group called Willits Economic LocaLization (WELL) to work on a plan. Their objectives are straightforward:

- Determining the current resource use in the community of Willits, California (energy, transportation, food, housing, etc.).

- Examining how the community can reduce its consumption of those resources imported.

- Visualizing local resources that can replace those imported from outside the community.

- Implementing this transition toward a localized economy.

After nearly two years of work mostly done by volunteers, in 2006 the group created and adopted formal guidance documents, including a governance document, a membership document, and a one-year strategic plan. These elements have served as a useful model to other communities interested in making their own sustainability plans.[58]

A nonprofit group called the Post Carbon Institute has made its mission to help communities organize themselves and come up with their own sustainability plans. Through their online Relocalization Network, community groups can share ideas, information, and inspiration with each other. As of July 2007, there are already 159 Post Carbon groups, and the network is growing rapidly. In addition, via the Post Carbon Cities initiative, they offer media on peak oil and response planning, as well as technical assistance and resources for municipalities interested in relocalization.

Through experimental projects such as Time Banks, where participants can exchange their services in time units rather than in money, and their Energy Farms, which attempt to discover and demonstrate sustainable local agriculture for food and fuel production, the Post Carbon Institute offers a wealth of tools and support to help communities plan their own futures.

THE HYDROGEN ECONOMY

Much has been made of the concept of a "hydrogen economy," because it offers the possibility of a portable fuel that can be generated from any number of sources and consumed without greenhouse gas emissions.

That's a major win-win against the twin devils of peak oil and global warming, and as such it has attracted the support of an unlikely alliance of environmentalists, technologists, politicians, and automakers.

It's important to realize that hydrogen is not a fuel source; it's an energy *carrier* like electricity. Hydrogen does not exist freely in the universe; it's always bound to something else. So it takes an investment of energy to free hydrogen from its existing arrangement and make it available as a stored fuel.

The hydrogen fuel cycle goes like this: Hydrogen is liberated from some source, compressed or liquefied for storage and transport, then "burned" in a device called a fuel cell, in which energy is captured from the hydrogen as it combines with oxygen from the air to form water. The captured energy can be used to power electric motors and generators, and the only emissions are pure water.

It's an elegant vision, and has captured the imagination of such luminaries as Stanford Ovshinsky, the brilliant founder of the advanced energy company Energy Conversion Devices (ECD Ovonics, NASDAQ: ENER). Hydrogen proponents imagine a future wherein the original hydrogen is generated by the electrolysis of water, using electricity generated from renewable sources. Thus the hydrogen fuel cycle would begin and end with plain water, and it would still offer portability, as well as a basis for a distributed clean, green energy cycle.

They envision homeowners generating their own renewable power (using solar, geothermal, micro-hydro, or whatever they've got), and turning it into hydrogen that they can store on-site, then consume in their hydrogen-powered cars or in the fuel cell stack that powers their home.

Unfortunately, the vision breaks down when we analyze the energy return on investment (EROI) of the process. According to the second law of thermodynamics, when energy is converted from one form into another, a little energy is lost in the process, usually as heat. Essentially every time you convert energy, you pay a tax.

EROI: The Hydrogen Buzzkill

Calculating the EROI of a hydrogen fuel cycle requires a good many assumptions about how it will be generated, transported, stored, and consumed. So different sets of assumptions can produce quite different results. In the aforementioned example of home-based hydrogen generation, where the hydrogen is generated and consumed in a single site, losses along the way are low. But when it is used in a vehicle, as hydrogen proponents suggest, losses are much higher.

Let's explore a typical six-step calculation of the EROI of the hydrogen fuel cycle for cars:[59]

1. Suppose we generate the hydrogen by the electrolysis of water. First we must rectify the grid's AC electricity into DC, at a cost of about 2 to 3 percent of the energy contained in the hydrogen.

2. Now we can electrolyze the water, but that process is only about 70 percent efficient, so we lose another 30 percent there.

3. Now we have hydrogen gas, but it takes up a lot of space. We could compress it to around 10,000 pounds per square inch (psi) to make it fit in a

reasonably sized tank, which costs another 15 percent. But even then, it would have only about one-fifth of the energy density of gasoline, and the pressurized tank needed to store it is very heavy, large, and expensive. So if we wanted to use it in a vehicle, we would have to liquefy the hydrogen by cooling it down to about –253°C, and keep it in a much smaller pressurized, insulated container instead. This process would cost another 30 to 40 percent of the energy in the hydrogen.

4. We lose some more potential energy during storage because hydrogen boils off above –253°C, so it's very difficult to keep it from escaping its container. In vehicles, about 3 to 4 percent of the hydrogen boils off every day. At least 10 percent of the hydrogen will boil off during delivery and storage.

5. Then we burn the hydrogen in a vehicle's fuel cell at an efficiency of about 50 percent (for a proton membrane fuel cell stack).

6. And finally, we lose another 10 percent of the energy that makes it to the electric motors driving the wheels, because they are only about 90 percent efficient.

In the end, about 80 percent of the original energy generated in order to produce the hydrogen is lost, for an EROI of 0.2. Since it clearly doesn't pay to have an energy regime with an EROI of less than 1.0, hydrogen-powered cars seem a permanent improbability.

There is also the issue of scale. How could we generate a sufficient amount of electricity to make enough hydrogen to power all those cars? To put the problem in perspective, it has been calculated that it would require 67 large nuclear reactors to produce enough hydrogen to fuel the UK's car fleet, and 100 nuclear reactors to displace all the UK's road transport. It's hard to imagine that happening, just as it's hard to imagine generating that much electricity via renewables just for transportation.[60]

Carbon Emissions Persist

There's another dirty little secret about hydrogen that is rarely mentioned by hydrogen hypers: The vast majority of hydrogen manufactured today is not made from the electrolysis of water, because of the energy inputs needed. Instead, it's made from natural gas, which is a ready and easily exploited feedstock for hydrogen production that can be transported more easily in liquid form. And that means that the hydrogen production does, in fact, produce carbon dioxide emissions, effectively nullifying the environmental benefits of fuel cells.

When natural gas is the feedstock, as it is today, the hydrogen fuel cycle amounts to going around the block to get to the back door, for nothing.

A final problem with the concept of a hydrogen economy is that we would essentially need a whole new infrastructure for it, from "wells to wheels." Nothing in our current energy infrastructure is compatible with hydrogen as fuel.

A major reason for that is that hydrogen is the smallest element, so it wants to escape from just about anything you use to contain it. Tanks, pipes, valves, and fittings all along the way leak, constantly. For another, it's highly reactive and makes metal brittle and prone to leaking. The storage and transport losses can be considerably worse than in the foregoing example.

Starting Over

To build a hydrogen economy, we would need to start over with *everything*—hundreds of thousands of miles of pipeline, 90,000 new pumps at service stations, 210 million vehicles: everything.

Given what we know about the peak oil situation, one wonders just how much of the remaining fossil fuel energy would be needed to replace all that stuff. For example, the amount of energy needed to construct an average car is estimated at the energy equivalent of 27 to 54 barrels of oil.[61] Replacing 210 million vehicles would therefore run somewhere between 5.6 and 11.3 billion barrels of oil, when the United States' entire oil usage is around 8 billion barrels per year. It's fair to say it would be a sizable chunk, a chunk we'd probably be better off using for food and shelter, or for making solar panels and wind turbines.

And then there is the old chicken-and-egg problem: Who is going to pony up the hundreds of billions (actually probably closer to the low trillions) of dollars to build all that infrastructure before the cars are in the showroom, and who's going to put hydrogen cars into a sufficient number of showrooms before the customer has easy access to a refueling station?

There are a few other alternative hydrogen infrastructures, but each has daunting challenges associated with it:

- Hydrogen could theoretically be produced on board a vehicle from liquid methanol or gasoline, but it's going to be difficult, inefficient, and expensive. Big R&D money would be needed for that direction.

- Hydrogen could be produced at local centers, but then we're back to the aforementioned problems of storage, transfer, and the lack of infrastructure.

- It could also be produced right at the fueling station, from methane gas or from water via electrolysis, but the cost of building such stations will be enormous and the infrastructure needs would be great (either to ship natural gas to the stations or to upgrade the grid to handle all that extra electricity). And again, who's going to make that investment before the cars are there?

Now, although it doesn't make sense as a transportation solution, in the right applications hydrogen can be a useful storage system. For example, a large commercial building equipped with a solar system and a fuel cell stack could generate, store, and use much of its own power with minimal losses along the way and no emissions. In such applications, hydrogen is smart. Consequently, we believe the future is bright for companies that focus on that market segment.

Investment Opportunities

We will probably never see a hydrogen economy, but certain applications could be viable. The biggest players are large conglomerates with many more business segments than just hydrogen—companies like Siemens Westinghouse, Cummins Inc., General Electric, Caterpillar, Ingersoll-Rand Company, and Kawasaki. But here are some more focused pure plays on hydrogen, which may be profitable investing opportunities.

FuelCell Energy, Inc. (NASDAQ: FCEL) manufactures fuel cell power plants for large, stationary power-generation applications for commercial, industrial, government, and utility customers. Its carbonate Direct FuelCell (DFC) power plants produce electricity electrochemically from fuels such as natural gas, methanol, diesel, biogas, coal gas, coal mine methane, and propane, and come in 300-kilowatt, 1.2-megawatt, and 2.4-megawatt sizes with between 45 percent and 47 percent efficiency.

Plug Power Inc. (NASDAQ: PLUG) is a development-stage company that makes multiple products for stationary fuel cell systems and fuel processing systems. The company's GenCore product is designed for uninterruptible power supply (UPS) applications (intermittent or backup power demands), and has been purchased by telecommunications carriers and utility customers in North and South America, Europe, Japan, and South Africa.

Ballard Power Systems Inc. (NASDAQ: BLDP) designs, develops, manufactures, and sells proton exchange membrane fuel cell products. One of the most interesting products is a residential fuel cell cogeneration technology currently being demonstrated in Japan. These systems use existing fuel supplies (natural gas or kerosene) to produce hydrogen, which is then converted into electricity and heat—providing for all the hot water needs of a typical Japanese home, plus a kilowatt of power (slightly less than half of the power needed for a typical two-bedroom home in the United States). Ballard also is working with DaimlerChrysler and Ford to develop fuel cell systems for buses, and makes carbon fiber products for the automotive and fuel cell industries.

Although it is more of a play on solar than it is on hydrogen, the aforementioned Energy Conversion Devices (ENER) is building fuel cells and solid forms of hydrogen storage, enabling technologies that make the hydrogen fuel cycle possible. The company expects to develop a full range of stationary, portable power and transportation applications, which can supplement the grid or work offline as portable, fossil-fuel-powered generators.

CHAPTER

13

A FUTURE ELECTRIC

Eighty-five percent of the energy we use comes from fossil fuels. That will wind down, and by and by we're going to have to live on that 15 percent [that is not from fossil fuels] and hopefully we can grow it above the 15 percent that it is now. But that is the dimension of the challenge that we face.

—U.S. REPRESENTATIVE ROSCOE BARTLETT

In the first half of the Age of Oil, oil was plentiful, cheap, and of high quality. Now we enter the second half, in which oil is much harder to find, harder and more expensive to produce, more expensive to refine into useful products, and of progressively lesser quality. Similar trends hold for natural gas, coal, and uranium.

And as we have seen, biofuels will never be more than a partial solution. According to a recent analysis[1] by petrochemist and biofuel engineer Robert Rapier, if we planted all four billion arable acres of land in the world with the most popular biodiesel feedstock, rapeseed, we could produce just under 30 million barrels per day of biodiesel, or just over a third of our present usage of petroleum. And when we take into account all the energy inputs to grow, harvest, and process the rapeseed into fuel, the net yield will be very low, or even negative. Clearly, a liquid fuel regime at the current scale is simply not tenable without oil.

So what sort of energy infrastructure can we hope to have in the future?

The answer is electric. Electricity can be generated from any renewable or nonrenewable source, it can be generated almost anywhere, and it can be emissions-free. If we could massively exploit the world's geothermal potential, for example, we could be running a good deal of our infrastructure on it, without contributing to global warming or otherwise contaminating the environment. Short of everyone taking up the energy lifestyle of the Amish (although it would be a great thing if they did), electricity must be the energy of the future. This is particularly true 80 to 100 years from now, when there will be very little production of today's most dominant fuels.

THE RAIL REVOLUTION, PART II

The low-hanging fruit in switching away from liquid fuels is to focus first on transportation. In the United States, about 70 percent of our total oil use goes to transportation (gasoline, diesel, jet, and boat fuel). If we could displace that portion of consumption, we could save the rest of the oil for uses such as plastics and petrochemicals, some of which can't be made from anything but oil.

A major step in reducing our use of transportation fuel is to switch back to rail, because it is far more efficient. Let's compare the energy requirements of different modes of transportation.

First, the requirements for passenger travel are shown in Table 13.1.

Now let's compare the values for freight, as shown in Table 13.2.

In the United States as of 2002, rail carried 28 percent of the freight miles while consuming 220,000 barrels per day of fuel. By comparison, trucks carried slightly more, at 32 percent of the freight miles, but burned nearly 10 times as much fuel, at 2.07 million barrels per day (about 10 percent of our total petroleum usage). And light commercial trucks consumed another 300,000 barrels per day. From a pure fuel efficiency standpoint, rail is often said to be three[2] to four[3] times as efficient as light trucks, but taking the data shown in Tables 13.1 and 13.2 into account, rail is actually more than eight times as efficient as trucking.[4]

According to a 2006 *Forbes* magazine interview with Gil Carmichael, the head of the Federal Railroad Administration under the first President Bush, "A double-stack freight train can replace as many as 300 trucks and achieve nine times the fuel efficiency of highway movement of the same tonnage volume. . . . Unlike highway expansion projects which require additional land, and which

TABLE 13.1   Comparison of U.S. Passenger Transportation Modes

Transport Mode	Average Passengers per Vehicle	Efficiency per Passenger	
Motorcycles	1.22	2,049 Btu/mi	56 mpg
Rail (Commuter)	33.4	2,571 Btu/mi	44 mpg
Rail (Intercity Amtrak)	17.2	2,935 Btu/mi	39 mpg
Rail (Transit Light & Heavy)	21.7	3,228 Btu/mi	35 mpg
Cars	1.57	3,549 Btu/mi	32 mpg
Air	90.4	3,587 Btu/mi	32 mpg
Personal Trucks	1.72	4,008 Btu/mi	28 mpg
Buses (Transit)	8.7	4,160 Btu/mi	27 mpg

Source: "Transportation Energy Data Book: Edition 26–2007," Center for Transportation Analysis (Oak Ridge National Laboratory), http://cta.ornl.gov/data/tedb26/Edition26_Chapter02.pdf.

TABLE 13.2   Comparison of U.S. Freight Transportation Modes

Transport Mode	Fuel Consumption (Btus per Ton Mile)
Class 1 Railroads	344
Domestic Waterborne	417
Heavy Trucks	3,357
Air Freight	9,600 (approx.)

Sources: "Transportation Energy Data Book: Edition 26–2007," Center for Transportation Analysis (Oak Ridge National Laboratory), http://cta.ornl.gov/data/tedb26/Edition26_Chapter02.pdf; "State Action Policies: Washington," the Environmental Protection Agency, http://yosemite.epa.gov/gw/StatePolicyActions.nsf/uniqueKeyLookup/MSTY5Q4MSV?OpenDocument; "Energy Efficiency Page — Transportation Sector," Energy Information Administration, http://www.eia.doe.gov/emeu/efficiency/ee_ch5.htm.

involve huge costs, prolonged delays, and increasing public opposition, many rail lines can double or triple today's capacity by adding track on rights-of-way the railroads already own."[5]

In fact, apart from motorcycles, rail is the cheapest form of transportation for both passengers and freight!

Big Investments in Rail

Perhaps that is why some of the richest and most successful investors in the world have been recently making huge investments in rail.

Bill Gates, the richest man in the world, has been accumulating shares of Canadian National Railway (NYSE: CNI) since 2000, making him its largest investor.

Legendary investor Warren Buffett is the second-richest man in the world[6] and the CEO of investment company Berkshire Hathaway Inc. In April 2007 the firm disclosed that it had become the biggest shareholder in Burlington Northern, with an 11 percent stake in the firm. Berkshire is now also among the 10 biggest shareholders of both Union Pacific Corporation (NYSE: UNP) and Norfolk Southern Corporation (NYSE: NSC), and its total investments in rail are thought to be around $4.5 billion.[7]

Carl Icahn, the 53rd-richest person in the world,[8] has taken a $122 million stake in CSX.[9] And investor George Soros, the 80th-richest person in the world, is reported to have taken positions in Norfolk Southern and Union Pacific.[10]

Electric Rail Potential

According to engineer Alan Drake, who has done extensive research on the potential of rail, and electrified rail in particular, rail can significantly reduce our consumption of diesel fuel. He believes that one to two million barrels a day of diesel fuel (five to 10 percent of our total oil usage) could be supplanted using just 1.4 percent of U.S. electrical production, and that switching half of our current truck freight to electric rail could save 6.3 percent of U.S. oil consumption.[11]

If electrified railroads also incorporated regenerative braking technology (as featured in GE's new groundbreaking hybrid locomotives), Drake calculates that the savings realized by switching freight loads from diesel-powered trucks to modern electric rail is 20 to 1.

Combined with more efficient cars, and increased production of electricity from renewables, shifting loads to electric rail could significantly reduce our oil consumption. But there would be many other benefits as well, from reducing greenhouse gas emissions, to reduced road congestion, to stopping the bleeding of U.S. dollars sent overseas for oil.

We need look no further than Europe for an example of how an electric transportation system can work. Most railways in Europe and Japan, and many in Russia, are now electric, as are many of the underground trains and trams elsewhere, such as the New York City subway and the BART train system in the San Francisco Bay Area. Under the UK's system, for example, between its 93 percent efficient grid transmission system and 95 percent efficient electric motors with regenerative braking, the entire system's efficiency is nearly 90 percent.[12]

For long-distance or intercity routes, high-speed electric trains can transport passengers nearly as quickly as air travel door-to-door. These trains, like the TGV in France, must be experienced to believe, transporting passengers and cargo smoothly at over 200 miles per hour in quiet comfort, with ample leather seats, no security or luggage hassles, no long waits in queues, or having to show up several hours in advance, and they take you right to the center of town. Such high-speed wheeled trains can reach over 350 mph, which is comparable to Japanese maglev (magnetic levitation) trains.

For the United States, the greatest savings potential of electrified rail would be in replacing car and light truck traffic with urban rail. Since 90 percent of our transportation energy comes from oil, we could reduce our oil consumption significantly by deploying everything from intercity commuter lines to local freight lines to everyday streetcars. Drake believes that with a supportive public policy, a crash urban rail building program could save 9 percent of our current transportation fuel consumption by 2020, with a corresponding 15 percent reduction in private auto travel.

By way of example, Drake calculates that 106 miles of subway and grade-separated rail in the Washington, D.C. metro area alone is "a 90,000 barrel/day oil field that never depletes but only grows a bit each year,"[13] and that such a rail system could easily offset 135,000 barrels a day of oil. That's nearly one percent of the United States' total petroleum usage for transportation, just by implementing rail in one major metropolitan area.

At just over half a million people, Washington, D.C. is only the nation's 27th largest city, and there are about 40 cities in the country with 400,000 people or more.[14] Do the math: By implementing a similar rail system to what Drake proposes for D.C. for all 40, we might eliminate some 40 percent of our transportation demand for oil!

Rail is clearly our lowest-energy option for the future, and the technology is as tried and true as it can be. Although only four U.S. cities currently have an electric trolleybus system (San Francisco, Seattle, Boston, and Dayton), they used to exist in dozens of cities. The oil crisis of the early 1970s revived public interest in electrified rail, but when the Saudis increased production and the price of oil fell again, those plans were scrapped.

Inner-city rail has long had a majority of political support in many cities, but it still faces significant hurdles on two fronts: the political and the financial. In case after case, from Miami's elevated Subway in the Sky to Seattle's expanded monorail plan, the plans are eventually derailed as mounting costs and uneven political support take their toll along the way to getting the projects started. NIMBYism, access to facilities, taxation implications, local jurisdictions, overlapping regulations, lack of usable easements, and a thousand other hurdles plague the path to a future running on rails.

This is why federal support is so essential, as it has been for the nations of Europe and Japan. Without the deep pockets of federal funding and the authority to claim eminent domain and build the new infrastructure where it makes the most sense, rail projects are often too big to be taken on by municipalities. Even a city the size of Los Angeles, with its hundreds of miles of freeways, was only able to self-fund a mere 73 miles of light rail metro system, carrying only 262,000 passengers per day in an area with nearly 10 million people.

The United States not only needs federal funding and regulatory support, but also vision to lead the country where it needs to go and overcome the hurdles along the way. This leadership is critical from the mayoral level all the way up to the presidential level.

France provides a good example of such leadership, with the 2006 announcement by President Jacques Chirac that "RATP and SNCF [the French railroads] will not have to use one drop of oil in 20 years." As of 2005 there were only five towns in France with a population larger than 100,000 that did not have a tram or plans for one.

Portland, Oregon, has always been one of the most progressive U.S. cities in terms of planning for the future and protecting the environment, and its leaders are already anticipating peak oil and considering what they can do about it. Commissioner Sam Adams oversees the Portland Office of Transportation, which is developing a 30-year rail transit plan for the city, and he envisions a future of electric streetcars for his city. "What would Portland look like if we implemented solutions to global warming and peak oil?" Adams asked. "It would look a lot like Portland circa 1920, a time when the main means of motion were your feet, streetcars, and bikes."[15]

Investment Opportunities

Investing in rail is probably best done via a long-term buy-and-hold strategy, and it would be wise to follow in the footsteps of the aforementioned mega-rich investors by simply buying shares of the big railroads: Burlington Northern (NYSE: BNI), Union Pacific (NYSE: UNP), Norfolk Southern (NYSE: NSC), and Canadian National Railway (NYSE: CNI).

And although General Electric is too large to be a pure play on rail, it is the largest manufacturer of railroad locomotives in the United States, including the world's first hybrid locomotive engines. And as we discussed in the previous chapter, it also has exposure to other profitable sectors post peak, such as more efficient appliances, wind generators, and other areas, so it could be a decent choice as well for the long-term investor.

ELECTRIFIED CARS

We have seen that electric rail could handle much of our freight transport needs, but what about personal transportation?

Several studies, such as a 10-year research project by the U.S. Department of Transportation, have explored the idea of electrified roads. Various designs have been proposed, from overhead electric cables such as those used on trolleybuses, to something like a life-sized slot car track. The cars would still need a modicum of battery power to get them between the home and the electric rail, but not nearly as much as an independently powered vehicle.

It has been calculated that on average, such a system could be as much as 80 percent efficient overall. Accordingly, 120 terawatt-hours (TWh) of electricity could supply all of Britain's road transport—the generation equivalent of 12 nuclear reactors, or just 30 percent of Britain's existing electricity production. This is far more realistic than the projected 100 additional nuclear reactors that would be required by a hydrogen-powered system of transportation.[16]

Plug-In Hybrid Revolution

We need not wait for an all-electric regime to run transportation on electricity, however. A small handful of all-electric cars have been produced, such as General Motors' EV-1, the story of which was vividly retold in the recent documentary film, *Who Killed the Electric Car?*

And now there is a new generation of electric vehicles on the way, such as those made by Tesla Motors. Although its high-performance sports car, the Tesla Roadster, fetches a whopping $92,000 for the base model, Tesla has plans to introduce other more affordable models, such as a $50,000 to $70,000 sedan and even a $30,000 model.

The key issue with all-electric cars has always been, and still remains, the battery systems. The battery packs available today are either too big and heavy or too expensive. However, the intensive research now under way on battery technologies may eventually lower the battery barrier. Companies such as the privately held A123 Systems have developed new lithium-ion batteries that can take a car 40 miles on a charge, which would be sufficient to power plug-in hybrid electric vehicles (PHEVs) for 70 percent of daily trips in the United States, delivering 100 mpg overall.[17]

Therefore, the most promising approach to substituting electricity for personal transportation in the near term is the plug-in hybrid electric vehicle, which is basically a souped-up gas-electric hybrid with a larger battery pack that can be plugged in and charged up from the grid—usually at night, when demand and grid power prices are low. You may recall from Chapter 5 that PHEVs are also a key prescription of James Woolsey and the green hawks. The advantage of such a system is that a typical short-distance round-trip on city streets could be made on battery power alone.

According to a July 2007 study[18] by the Electric Power Research Institute (EPRI) and the Natural Resources Defense Council (NRDC), billed as "the most comprehensive environmental assessment of electric transportation to date," the potential benefits of PHEVs are significant.

The researchers used computer models to simulate the carbon emissions under various scenarios, varying the rate of adoption of the new vehicles and the type of fuel used by utilities.

The study found that shifting 60 percent of American car trips to plug-in hybrids by 2050 would lead to an increase in electricity usage of just 7 percent to 8 percent, but would displace the need for 3 to 4 million barrels of oil per day by 2050—more than twice the United States' imports from Saudi Arabia.

Interestingly, they also found that switching to PHEVs would reduce greenhouse gases, *no matter what energy source was used to produce the electricity,* because PHEVs generated 40 percent to 65 percent less greenhouse gas emissions than gas-fueled vehicles, and 7 percent to 46 percent less than conventional hybrids. Other air pollutants such as nitrogen oxide, sulfur dioxide, and ozone would also be reduced in most regions, but particulate matter emissions from the increased burning of coal could rise.

ALL-ELECTRIC

It's easy to see how an all-electric economy could be the only possible, practical response to the peaking of our traditional forms of energy. Not only does it open the door to emerging and enormous renewable resources like geothermal, solar, wind, and marine energy, but it has the potential to eliminate most of the carbon emissions of the fossil-fueled regime.

About the only thing we can't do with electricity is run airplanes or boats,[19] although boats can use nuclear and sail-powered drive systems. However, if we switched over all other loads to electricity, there should be plenty of liquid fuels to go around for boating and flying for many decades to come—albeit at higher prices.

Imagine what could be achieved if, instead of spending half a trillion dollars per year on oil, we spent it on solar, wind, geothermal, and tidal generation; on smart grids and microgrids; on electrified rail and electric cars, even electrified roads; and on more efficient electric appliances and small devices self-powered by solar energy. Calculating the potential of such a transformation at this point would require so many assumptions about the future that it's probably not worth attempting, but having exhausted all other alternatives in the foregoing analysis, it seems the only logical way forward. Most analysts who are aware of the energy issues that underpin "peak everything" have arrived at this same conclusion, even petroleum geologists.

The future, inasmuch as there is one, will be electric.

EPILOGUE

WHY WE'RE ENERGY OPTIMISTS

The challenges before us are indeed daunting and unprecedented, but we have at least an inkling of the way forward.

It was our goal with this book to present a comprehensive view of the current energy landscape. From renewable sources like wind, solar, and geo-thermal to old standbys in the energy complex like oil and nuclear, everything is on the table as a potential solution to the current crisis.

It was also our intention to present the pressure points in the energy market that will impact energy policy. Whether it's talk of preventing or slowing global warming or terrorism, everything we do now entails an energy consideration.

Let's attempt to summarize what we have learned in this study.

A HARSH REALITY

According to our best, most realistic estimates, here's how things stand globally:

Oil: Peaking some time in the next three years, possibly already past the peak.

Gas: Peaking some time in the next three to 13 years.

Coal: Peaking some time in the next 13 years.

Nuclear: Probably peaking some time in the next 10 years, with lots of variables, but its use won't increase substantially.

Tar sands and oil shale: Tar sands production may grow from approximately 1.5 mbpd today to some 5 mbpd by 2030, but it will be unable to even compensate for the decline of a handful of mature oil reservoirs. Oil shale will never be a significant source of fuel.

Hydropower: All of the good resources have already been tapped, and due to reduced water flows (thanks to global warming) and environmental concerns, hydropower is in permanent decline. Indeed, for environmental reasons, the trend is toward shutting down and dismantling hydro plants.

Biofuels: Low net energy return guarantees that biofuels, too, will remain minor players, unable to compensate for the immense loss of energy that oil peaking represents, at least for the near future. Biofuels do have some room to grow, so to speak, but they will probably remain special-purpose fuels and a relatively small part of the overall fuel mix.

All renewables: All other renewables (solar, wind, tidal, wave, and geo-thermal combined) currently provide around 1 percent of the total energy mix. And making all that renewable energy equipment relies heavily on fossil fuels, for mining, smelting, fabricating, shipping, installing, and grid infrastructure.

Even at the current rates of growth, these energy sources won't be able to make up the loss of energy from the peaking of fossil fuels. The quantities of energy we're talking about, and the time (and energy) that it takes to deploy them, are simply too vast. The CEO of Royal Dutch/Shell, Jeroen van der Veer, believes that even after accounting for technological breakthroughs, renewables could only make up about 30 percent of the total energy supply by midcentury,[1] but we think that is optimistic.

In our estimation, it would be amazing to generate 10 percent from renewables by 2020, and up to 20 percent by midcentury. Whatever their contribution, it will be crucial, but we would be surprised if it could even compensate for the loss of fossil fuel energy over the same period.

When all possible energy sources are taken into account, as well as the inherent limits of each one, it becomes clear that energy independence, meaning freedom from imported oil and gas, isn't a practical possibility for the foreseeable future.

A 2006 study sponsored by the Council on Foreign Relations ("National Security Consequences of U.S. Oil Dependency") reached the same conclusion: "During the next twenty years (and quite probably beyond) it is infeasible to eliminate the nation's dependence on foreign energy sources."[2]

FORESIGHT IS 2020

Taking all of the aforementioned production models into account, it looks like *all major sources of energy* that we use today will peak right around 2020 to 2025. That probably includes all renewables, because constrained availability of the other fuels will limit our ability to make more renewable energy machines.

All fossil fuels, plus nuclear fission, will decline much more rapidly than they scaled up, and will be pretty much kaput by the end of the twenty-first century. After "peak everything," we will have to build any additional renewable energy infrastructure using only renewable energy and manual labor. If we should reach the end of the twenty-first century without creating any radical new energy technologies that can make up for the loss of fossil fuels, then we'll be forced to live within the budget of annual solar income and biomass.

But it will be very difficult to make new wind turbines and solar panels and so on using only renewable energy. Imagine mining metals, transporting ore, and running a smelter and a metal shop using only electricity from renewable energy and human or animal labor! One must wonder just how much renewable energy technology can be created using only renewable energies. How much of a renewable-energy-powered manufacturing base will we have by the time we lose access to cheap fossil fuels for good?

The scenario might be a bit different if somebody actually succeeds (and soon) in building pebble-bed nuclear reactors or fusion reactors on a commercial scale, or if a way is found to make cellulosic ethanol cheaply at commercial scale; but at this point in time, none of those things seem likely.

What does seem likely is that energy depletion has the potential to cause global conflict.

At this point we must consider the case amply proven that *there are no supply-side solutions* to the problem of fossil fuel peak. Trying to maintain business as usual by increasing energy supply may be possible in the short term. But in the long term, it is not only impossible; it's suicidal! The longer our energy consumption is allowed to grow, to meet the demands of growing population and growing economies, the greater will be our overhang as we pass the point of peak energy, and the more difficult will be the post-peak adjustment.

Indeed, as Stanley Jevons observed all the way back in 1865, increases in efficiency generally lead to increased, not decreased, consumption, as freed capital makes it possible to scale up one's activities. This dynamic has since come to be known as the Jevons Paradox.[3]

Clearly, the prudent course of action is to reduce our energy demand aggressively, in order to make the remaining fuel last as long as possible and give us as much time as possible to adjust to a regime of declining, rather than increasing, energy supplies.

But human history has precious few examples of heeding such foresight and proactively preparing for the future. Instead, we invariably cling to the present with a white-knuckled grip and try to ward off undesirable changes as long as possible—precisely what we should *not* do if we want to minimize the pain and chaos of the future.

The world is in no way prepared for the coming changes. The first world is massively addicted to fossil fuels in every way, and the developing world is rapidly going in the same direction.

All of the world's economies depend on continuous growth to be considered healthy, and none are doing any serious planning for a world of declining energy. When an economic growth rate under 2 percent annually is considered a depression, what will we call a reality in which we have *negative* growth rates, and how will we deal with it?

This is truly the greatest challenge we have ever faced.

The Next Greatest Generation?

But this isn't the first time we have faced a major challenge.

Sixty-odd years ago, America responded to Hilter's threat with an unprecedented mobilization of manufacturing muscle and good old American ingenuity, creating a powerful war machine in very short order and winning the war. Those young men and women earned their reputation as the "Greatest Generation."

Now American business has another great security challenge at its feet: Can it find a way forward for the lumbering U.S. economy?

Can we be the next Greatest Generation by greening not just our military, but our entire infrastructure?

The similarity of World War II to the present-day twin challenges of energy supplies and global warming has also apparently occurred to Britain's Prince Charles, who said: "We can do it. Just think what they did in the last war. Things that seemed impossible were achieved almost overnight."

Our ability to execute on advanced and alternative energy technologies, and to do more with less, is what will make it or break it now for the Land of the Free.

The very security, prosperity, and liberty of our great country depend on it.

NEVER SELL SHORT HUMANITY

If there's one thing we've learned in our study of these subjects, it's to never sell short humanity. When sufficiently aroused, we have an amazing ability to come up with creative solutions and change our behaviors. Nothing is ever set in stone.

And that's the true moral of this story: Every crisis—no matter how dismal it looks—contains the blueprint for its own solution.

And peak oil is no different.

As you read this, investors, academicians, and entrepreneurs are racing to find and create the next great energy source.

The market is responding accordingly to higher oil prices.

Back in 2003, when we first began to study peak oil in earnest, we would have never imagined that in just three years we'd see everybody from prime ministers to CEOs to CIA and Pentagon heads making energy security and global warming their top priorities. Hardly anybody was even thinking about biofuels. We'd have scoffed at the notion that entire countries would agree to phase out incandescent lightbulbs. And yet, here we are. And the renewable energy industry is in better shape than ever.

We have some major challenges ahead. We have to change assumptions that everyone alive today has always taken for granted, like economies that constantly expand, populations that grow unchecked, and endless supplies of cheap fossil fuels.

If you live for another 20 years, you will be around to see the beginning of the end of the Energy Man phase of human history. How will you prepare for that? Those who were born at the turn of the new century will be in their college years when we reach peak energy; what will their adulthoods be like?

The low-hanging fruit right now is clearly efficiency—not just swapping out our lightbulbs, but improving fuel economy, improving insulation, changing the ways we make buildings, and reconfiguring entire communities, all with the goal of relocalization. The more food and energy that people can grow for themselves, the better.

Solar power makes economic sense for just about anybody now, so it's taking off. Wind and geothermal power are also set for enormous growth. Biofuels clearly have a growing role, and innovations in transportation are popping up like daisies. Other, more distant solutions are out there, too, beckoning for the large stream of R&D money that's rapidly flowing toward them.

The dimmer the reality of fossil fuels is, the brighter the future is for renewables. But we've got a lot of work to do. There is no time to lose.

Now put this book down, go out there, install some solar panels on your house, and learn how to grow a decent tomato. You won't regret it.

APPENDIX A

ENERGY UNITS AND EQUIVALENCES TABLES

TABLE A.1   **Typical Heat Values of Fuel Sources**

Brown Coal	9.7 MJ/kg
Straw and Grain	14 MJ/kg
Firewood (Dry)	16 MJ/kg
Black Coal (NSW & Qld)	24–30 MJ/kg
Black Coal (SA & WA)	13–20 MJ/kg
Rapeseed Oil	37 MJ/kg
Natural Gas	39 MJ/m^3
Crude Oil	45–46 MJ/kg
Natural Uranium—in Light Water Reactor	443,000 MJ/kg
Enriched Uranium (3.5%)—in Light Water Reactor	3,456,000 MJ/kg
Uranium—in Fast Breeder Reactor	24,000,000 MJ/kg

MJ = Megajoules.

Source: Dr. Tad W. Patzek, Professor of Geoengineering, University of California at Berkeley, sources cited on his web page: http://petroleum.berkeley.edu/patzek/ce24/Spring2003/heatvalues.htm.

TABLE A.2 Typical Heat Values of Finished Fuels

Jet Fuel	135,000 Btu/gallon
Compressed Natural Gas	138,700 Btu/gallon
Aviation Gasoline	120,200 Btu/gallon
Distillate Fuel	138,700 Btu/gallon
Automotive Gasoline	125,000 Btu/gallon
Residual Fuel	149,700 Btu/gallon
Diesel Motor Fuel	138,700 Btu/gallon
Natural Gas	1,031 Btu/ft[a]
Electricity 1kWh	3,412 Btu[a]

[a]Negating electrical system losses. To include approximate electrical system losses, multiply this conversion factor by 3.

Source: Dr. Tad W. Patzek, Professor of Geoengineering, University of California at Berkeley, sources cited on his web page: http://petroleum.berkeley.edu/patzek/ce24/Spring2003/heatvalues.htm.

TABLE A.3 Energy Unit Equivalences

1 barrel of oil equivalent $=$ 5.80 MBtu
1 tonne oil equivalent $=$ 41.868 GJ $=$ 39.68 MBtu
1 Mbd $=$ 2 quad/yr
1 calorie (mean) $=$ 4.1900 J
1 Btu $=$ 251.9958 calories $=$ 1,055.87 J
1 kilowatt-hour (kWh) $=$ 3.6 $\times$ 10^6 J $=$ 3,412 Btu
1 quad $=$ 109 MBtu $=$ 10^{15} Btu $=$ 1.055 EJ
1 exajoule (EJ) $=$ 10^{18} J
1 terawatt-year (TWyr) $=$ 8.76 $\times$ 10^{12} kWh

Source: American Physical Society, "Energy Units," www.aps.org/policy/reports/popa-reports/energy/units.cfm.

TABLE A.4 Comparative Thermal Values of Various Fuels

To find the comparative thermal value of one fuel to another, look up the first fuel in the left-hand column, and get its Btu value. Then find that value in the top row, and look down the corresponding column to find the Btu equivalence of the other fuel.

Thermal Value	1,000,000 Btu 1 MMBtu	24,000,000 Btu 24 MMBtu	91,600 Btu 91.6 MBtu	125,000 Btu 125 MBtu	139,000 Btu 139 MBtu	150,000 Btu 150 MBtu	3,412,000 Btu 3.412 MMBtu
Natural Gas 1,000 Btu/cu ft.	1,000 cu ft 1 Mcf	24,000 cu ft 24 Mcf	91.6 cu ft	125 cu ft	139 cu ft	150 cu ft	3,412 cu ft
Coal 12,000 Btu/lb	83.333 lbs	2,000 lbs 1 ton	7.633 lbs	10.417 lbs	11.583 lbs	12.5 lbs	284.3 lbs
Propane 91,600 Btu/gal	10.917 gal	262 gal	1 gal	1.365 gal	1.517 gal	1.638 gal	37.3 gal
Gasoline 125,000 Btu/gal	8 gal	192 gal	0.733 gal	1 gal	1.112 gal	1.2 gal	27.3 gal
Fuel Oil #2 139,000 Btu/gal	7.194 gal	172.662 gal	0.659 gal	0.899 gal	1 gal	1.079 gal	24.5 gal
Fuel oil #6 150,000 Btu/gal	6.666 gal	160 gal	0.611 gal	0.833 gal	0.927 gal	1 gal	22.7 gal
Electricity 3,412 Btu/kWh	293.083 kWh	7034 kWh	26.846 kWh	36.635 kWh	40.739 kWh	43.962 kWh	1,000 kWh 1 MW

Source: Dr. Tad W. Patzek, Professor of Geoengineering, University of California at Berkeley; sources cited on his web page: http://petroleum.berkeley.edu/patzek/ce24/Spring2003/heatvalues.htm.

APPENDIX B

TOP OIL PRODUCERS AND PEAK PRODUCTION

TABLE B.1 Top Oil Producers and Peak Production (2006)

Country	Peak Year	Peak Rate (Million barrels/day)	Current Rate (Million barrels/day)	Change '05–'06 (1000's barrels/day)	Trend	Comments
Saudi Arabia*	N/A		10.9	–255	→	Saudi Arabia says steep decline is voluntary cutback; we'll see.
Russia	1987	11.5	9.8	217	←	Russia repeaks in 2–4 years; growth spurt almost over.
United States	1971	11+/–	6.9	–24	→	Gulf of Mexico 2006 comeback partially offset other declines.
Iran*	1974	6.06	4.3	75	—	Slow gains/flat; Iran won't repeak; nukes 1 nationalism.
Mexico	2004	3.8	3.7	–77	→	Cantarell field in permanent decline, –17% annually.
China	N/A		3.7	57	←	China probably will peak and flatten within two years.
Canada	N/A		3.1	106	←	Canada's conventional oil peaked years ago; oil sands up.
United Arab Emirates*	N/A		3	218	←	UAE talks increase; what's in their best interest?
Venezuela*	1970	3.6?	2.8	–103	→	Resource nationalism poster child; Chavez-driven dip.
Norway	2001	3.42	2.8	–191	→	Norwegian North Sea steadily declining; –19% in five years.

TOP TEN: 62% OF TOTAL   51   23

Country	Year	Peak	Production	Net	Trend	Notes
Kuwait*	1972	3.28	2.7	61	←	Burghan Field, world's second largest, has peaked.
Nigeria*	N/A		2.46	-120	→	Nigeria = basket case. Deepwater, violence both grow.
Algeria*	N/A		2.02	-11	—	Algeria has room to grow; cut for OPEC quota last year.
Iraq*	1979	3.48	2	166	—	Civil war hurting infrastructure; can't bounce back fast.
Libya*	1970	3.32	1.84	84	←	Libya can increase, but new peak unlikely.
Brazil	N/A		1.81	94	←	Still growing; excludes cane ethanol. Self-sufficient.
United Kingdom	1999	3	1.64	-173	→	Production down 44% since 1999. Prognosis: terminal.
Kazakhstan	N/A		1.43	70	←	Kazaks have tripled production over past decade.
Angola*	N/A		1.41	176	←	Angola rising star; has doubled over past decade.
Qatar*	N/A		1.13	107	←	Qatar doubled over past decade; large NGL gains continue.
NEXT TEN (11–20): 23% OF TOTAL			18.4	454		

(Continued)

TABLE B.1 Continued

Country	Peak Year	Peak Rate (Million barrels/day)	Current Rate (Million barrels/day)	Change '05–'06 (1000's barrels/day)	Trend	Comments
Indonesia*	1977	1.69	1.07	–58	→	OPEC member used to export; now net importer.
India	N/A		0.81	23	—	India flat near 800,000 bpd. Imports rising.
Malaysia	2004?	0.79	0.75	–20	→	Malaysia doubled since 1985; now declining. On watch list.
Oman	2001	0.96	0.74	–36	→	Oman: 23% decline since 2001.
Argentina	1998	0.89	0.72	–9	→	Argentina's steady decline continues.
Egypt	1993	0.95	0.68	–18	→	Egypt yields new gas finds, but not much new oil.
Azerbaijan	N/A		0.65	202	←	Zooming up the chart; new pipeline allows big exports.
Colombia	1999	0.84	0.56	4	—	Colombians still beset by narcoterrorists and rebels.
Ecuador	N/A		0.55	4	—	Up only 1% past two years. Internal politics volatile.
Australia	2000	0.81	0.54	–10	→	A 2007 rebound is break in long decline trend.
NEXT TEN (21–30): 9% OF TOTAL			7.1	82		

	Year					
Syria	1995	0.6	0.42	-41	→	Syria down 28% since 2001, 9% drop last year alone.
Sudan	N/A		0.4	42	←	Sudanese violence persists; new OPEC member soon.
Yemen	2001	0.47	0.39	-36	→	Yemen halted decline, could be one-year reprieve.
Vietnam	2004?	0.43	0.37	-31	→	Vietnam suffered two-year decline of 14%. Trend?
Equatorial Guinea	N/A		0.36	2	—	E. Guinea producing for 13 years; growth spurt over?
Denmark	2004	0.39	0.34	-35	→	One-year decline of 9% in 2006.
Thailand	N/A		0.29	21	←	Thailand should still see modest growth.
Congo	1999	0.29	0.26	16	—	Congo's small two-year gain brings it back to plateau.
Gabon	1997	0.37	0.23	-2	→	Gabon, former OPEC nation, flat spot during decline.
Brunei	1979	0.24	0.22	15	—	Brunei flat five years, then a little growth; new peak?
NEXT TEN (31–40):	**4% OF TOTAL**		3.28	-49		*Nations 31–40 total produce little more than Canada.*

(*Continued*)

TABLE B.1 Continued

Country	Peak Year	Peak Rate (Million barrels/day)	Current Rate (Million barrels/day)	Change '05–'06 (1000's barrels/day)	Trend	Comments
Trinidad & Tobago	1978	0.23	0.17	3	—	Dipped 25% 1985–1998. Recent uptrend.
Turkmenistan	2003?	0.2	0.16	−29	→	Sudden 15% drop last year.
Chad	N/A	N/A	0.15	−20	→	Producing only three years; geopolitical hic-cup = one-year drop?
Uzbekistan	1992	0.19	0.13	−1	→	Could repeat, but unlikely: down 1/3 past six years.
Peru	1983	0.2	0.12	5	←	Peru bounced back in 2005, 2006; watch for nationalism.
Italy	N/A	0.12	0.11	−6	—	Near the bottom ranking, but new peak in 2005.
Romania	1976	0.3	0.11	−9	→	World's first oil wells drilled here in 1854.
Tunisia	1984	0.12	0.07	−5	—	Only Tunisia cares about small decline.
Cameroon	1988	0.18	0.06	5	→	Only Cameroon cares about small increase.
ALL THE REST	N/A		0.75	5	→	"Everybody else" trending down, too small to matter.
NEXT TEN (41–50):	**2% OF TOTAL**		1.83	1.83		*Remaining nations produce same as Libya.*
TOTAL			81.66	511.83		

* = OPEC Member

Data source: British Petroleum, using 2006 data. Includes crude oil, shale oil, oil sands, and natural gas liquids (NGLs); excludes biomass. Comments and data aggregation by Steve Andrews and Randy Udall, ASPO-USA, *Peak Oil Review* 2, no. 23, June 18, 2007, www.aspo-usa.com/. Revised by Chris Nelder.

APPENDIX C
ENERGY MIX CHARTS

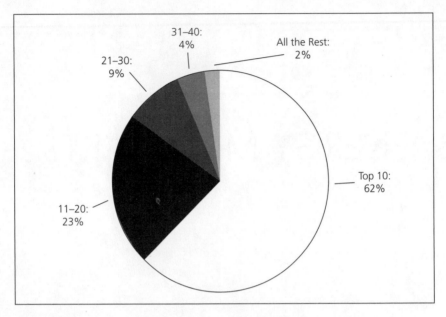

FIGURE C.1   *Oil-Producing Nations by Share of Total*

Source: Chart created from data provided in Appendix B.

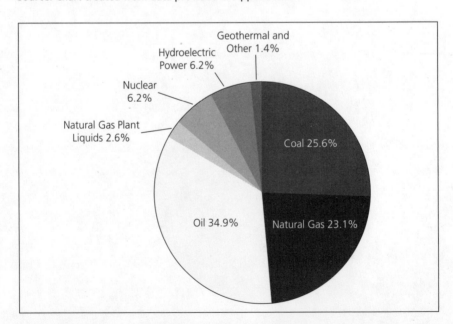

FIGURE C.2   *World Energy Production by Source, 2004*

Source: EIA, "World Primary Energy Production by Source, 1970–2004," www.eia.doe
.gov/emeu/aer/txt/stb1101.xls.

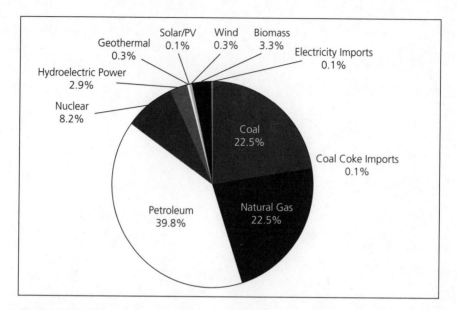

FIGURE C.3 *U.S. Energy Consumption by Source, 2006*

Source: EIA, "U.S. Energy Consumption by Source, 1970–2004," www.eia.doe.gov/
emeu/aer/txt/stb0103.xls.

GLOSSARY

bbl: Barrel (42 gallons).

boe: Barrels of oil equivalent.

bpd: Barrels per day.

Btu: British thermal unit (a measure of heat energy).

C+C: Crude oil + lease condensates.

DOE: U.S. Department of Energy.

dry gas (dry natural gas): "Natural gas which remains after the liquefiable hydrocarbon portion has been removed from the gas stream (i.e., gas after lease, field, and/or plant separation); and any volumes of nonhydrocarbon gases have been removed where they occur in sufficient quantity to render the gas unmarketable. Note: Dry natural gas is also known as consumer-grade natural gas. The parameters for measurement are cubic feet at 60 degrees Fahrenheit and 14.73 pounds per square inch absolute." (*Source:* DOE, www.eia.doe.gov/emeu/iea/glossary.html#DryNaturalGas)

EIA: Energy Information Administration, part of the U.S. Department of Energy, which keeps data and statistics on energy.

EUR: Estimated ultimately recoverable (equivalent to URR).

exajoule (EJ): 1 EJ = 10^{18} J.

Gb: Billion barrels.

GW: Gigawatts; 1 GW = 1 billion watts.

IEA: International Energy Agency, an intergovernmental body created after the oil shocks of the 1970s to coordinate the West's reaction to energy crises.

joule (J): Unit of energy equivalent to the work done in lifting a one-newton weight a distance of one meter.

kW: kilowatt (a measure of electrical energy); 1,000 watts.

kWh: kilowatt-hour (i.e., a kilowatt of energy consumed or generated for one hour).

mbpd: Million barrels per day.

MW: Megawatt.

NGL: Natural gas liquids (lease condensate + NGPL).

NGPL: Natural gas plant liquids.

quad: Quadrillion Btus.

Tb: Trillion barrels.

TWh: terawatt-hour, or one billion kilowatt-hours.

URR: Ultimate recoverable resource (equivalent to EUR).

watt: A measure of electrical energy, equivalent to one ampere flowing under a pressure of one volt at unity power factor.

NOTES

Introduction

1. *Source:* The Wolf at the Door, "The Beginner's Guide to Peak Oil." http://wolf.readinglitho .co.uk/mainpages/oilproducts.html.
2. Australian Broadcasting Corporation, transcript of interview with Roger Bezdek, June 19, 2007. www.abc.net.au/lateline/business/items/200706/s1956166.htm.

Chapter 1   December 2005: The Month the Devil Wept His Trillionth Tear

1. Matthew R. Simmons' slide deck, "Energy Market Outlook," April 26, 2007, Investment Adviser Association 2007 Annual Conference, www.simmonsco-intl.com/files/Investment%20Advisers %20Association%20April%2026.pdf.
2. Simmons' remarks at ASPO-USA First World Oil Conference, November 10, 2005. Notes by Chris Nelder, www.getreallist.com/article.php?story=20060829200211917.
3. Tom Petrie, "A Strategic Perspective on 21st Century Energy Challenges," a presentation to the Institute of International Education, June 18, 2007. As cited by Steve Andrews, *Peak Oil Review,* June 25, 2007.
4. Brian Bender, "Pentagon Study Says Oil Reliance Strains Military," *Boston Globe,* May 1, 2007, www.boston.com/news/nation/washington/articles/2007/05/01/pentagon_study_says_oil_ reliance_strains_military/?page=2.

Chapter 2   What Is Peak Oil?

1. William M. White, *Geochemistry,* an on-line textbook by Cornell University, Ch. 14, http://www .geo.cornell.edu/geology/classes/Chapters/Chapter14.pdf.
2. Johnathan Billig and Anna Iroff, "How Oil Is Formed and Found," www.columbia.edu/~ari2102/ Oil%20Formation/Oil%20Formation2.html.
3. Kenneth S. Deffeyes, *Beyond Oil* (New York: Hill & Wang, 2005).
4. William M. White, *Geochemistry.*
5. Energy Story, "Fossil Fuels—Coal, Oil and Natural Gas," www.energyquest.ca.gov/story/ chapter08.html.
6. Colin Campbell interview in the documentary film *A Crude Awakening.*
7. "Letter to Members" from the National Academy of Sciences, Volume 19, Number 4, April 1990, http://www.hubbertpeak.com/hubbert/tribute.htm.
8. Centre for Energy, "What Is Oil?" www.centreforenergy.com/generator.asp?xml=%2Fsilos% 2Foil%2FoilOverview01XML.asp&Template=1,1.
9. OPEC Monthly Oil Market Report, August 2005, http://www.opec.org/home/Monthly%20Oil% 20Market%20Reports/2005/pdf/MR082005.pdf.

10. Energy Information Administration FAQ, "Pricing Differences Among Various Types of Crude Oil," July 2006. http://tonto.eia.doe.gov/ask/crude_types1.html.

11. Ibid.

12. W. L. Littlejohn, "Further to the Future of Saudi Oil," *Aramco Expats*, March 6, 2004, http://www.peakoil.com/printout1556.html.

13. Colin J. Campbell and Jean H. Laherrère, "The End of Cheap Oil," *Scientific American*, March 1998.

14. Ibid.

15. International Energy Agency, *World Energy Outlook 2004*.

16. World Resources Institute, "Estimated Ultimately Recoverable Oil," http://pubs.wri.org/pubs_content_text.cfm?ContentID=380.

17. Reserves revisions from Fredrik Robelius, "Giant Oil Fields—The Highway to Oil," PhD dissertation for Uppsala University, Sweden, March 2007, www.diva-portal.org/diva/getDocument?urn_nbn_se_uu_diva-7625-1__fulltext.pdf.

18. Ahmed Jarallah, "Kuwait Oil Reserves Secret for National Security; Shuwayib Head of KPC," *Arab Times*, May 13, 2007, www.arabtimesonline.com/arabtimes/kuwait/Viewdet.asp?ID=10301&cat=a.

19. ASPO Newsletter 78, item 827, June 2007. www.aspo-ireland.org/contentFiles/newsletterPDFs/newsletter78_200706.pdf.

20. ASPO Newsletter 79, item 832, July 2007, www.aspo-ireland.org/contentFiles/newsletterPDFs/newsletter79_200707.pdf.

21. Phil Hart and Chris Skrebowski, "Peak Oil: A Detailed and Transparent Analysis," May 30, 2007, www.philhart.com/CERA_SPE_debate.

22. Ibid.

23. World Resources Institute, "Estimated Ultimately Recoverable Oil," http://pubs.wri.org/pubs_content_text.cfm?ContentID=380.

24. David Woodward, "2020 Vision, A Look at the Oil Industry in the 21st Century," *Middle East Well Evaluation Review*, November 14, 1993.

25. Energy Information Administration, "World Oil Reserves by Region," January 1, 2005, www.eia.doe.gov/pub/oil_gas/petroleum/analysis_publications/oil_market_basics/sup_image_reserves.htm.

26. World Resources Institute, "Estimated Ultimately Recoverable Oil," http://pubs.wri.org/pubs_content_text.cfm?ContentID=380.

27. Robelius, "Giant Oil Fields."

28. ASPO Newsletter 78, June 2007, www.aspo-ireland.org/contentFiles/newsletterPDFs/newsletter78_200706.pdf.

29. PowerSwitch Energy Awareness, "PIRA: Non-OPEC Conventional Crude peaked in 2006," April 28, 2007, http://www.powerswitch.org.uk/portal/index.php?option=com_content&task=view&id=2172&Itemid=2.

30. ASPO Newsletter 77, May 2007, www.aspo-global.org/newsletter/ASPOGlobal_Newsletter77.pdf.

31. "Lease condensates: A mixture consisting primarily of pentanes and heavier hydrocarbons which is recovered as a liquid from natural gas in lease separation facilities. This category excludes natural gas plant liquids, such as butane and propane, which are recovered at downstream natural gas processing plants or facilities." Energy Information Administration Glossary, www.eia.doe.gov/glossary/glossary_l.htm.

32. Tony Eriksen, "Updated World Oil Forecasts, including Saudi Arabia," August 5, 2007, http://www.theoildrum.com/node/2716#more.

33. Ali Samsam Bakhtiari, "The Century of Roots," April 2007, http://www.sfu.ca/~asamsamb/THE%20%20CENTURY%20%20OF%20%20ROOTS/THE%20%20CENTURY%20%20OF%20%20ROOTS.htm.

34. ASPO Newsletter 77, May 2007, www.aspo-global.org/newsletter/ASPOGlobal_Newsletter77.pdf.

35. Rembrandt Koppelaar, *Oilwatch Monthly*, June 2007, ASPO Netherlands, www.peakoil.nl/wp-content/uploads/2007/06/oilwatch_monthly_june_2007.pdf.

36. Export data from EIA, "Top World Oil Net Exporters," 2006, www.eia.doe.gov/emeu/cabs/topworldtables1_2.html.

37. Koppelaar, *Oilwatch Monthly*.

38. The Oil Drum, comment on "Net Oil Exports and the 'Iron Triangle,'" www.theoildrum.com/node/2767#comment-213072.

39. Rembrandt Koppelaar, "Will OPEC increase supply in the 2nd half of 2007? Or has Ghawar peaked?" The Oil Drum, June 21, 2007, http://europe.theoildrum.com/node/2670.

40. "OPEC Rigidity Will Bleed Oil Markets—IEA," *Business Report*, June 12, 2007, www.busrep.co.za/index.php?from=rss_Business%20Report&fArticleId=3880752.

41. OPEC, "Statement by HE Abdalla Salem El-Badri, Secretary General of OPEC, on Oil Market Fundamentals," June 14, 2007, www.opec.org/opecna/Press%20Releases/2007/pr052007.htm.

42. "OPEC Crude Oil Production (Excluding Lease Condensate), 1997–Present," *International Petroleum Monthly*, Energy Information Administration, www.eia.doe.gov/emeu/ipsr/t12.xls.

43. Dave Cohen, "A Paradigm Shift," June 20, 2007, www.aspo-usa.com/index.php?option=com_content&task=view&id=155&Itemid=76.

44. The Oil Drum, June 21, 2007, www.theoildrum.com/node/2670#comment-203906.

45. Associated Press, "Oil majors replace less than 100 percent of reserves, report says," International Herald Tribune, June 21, 2007, http://www.iht.com/articles/ap/2007/06/21/business/NA-FIN-US-Oil-Reserve-Replacements.php.

46. Ibid.

47. "Deep Output Overtakes Shallow," *Explorer*, September 2004, www.aapg.org/explorer/2004/09sep/gom_deepwater.cfm.

48. " 'Nice Quarter' for Transocean," *Houston Chronicle*, October 31, 2007, www.chron.com/disp/story.mpl/business/energy/5262879.html.

49. "ExxonMobil Announces Drilling of World-Record Well," Sakhalin-1 Project press release, April 23, 2007, http://www.sakhalin1.com/en/news/press/20070423.asp.

50. The Oil Drum, "Peak Oil Overview," June 2007, www.theoildrum.com/node/2693.

51. Energy Information Administration, "Accelerated Depletion: Assessing Its Impacts on Domestic Oil and Natural Gas Prices and Production," Appendix G, July 2000, http://www.eia.doe.gov/oiaf/servicerpt/depletion/pdf/sroiaf(2000)04.pdf.

52. Matthew R. Simmons, "Is the World Supply of Oil and Gas Peaking?" *International Petroleum Week*, February 13, 2007, www.simmonsco-intl.com/files/IP%20week%20talk.pdf.

53. Paul Roberts, *The End of Oil* (Boston: Houghton Mifflin, 2004), 62.

54. Matt Chambers, "Dubai Crude Output Dn Rapidly as Govt Makes to Crimp Decline," *Dow Jones Newswire*, July 15, 2007, www.zawya.com/Story.cfm/sidDN20070715000464/secIndustries/pagOil%20&%20Gas#DN20070715000464.

55. International Energy Agency, "Medium Term Oil Market Report," July 2007, http://omrpublic .iea.org/mtomr.htm.

56. Ibid.

57. Mella McEwen, "Despite Belief in Peak Oil, Pickens Still Believes in Oil and Gas," April 5, 2007, www.mywesttexas.com/site/news.cfm?newsid=18171403&BRD=2288&PAG=461&dept _id=475626&rfi=6.

58. "AP Interview: T. Boone Pickens Says Global Oil Production Has Reached its Peak," *International Herald Tribune*, March 1, 2007, www.iht.com/articles/ap/2007/03/01/africa/ME-FIN-Pickens-Oil-Peak.php.

59. ASPO-USA *Peak Oil Review* 2, no. 17, May 7, 2007.

60. David Cohen, "Exaggerated Oil Recovery," ASPO-USA, July 19, 2007, http://www.aspo-usa .com/index.php?option=com_content&task=view&id=177&Itemid=91.

61. Hall & Cleveland, 1981; Hall, Powers & Schoenberg, in press.

62. Euan Mearns, "Ghawar Reserves Update and Revisions," The Oil Drum: *Europe,* May 2, 2007, http://europe.theoildrum.com/node/2507.

63. Stuart Staniford, "Saudi Arabian Oil Declines 8% in 2006," The Oil Drum, March 2, 2007, www .theoildrum.com/node/2325.

64. Chris Nelder's notes from the first ASPO-USA Conference, November 10, 2005, Denver, CO, www.getreallist.com/article.php?story=20060829200211917.

65. F. Jay Schemf, "Simmons hopes he's wrong. Leading energy analyst believes Saudi Arabia's crude oil supply near peak; calls for greater global reserve transparency to anticipate 'cataclysm,'" *Petroleum News* 9, no. 31, August 1, 2004, www.petroleumnews.com/pnads/238338932 .shtml.

66. Documentary filmmaker James Fox, in personal conversation with Chris Nelder.

67. Matthew R. Simmons' slide deck, "Energy Market Outlook," April 26, 2007, Investment Adviser Association 2007 Annual Conference, www.simmonsco-intl.com/files/Investment%20Advisers %20Association%20April%2026.pdf.

68. ASPO Newsletter 77, May 2007, www.aspo-global.org/newsletter/ASPOGlobal_Newsletter 77.pdf.

69. Tom Standing, "BP's Recent Production Data, and a Different View of Future World Oil Production Trends," ASPO, July 1, 2007, www.aspo-usa.com/index.php?option=com_content&task= view&id=160&Itemid=76.

70. *Open Sources Information,"* National Oil Companies: Oil's Dark Secret," August 11, 2006, www .opensourcesinfo.org/journal/2006/8/13/national-oil-companies-oils-dark-secret.html.

71. "Really Big Oil," *The Economist*, August 10, 2006, http://www.economist.com/opinion/display story.cfm?story_id=7276986.

72. Tom Petrie, "A Strategic Perspective on 21st Century Energy Challenges," a presentation on June 18, 2007, in Denver, to the Institute of International Education, as cited in *Peak Oil Review* June 25, 2007. Notes by Steve Andrews.

73. "Really Big Oil" *The Economist*.

74. RTÉ One video presentation, *Future Shock: End of the Oil Age*, June 18, 2007, www.rte.ie/tv/ futureshock/av_20070618.html.

75. ASPO Newsletter 77, May 2007, www.aspo-global.org/newsletter/ASPOGlobal_Newsletter77.pdf.

76. Matthew Simmons, "The World's Giant Oilfields," Simmons & Company International, www .nps.edu/cebrowski/Docs/energy/giantoilfields.pdf.

77. Tony Hayward, "Securing the Future—An Oil Company Perspective," *SperoNews*, June 13, 2007, www.speroforum.com/site/article.asp?idCategory=34&idsub=174&id=9897&t=Securing+the+future+-+An+oil+company+perspective.

78. ASPO Newsletter 77, May 2007.

79. Ibid.

80. RTÉ One video presentation, *Future Shock: End of the Oil Age*.

81. Jim Jubak, "The Oil Squeeze Has Just Begun," *MSN Money*, July 17, 2007, http://articles.moneycentral.msn.com/Investing/JubaksJournal/TheOilSqueezeHasJustBegun.aspx?page=2.

Chapter 3 Wanted: Five New Saudi Arabias

1. *Gulf Times*, "Oil Demand Seen Rising, Piling Pressure on OPEC," June 13, 2007, www.gulf-times.com/site/topics/article.asp?cu_no=2&item_no=154842&version=1&template_id=48&parent_id=28.

2. "Will You Join Us?" www.willyoujoinus.com/issues/population/, citing World Population 1950–2050, U.S. Census Bureau, www.census.gov/ipc/www/worldpop.html.

3. John W. Schoen, "How Long Will the World's Oil Last?" *Energy Bulletin*, September 8, 2004, www.energybulletin.net/2007.html.

4. Energy Information Administration, "International Energy Outlook 2007," May 2007, www.eia.doe.gov/oiaf/ieo/pdf/0484(2007).pdf.

5. Matthew R. Simmons' slide deck, "Energy Market Outlook," April 26, 2007, Investment Adviser Association 2007 Annual Conference, www.simmonsco-intl.com/files/Investment%20Advisers%20Association%20April%2026.pdf.

6. "Population and Energy," Die Off, http://dieoff.org/page199.htm.

7. Daniel Howden, "World Oil Supplies Are Set to Run Out Faster Than Expected, Warn Scientists," *Independent*, June 14, 2007, http://news.independent.co.uk/sci_tech/article2656034.ece.

8. Greg Morcroft, "U.S. Wealth Growth Rate Slows; China, India Pick Up Pace," *MarketWatch*, June 20, 2006, www.marketwatch.com/news/story/us-wealth-growth-rate-slows/story.aspx?guid=%7B3A300741-A171-4979-A7BF-E111D6CBB001%7D.

9. Milton Copulos, "Averting Disaster of Our Own Design," *EvWorld*, March 30, 2006, www.evworld.com/article.cfm?storyid=1003.

10. Energy Information Administration, "China's Energy Demand Now Exceeds Domestic Supply," www.eia.doe.gov/emeu/cabs/china/part2.html.

11. *China Daily*, "Quenching China's Thirst for Oil," June 19, 2007, www.chinadaily.com.cn/bizchina/2007-06/19/content_897795.htm.

12. Paul Rogers, "The United States and Africa: Eyes on the Prize," *Open Democracy*, March 15, 2007, www.opendemocracy.net/conflict/us_africa_4438.jsp.

13. OPEC, "World Oil Demand," May 17, 2006, www.gulfoilandgas.com/webpro1/main/mainnews.asp?id=2952.

14. Thomas L. Friedman, "The Power of Green," *New York Times*, April 15, 2007, www.energybulletin.net/28602.html.

15. Energy Information Administration, "International Energy Outlook 2006," Report DOE/EIA-0484(2006), June 2006, www.eia.doe.gov/oiaf/ieo/oil.html.

16. Energy Information Administration, "International Energy Outlook May 2007."

17. Copulos, "Averting Disaster."

18. Energy Information Administration, "Top World Oil Producers and Consumers," www.eia.doe .gov/emeu/cabs/topworldtables1_2.html.

19. Keith Bradsher and David Barboza, "Pollution from Chinese Coal Casts a Global Shadow," *New York Times,* June 11, 2006, www.nytimes.com/2006/06/11/business/worldbusiness/11chinacoal .html?ex=1307678400en=e9ac1f6255a24fd8ei=5088partner=rssnytemc=rss&pagewanted=all.

20. Data by BP, reference furnished by Steve Andrews, ASPO-USA, in *Peak Oil Review* 2, no. 20, May 28, 2007.

21. Bradsher and Barboza, "Pollution from Chinese Coal."

22. Alan Herro, "Chinese Air Pollution Crosses Pacific, Reaches Western United States," Mines and Communities Website, March 30, 2007, www.minesandcommunities.org/Action/press1423.htm.

23. Richard McGregor, "750,000 a Year Killed by Chinese Pollution," *Financial Times,* July 2, 2007, www.ft.com/cms/s/8f40e248-28c7-11dc-af78-000b5df10621.html.

24. Energy Edge Limited, "Coal of the Future," February 2007, http://ie.jrc.cec.eu.int/publications/ scientific_publications/2007/EUR22644EN.pdf.

25. World Coal Institute, "Coal Facts 2007," www.worldcoal.org/pages/content/index.asp? PageID=188.

26. Quentin Sommerville, "China Car Firm Gears Up for Booming Sales," *BBC News,* March 25, 2007, http://news.bbc.co.uk/2/hi/business/6364195.stm.

27. Copulos, "Averting Disaster."

28. "China Overtakes US as Top CO_2 Emitter—Dutch Agency," Reuters, June 20, 2007, www.alertnet .org/thenews/newsdesk/L20802191.htm.

29. Copulos, "Averting Disaster."

30. "India May Raise Lenders' Reserve Limit as U.S. Plans Rate Cut," Bloomberg, October 31, 2007, www.bloomberg.com/apps/news?pid=20601091&sid=afO403M3pdpE&refer=india.

31. "Chris Skrebowski on Alarming New Peak Oil Report (transcript)," Global Public Media, October 23, 2007, http://globalpublicmedia.com/transcripts/2820.

32. ABC Radio National, "Peak Oil Transcript," October 8, 2006, www.abc.net.au/rn/nationalinterest/ stories/2006/1754565.htm.

33. Energy Information Administration, 2007.

34. Energy Information Administration, "International Energy Outlook 2006."

35. All data in this section is from EIA for 2006. These numbers will not add up for the casual reader, however, due to the particular definitions of what is included in each of these numbers. We use them here as a general illustration of the supply balance for the United States. Please refer to the EIA for additional explanation of the details.

36. At first glance, the data in the Top 10 Exporters table may not seem to mesh with other data in this chapter. This is in part due to different data sources, and in part due to different definitions of what is being counted. Total rationalization of oil data is often nearly impossible, unfortunately. Please refer to the respective agencies for a more detailed explanation of these numbers.

37. ASPO Canada, "EIA Country Analysis Briefs: Canada," May 9, 2007, http://aspocanada.ca/eia-country-analysis-briefs-canada.html.

38. According to the Canadian Association of Petroleum Producers, 2005 reserves were 5.21 billion barrels of conventional crude reserves, less two years' production at 1.364 million barrels per day gives 4.2 billion barrels of conventional crude reserves in 2007, www.capp.ca/raw.asp?x=1&dt= NTV&e=PDF&dn=112818.

39. ASPO Canada, "EIA Country."

40. The Oil Drum, July 10, 2007, www.theoildrum.com/node/2755#comment-211394.

41. Fredrik Robelius, "Giant Oil Fields."

42. Constance Ikokwu, "$16bn Lost in N'Delta, Says US Report," *This Day,* July 19, 2007, www .thisdayonline.com/nview.php?id=84001.

43. Juliana Taiwo, "Gov Alerts NNPC Over Textile Workers' Fate," *This Day (Lagos),* July 16, 2007, http://allafrica.com/stories/200707160238.html.

Chapter 4 $480 a Barrel: The True Value of Oil

1. Richard T. Stuebi, "What Is Energy Worth?" *Clean Tech Blog,* November 27, 2006, www .cleantechblog.com/2006/11/what-is-energy-worth.html.

2. Stuebi, "What is Energy Worth?"

3. Michael T. Klare, "Pentagon vs. Peak Oil," *AlterNet,* June 15, 2007, www.alternet.org/ environment/54195/.

4. Ibid.

5. Bryan Bender, "Pentagon Study Says Oil Reliance Strains Military," *Boston Globe*, May 1, 2007, www.boston.com/news/nation/washington/articles/2007/05/01/pentagon_study_says_oil_ reliance_strains_military/?page=2 on the "Transforming the Way DoD Looks at Energy" study by LMI Government Consulting quoting Milton R. Copulos.

6. Bill Moore, "Hidden Cost of Our Oil Dependence," *EvWorld,* April 23, 2006, www.evworld .com/article.cfm?storyid=1018.

7. Ibid.

8. Milton Copulos, "Averting Disaster of Our Own Design," *EvWorld,* March 30, 2006, www .evworld.com/article.cfm?archive=1&storyid=1003&first=4957&end=4956.

9. International Center for Technology Assessment, "'Real Price of Gasoline' Report Reveals Actual Cost of Gas to Consumers Is as High as $15.14 per Gallon," November 16, 1998, www.icta.org/ press/release.cfm?news_id=12.

10. Union of Concerned Scientists, "Clean Vehicles, Subsidizing Big Oil," www.ucsusa.org/clean_ vehicles/fuel_economy/subsidizing-big-oil.html.

11. Richard Black, "Climate 'Makes Oil Profit Vanish,'" *BBC News,* February 9, 2006, http://news .bbc.co.uk/2/hi/science/nature/4699354.stm.

12. Earth Policy Institute, "Carbon Dioxide Emissions by Top Ten Emitting Countries, 2005," www. earth-policy.org/Indicators/CO2/2006_data.htm#table1.

13. Cutler J. Cleveland, "Biophysical Economics," *Encyclopedia of Earth,* September 14, 2006, www.eoearth.org/article/Biophysical_economics.

14. Ibid.

15. Cutler J. Cleveland, Robert Costanza, Charles A.S. Hall, and Robert Kaufmann, "Energy and the U.S. Economy: A Biophysical Perspective," *Science* 225: 890–897 (1984).

Chapter 5 The Pentagon Prepares for Peak Oil

1. Bryan Bender, "Pentagon Says Oil Won't Last," *Boston Globe,* May 1, 2007, www.telegram .com/apps/pbcs.dll/article?AID=/20070501/NEWS/705010616/1116.

2. Luke Burgess, "Insider Information: What the Military Doesn't Want You to Know about its Oil Consumption," *Energy and Capital,* July 11, 2006, http://www.energyandcapital.com/articles/ oil-consumption-military/237.

3. Ronald O'Rourke, "Navy Ship Propulsion Technologies: Options for Reducing Oil Use—Background for Congress," CRS Report for Congress, December 2006, www.fas.org/sgp/crs/weapons/RL33360.pdf.

4. Dan Murphy, "New Saudi Tack on Al Qaeda," *Christian Science Monitor*, April 30, 2007, www.csmonitor.com/2007/0430/p06s02-wome.html.

5. George P. Shultz and R. James Woolsey, "Oil and Security," Committee on the Present Danger Policy Paper, August 5, 2005, http://web.archive.org/web/20070403101414/http://www.fightingterror.org/pdfs/O&S8-5-05.pdf

6. "Rich Nations Accused of 'Green Imperialism' on Climate Change," *China Post*, June 25, 2007, www.chinapost.com.tw/news/113358.htm.

7. Ibid.

8. Ibid.

9. Christopher L.Weber and H. Scott Matthews, "Embodied Environmental Emissions in U.S. International Trade, 1997–2004," *Environmental Science and Technology*, June 2007.

10. "Rich Nations," *China Post*, www.chinapost.com.tw/news/113358.htm.

11. "We find ourselves dependent on imports from people who, by and large, are hostile to us. It makes [energy independence] a national security imperative."—Frank Gaffney, speaking at the American Council on Renewable Energy (ACORE) conference, December 2004, www.renewableenergyaccess.com/rea/news/story?id=19841.

Chapter 6 Twilight for Fossil Fuels

1. American Gas Association, "Most Frequently Asked Questions: Natural Gas Supply and Prices," Winter 2006–2007, http://www.aga.org/NR/rdonlyres/C298FEAE-5CEB-4AAA-8FAD-B4FCEC053713/0/0710FAQ.PDF

2. Kellia Ramares, "Will FERC Force LNG on Unwilling Communities?" *Global Public Media*, July 22, 2007, http://globalpublicmedia.com/transcripts/440 citing David Hughes, a research geologist with the Geological Survey of Canada.

3. J. David Hughes, "Natural Gas in North America: Should We Be Worried?" October 26, 2006, www.aspo-usa.com/fall2006/presentations/pdf/Hughes_D_NatGas_Boston_2006.pdf.

4. Ibid.

5. Personal correspondence, July 13, 2007.

6. Hughes, "Natural Gas in North America."

7. "High Risk of Underinvestment in Power Generation in Current Climate of Uncertainty," IEA press release, May 3, 2007, www.iea.org/Textbase/press/pressdetail.asp?PRESS_REL_ID=224.

8. National Energy Technology Laboratory (U.S. Department of Energy), "All About Hydrates–Necessary Conditions for Methane Hydrate Formation," http://www.netl.doe.gov/technologies/oil-gas/FutureSupply/MethaneHydrates/about-hydrates/conditions.htm.

9. United States Geological Survey, Minerals Management Service, "Methane Gas Hydrates," last updated January 15, 2004. http://geology.usgs.gov/connections/mms/joint_projects/methane.htm.

10. Using a conversion factor of 5,658.53 cubic feet of natural gas to 1 barrel of oil equivalent. Society of Petroleum Engineers, "Unit Conversion Factors," http://www.spe.org/spe-app/spe/industry/reference/unit_conversions.htm.

11. United States Geological Survey, Minerals Management Service, "Methane Gas Hydrates," last updated January 15, 2004, http://geology.usgs.gov/connections/mms/joint_projects/methane.htm.

12. MH21 Research Consortium, Japan Oil, Gas and Metals National Corporation, "Japan's Methane Hydrate Exploitation Program," July 2001, http://www.mh21japan.gr.jp/english/mh21/02keii.html.

13. Embassy of the People's Republic of China in Australia, "Nation plans large-scale investment in new energy," August 24, 2006. http://au.china-embassy.org/eng/xw/t268807.htm.

14. Milton Copulos, "Averting Disaster of Our Own Design," testimony before the Senate Foreign Relations Committee, March 30, 2006, *EvWorld*, www.evworld.com/article.cfm?archive=1&storyid=1003&first=12951&end=12950.

15. Ibid.

16. Energy Watch Group, "Coal: Resources and Future Production," March 2007, http://www.energywatchgroup.org/fileadmin/global/pdf/EWG-Coalreport_10_07_2007.pdf.

17. National Academy of Sciences, "Coal Research and Development to Support National Energy Policy," June 2007, http://dels.nas.edu/dels/rpt_briefs/coal_r&d_final.pdf.

18. Matthew L. Wald, "Science Panel Finds Fault with Estimates of Coal Supply," *New York Times,* June 21, 2007, www.nytimes.com/2007/06/21/business/21coal.html?ref=business.

19. Jeremy Gilbert, presentation to the ASPO Third Annual Oil Conference, Houston, TX, October 18, 2007. Notes by Chris Nelder, www.getreallist.com/resources/ASPO_Houston_10-07_cnelder.pdf.

20. Dr. Peter W. Becker, "The Role of Synthetic Fuel in World War II Germany," *Air University Review*, July–August 1981, www.airpower.maxwell.af.mil/airchronicles/aureview/1981/jul-aug/becker.htm.

21. U.S. Department of Energy, "The Early Days of Coal Research," www.fe.doe.gov/aboutus/history/syntheticfuels_history.html.

22. ABC Money.co.uk, "Coal-to-liquid fuel plant plan advances," May 31, 2007, http://www.abcmoney.co.uk/news/31200780608.htm.

23. Steve Andrews' notes from Tom Petrie, "A Strategic Perspective on 21st Century Energy Challenges," a presentation on June 18, 2007, in Denver, to the Institute of International Education, as cited in *Peak Oil Review*, June 25, 2007.*"*

24. James Hamilton, "Oil Shale Hits a Freeze," *Econbrowser*, June 17, 2007, www.econbrowser.com/archives/2007/06/oil_shale_hits.html.

25. Nancy Lofholm, "Shell Shelves Oil-Shale Application to Refine Its Research," *Denver Post*, June 16, 2007, www.denverpost.com/ci_6155257?source=rss.

26. The Oil Drum, June 19, 2007, www.theoildrum.com/node/2666#comment-203085.

27. Richard Heinberg, *The Party's Over* (n.p.: New Society Publishers, 2nd printing, pap., ca. 2003), 33.

28. Hall, et al., "Hydrocarbons and the Evolution of Human Culture," Nature Publishing Group, 2003, www.hubbertpeak.com/cleveland/OilAndCulture.pdf.

29. "Outstanding Investments" newsletter, June 2007, vol. 7, issue 6.

30. Hall, et al., "Hydrocarbons and Evolution."

31. Charles Hall, et al., presentation to the ASPO Third Annual Oil Conference, Houston, TX, October 18, 2007. Notes by Chris Nelder, www.getrealist.com/resources/ASPO_Houston_10-07_cnelder.pdf.

32. C. Raffensperger and J. Tickner (eds.), *Protecting Public Health and the Environment: Implementing the Precautionary Principle* (Washington, DC: Island Press, 1999).

33. NASA press release, "Research Finds That Earth's Climate Is Approaching 'Dangerous' Point," May 30, 2007, www.giss.nasa.gov/research/news/20070530/.

Chapter 7 Tar Sands: The Oil Junkie's Last Fix

1. Canadian Association of Petroleum Producers oil sands data 1999–2006, www.capp.ca/raw.asp? x=1&dt=NTV&e=PDF&dn=112820.

2. Jean H. Laherrère, "Tar Sands and Shale Oil Addendum to: Peak Oil Production and the Implications to the State of Connecticut Report to Legislative Leaders and the Governor," December 2007, http://www.housedems.ct.gov/Backer/TSandOSfina.pdf.

3. "Doing Some Digging—The Dirt on Oil Sands," *Canadian Mining Journal,* March 22, 2006, http://www.canadianminingjournal.com/esource/ctalink.asp?id=11035715.

4. Attribution: Dr. Jean-Marie Bourdaire.

5. Bengt Söderbergh, Fredrik Robelius, and Kjell Aleklett, "A Crash Program Scenario for the Canadian Oil Sands Industry," Uppsala University, June 8, 2006, www.peakoil.net/uhdsg/20060608EPOSArticlePdf.pdf.

6. Ibid.

7. Canadian Association of Petroleum Producers oil sands data 1999–2006, www.capp.ca/raw.asp? x=1&dt=NTV&e=PDF&dn=112820. Production was 383 kb/d of synthetic crude from mining and 609 kb/d bitumen; in 1998, the numbers were 308 kb/d synthetic, and 282 kb/d bitumen. Increase for synthetic is 3 percent per year; increase for bitumen is 11 percent per year. Overall, the increase is 8 percent per year.

8. Naomi Klein, "Baghdad Burns, Calgary Booms," *Nation,* May 31, 2007, www.thenation.com/doc/20070618/klein.

9. Energy Information Administration/*Natural Gas Monthly,* "U.S. Natural Gas Imports and Exports, 2005–2007," *Natural Gas Monthly,* September 2007, www.eia.doe.gov/pub/oil_gas/natural_gas/data_publications/natural_gas_monthly/current/pdf/table_04.pdf.

10. Byron W. King, "2006 Boston ASPO: The Canadian Tar Sands," *Whiskey and Gun Powder,* November 13, 2006, www.whiskeyandgunpowder.com/Archives/2006/20061113.html.

11. Andrew Nikiforuk, "An Inconvenient Swede," *Canadian Business Online,* October 9–22, 2006, www.canadianbusiness.com/markets/commodities/article.jsp?content=20061009_81365_81365.

12. World Business Council for Sustainable Development, "Not Enough Water for Oil Sands: Report," January 16, 2007, http://tinyurl.com/26rb3p.

13. Nikiforuk, "Inconvenient Swede."

14. Civitatensis, "To Nuke or Not to Nuke," www.civitatensis.ca/archives/2007/03/29/2049.

15. King, "2006 Boston ASPO."

16. Bengt Söderbergh, Fredrik Robelius, and Kjell Aleklett, "A Crash Program Scenario for the Canadian Oil Sands Industry."

17. Martin Mittelstaedt, "Choke Point for Oil Sands May Be Water Shortage," *The Globe and Mail,* www.theglobeandmail.com/servlet/story/RTGAM.20070511.wtarsands11/BNStory/Business/.

18. University of Toronto and University of Alberta, "Running out of Steam? Oil Sands Development and Water Use in the Athabasca River-Watershed: Science and Market Based Solutions," May 2007, www.ualberta.ca/~ersc/water.pdf.

19. *Rolling Stone,* July 2006.

20. Chris Nelder's notes from the ASPO-USA First World Oil Conference, December 17, 2005, www.getreallist.com/article.php?story=20060829200211917.

21. Bobby Magill, "*Grand Junction Sentinel* (Colorado): Experts: Withdrawal No Reason to Doubt Shell's Oil Shale Technology," Royal Dutch Shell Plc, July 5, 2007, http://royaldutchshellplc

.com/2007/07/05/grand-junction-sentinel-colorado-experts-withdrawal-no-reason-to-doubt-shella%e2%80%99s-oil-shale-technology/.

22. Ibid.

Part III Energy after Oil

1. Richard Heinberg, "Museletter #179: Burning the Furniture," *Global Public Media,* March 22, 2007, http://globalpublicmedia.com/richard_heinbergs_museletter_179_burning_the_furniture.

2. Graphic, "Total World Electricity Generation (% by fuel 2004)," World Coal Institute, www.richardheinberg.com/files/worldconsumption.gif.

Chapter 8 The Renewable Revolution

1. "Renewable energy could power half the nation," May 2, 2007, CNNMoney.com, http://money.cnn.com/2007/05/02/news/economy/renewables/index.htm.

2. "Sunlit Uplands," *Economist,* May 31, 2007, www.economist.com/surveys/displaystory.cfm?story_id=9217928.

3. Pew Center on Global Climate Change, "States with Renewable Portfolio Standards," August 2007, www.pewclimate.org/what_s_being_done/in_the_states/rps.cfm.

4. Sam Azzouni, "Oil and Gas Execs Say Focus on Renewable Energy Sources Key to Addressing Declining Oil Reserves, KPMG Survey Finds," KPMG LLP, May 11, 2007, www.prnewswire.com/cgi-bin/stories.pl?ACCT=104&STORY=/www/story/05-11-2007/0004586351.

5. Development committee (Joint Ministerial Committee of the Boards of Governors of the Bank and the Fund on the Transfer of Real Resources to Developing Countries), "Clean Energy for Development Investment Framework: The World Bank Group Action Plan," March 6, 2007, http://siteresources.worldbank.org/EXTSDNETWORK/Resources/DC2007-0002(E)-Clean-Energy.pdf?resourceurlname=DC2007-0002(E)-CleanEnergy.pdf.

6. U.S. Department of Energy, "Alternative & Advanced Fuels–Biodiesel Production," http://www.eere.energy.gov/afdc/fuels/biodiesel_production.html.

7. Ibid.

8. U.S. Department of Energy, "Alternative & Advanced Fuels–Biodiesel Benefits," http://www.eere.energy.gov/afdc/fuels/biodiesel_benefits.html.

9. Iowa State University, "What is biodiesel?" http://www3.me.iastate.edu/biodiesel/Pages/biodiesel1.html.

10. Joel Rose, "Company Makes Biodiesel from Restaurant Waste," NPR, December 6, 2007, www.npr.org/templates/story/story.php?storyId=6585629.

11. Ron Kotrba, "Food Waste to Fuel Tanks," *Biodiesel,* November 2006, www.biodieselmagazine.com/article.jsp?article_id=1251.

12. Susan Moran, "Biodiesel Comes of Age as the Demand Rises," *New York Times,* September 12, 2006, www.nytimes.com/2006/09/12/business/smallbusiness/12bio.html?ex=1315713600&en=0f141e75db5758b0&ei=5088&partner=rssnyt&emc=rss.

13. Ibid.

14. Ibid.

15. National Biodiesel Board, "Commonly Asked Questions," http://www.biodiesel.org/pdf_files/fuelfactsheets/CommonlyAsked.PDF.

16. From interview with Jeff Siegel on *TFN Smart Trading Action Alert* with Laura Cadden, Taipan Financial News, May 10, 2007.

17. Elizabeth Svoboda, "The Greenest Green Fuel," *Popular Science,* 2005, www.popsci.com/ popsci/printerfriendly/science/ee6d4d4329703110vgnvcm1000004eecbccdrcrd.html.

18. American Coalition for Ethanol, "U.S. Ethanol Production," http://www.ethanol.org/index .php?id=37&parentid=8.

19. U.S. Department of Energy, "Alternative & Advanced Fuels: Ethanol Production," http://www .eere.energy.gov/afdc/fuels/ethanol_production.html.

20. Ryan Keefe, Jay Griffin, and John D. Graham, "The Benefits and Costs of New Fuels and Engines for Cars and Light Trucks," November 2007, Pardee RAND Graduate School, http://www.rand .org/pubs/working_papers/2007/RAND_WR537.pdf

21. Hal Brenton, "Ethanol Demand Turns Corn into a Growing Cash Crop," *Seattle Times*, November 14, 2006, http://seattletimes.nwsource.com/html/businesstechnology/2003305110_biofuel15 .html.

22. Laura Meckler, "Fill Up with Ethanol? One Obstacle Is Big Oil," *Wall Street Journal*, April 2, 2007, reprinted at www.consumerwatchdog.org/energy/nw/?postId=7641.

23. Daniel J. Weiss and Nat Gryll, "Flex Fuel Bait and Switch," Center for American Progress, June 18, 2007, www.americanprogress.org/issues/2007/06/flexfuel.html.

24. "Fill Up with Ethanol? One Obstacle Is Big Oil," *Wall Street Journal*, April 3, 2007, http://online .wsj.com/article/SB117547886199856472.html.

25. "E85 Stations," http://e85vehicles.com/e85-stations.htm.

26. Patrick Mazza, "Biofuel Breakthroughs & Cellulosic Fuels Revolution," *Renewable Energy Access,* May 28, 2007, www.renewableenergyaccess.com/rea/news/reinsider/story?id=48637.

27. Ibid.

28. Stephen Long, "Miscanthus—A Solution to U.S. Dependence on Foreign Oil?" University of Illinois, *ACES News*, April 25, 2006, www.aces.uiuc.edu/news/stories/news3623.html.

29. Mazza, "Biofuel Breakthroughs," www.renewableenergyaccess.com/rea/news/printstory;jsessio nid=4AEA3C078CEB37FC687D14ABAA58140B?id=48637.

30. Range Fuels, "Range Fuels Awarded Permit to Construct the Nation's First Commercial Cellulosic Ethanol Plant," www.rangefuels.com/Range-Fuels-awarded-permit-to-construct-the-nations-first-commercial-cellulosic-ethanol-plant.

31. Mascoma, "Market Leadership," www.mascoma.com/welcome/market_leadership.html.

32. Verenium press release, "Verenium Corporation Announces Milestone Payment to the University of Florida for Cellulosic Ethanol Technology License," July 19, 2007, http://ir.verenium.com/ phoenix.zhtml?c=81345&p=irol-newsArticle&ID=1028358&highlight=.

33. FPL Energy, "FPL Energy Enters into Agreement with Citrus Energy for First of Its Kind Ethanol Plant," July 19, 2007, www.fplenergy.com/news/contents/2007/071907.shtml.

34. Mazza, "Biofuel Breakthroughs."

35. Christine Sismondo, "Children of the Corn," *Michael Pollan*, May 14, 2006, www.michaelpollan .com/press.php?id=51.

36. Tom Philpott, "Feeding the Beast," *Grist,* December 13, 2006, www.grist.org/comments/ food/2006/12/13/fuel_vs_food/.

37. Jason Hill, Erik Nelson, David Tilman, Stephen Polasky, and Douglas Tiffany, "Environmental, Economic, and Energetic Costs and Benefits of Biodiesel and Ethanol Biofuels," Proceedings of the National Academy of Sciences of the United States of America, July 12, 2006, www.pnas .org/cgi/content/full/103/30/11206.

38. "The Hungry Planet," September 3, 2006, Independent.co.uk, http://www.independent.co.uk/ environment/the-hungry-planet-414479.html.

39. Kyle Swanson, "Life in a Grass House," The Oil Drum, March 7, 2006, www.theoildrum.com/story/2006/3/7/03949/82426.

40. Tom Doggett, "Ethanol to Take 30 pct of U.S. Corn Crop in 2012: GAO," Reuters, June 11, 2007, www.reuters.com/article/scienceNews/idUSN1149215820070611.

41. Renewable Fuels Association, "Industry Statistics: 2007 Monthly U.S. Fuel Ethanol Production/Demand," www.ethanolrfa.org/industry/statistics/#B.

42. Energy Information Administration, "October Is Just the Beginning," October 11, 2007, http://tonto.eia.doe.gov/oog/info/twip/twip.asp.

43. "America's Growing Addiction to Corn," June 11, 2007, CNNMoney.com, http://money.cnn.com/2007/06/11/news/economy/bc.usa.ethanol.corn.reut/?postversion=2007061116.

44. White House press release, "Fact Sheet: Energy Independence and Security Act of 2007," December 19, 2007, http://www.whitehouse.gov/news/releases/2007/12/20071219-1.html.

45. Carolyn Pritchard, "Climate: The Food Chain's Weakest Link," republished by The Heat Is Online from MarketWatch, May 17, 2007, www.heatisonline.org/contentserver/objecthandlers/index.cfm?ID=6419&Method=Full.

46. "The Great Yellow Hope," May 24, 2006, New York Times, http://pollan.blogs.nytimes.com/2006/05/24/the-great-yellow-hope/.

47. Matthieu Auzanneau, "Sans l'or noir irakien, le marché pétrolier fera face à un "mur" d'ici à 2015," Le Monde, June 27, 2007, www.lemonde.fr/web/article/0,1-0,36-928476,0.html.

48. Translated by "Asebius" at The Oil Drum, http://europe.theoildrum.com/node/2721.

49. Tad Patzek, "Why Cellulosic Ethanol Will Not Save Us?" VentureBeat, November 5, 2006, http://venturebeat.com/2006/11/05/why-cellulosic-ethanol-will-not-save-us/.

50. Ibid.

51. International Monetary Fund, "World Economic Outlook: Spillovers and Cycles in the Global Economy," April 2007, www.imf.org/external/pubs/ft/weo/2007/01/index.htm.

52. Biopact, "Mexican Farmers Switch from Agave to Maize Because of Ethanol Boom," May 30, 2007, http://biopact.com/2007/05/mexican-farmers-switch-from-agave-to.html.

53. John Vidal, "Global Rush to Energy Crops Threatens to Bring Food Shortages and Increase Poverty, Says UN," Guardian, May 9, 2007, www.guardian.co.uk/frontpage/story/0,,2075458,00.html.

54. Moira Herbst, "Ethanol's Growing List of Enemies," BusinessWeek, March 19, 2007, www.businessweek.com/bwdaily/dnflash/content/mar2007/db20070316_016207_page_2.htm.

55. Alexei Barrionuevo, "Archer Daniels to Look Beyond Corn for Fuel Sources," New York Times, November 9, 2006, www.nytimes.com/2006/11/09/business/09adm.html?n=Top%2fReference%2fTimes%20Topics%2fSubjects%2fE%2fEthanol.

56. Wheat futures chart, www.freecharts.com/Commodities.aspx?page=chart&sym=WZ7.

Chapter 9 Endless Energy: Here Comes the Sun

1. Cutler J. Cleveland, "Energy Quality, Net Energy, and the Coming Energy Transition," Department of Geography and Center for Energy and Environmental Studies, Boston University, http://web.mit.edu/2.813/www/2007%20Class%20Slides/EnergyQualityNetEnergyComing-Transition.pdf.

2. Solar Energy Industries Association, "Concentrating Solar Power," www.seia.org/solartypes.php#csp.

3. Solar Energy Industries Association, "Solar Water Heating," www.seia.org/solartypes.php#swh.

4. U.S. Department of Energy, Energy Efficiency and Renewable Energy, "Report: U.S. Solar Cell Market Increased 33 Percent in 2006," March 28, 2007, www1.eere.energy.gov/solar/news_detail.html?news_id=10675.

5. Renewable Energy Access, "PV Costs to Decrease 40% by 2010," May 23, 2007, www.renewableenergyaccess.com/rea/news/story?id=48624.

6. World Watch Institute, "Solar Power Set to Shine Brightly," May 22, 2007, www.worldwatch.org/node/5086.

7. Solar Energy Industries Association, "Solar Energy Types," www.seia.org/solartypes.php.

8. Amanda Crowell, "A Bright Future for Solar Energy," *Research Horizons, Georgia Institute of Technology,* http://gtresearchnews.gatech.edu/reshor/rh-sf97/solar.htm.

9. Daniel M. Kammen, "The Rise of Renewable Energy," *Scientific American,* September 2006, vol. 295, no. 3.

10. U.S. Department of Energy, "Report: U.S. Solar Cell Market."

11. *Economist,* "Cleaning Up," May 31, 2007, www.economist.com/opinion/displayStory.cfm?Story_ID=9256652.

12. World Watch Institute, "Solar Power Set to Shine Brightly."

13. Paul Preuss, "Research at Advanced Light Source Promises Improved Solar Cell Efficiency," *Berkeley Lab,* October 3, 1997, www.lbl.gov/Science-Articles/Archive/pure-solar-cells.html.

14. Lisa Zyga, "40% Efficient Solar Cells to Be Used for Solar Electricity," *Physorg,* June 1, 2007, www.physorg.com/news99904887.html.

15. Phil LoPiccolo, "Applied Sees Sparkling Growth with Solar Plans," *WaferNews,* http://sst.pennnet.com/Articles/Article_Display.cfm?ARTICLE_ID=272075&dcmp=WaferNEWS.

16. Dr. Charles Gay, "The Solar Industry Continues to Gain Momentum," *Renewable Energy Access,* January 22, 2007, www.renewableenergyaccess.com/rea/news/reinsider/story;jsessionid=CC52AA008F8B4511820D723933B1C970?id=47178.

17. U.S. Department of Energy, "Report: U.S. Solar Cell Market."

18. "Fast Solar Energy Facts," March 2007, www.solarbuzz.com/FastFactsIndustry.htm.

19. Kammen, "The Rise of Renewable Energy."

20. Paul Preuss, "An Unexpected Discovery Could Yield a Full Spectrum Solar Cell," *Berkeley Lab,* November 18, 2002, www.lbl.gov/Science-Articles/Archive/MSD-full-spectrum-solar-cell.html.

21. Nanosolar's thin-film cells are produced by a process that in many ways resembles printing. Light-sensitive semiconductor particles are mixed into a kind of ink, which is printed onto a thin substrate of metal foil that is continuously pulled off a series of rolls. This highly efficient roll-to-roll technology makes it possible to produce a large volume of solar cells in a relatively small manufacturing space, further reducing costs, http://biz.yahoo.com/hbusn/061030/102606_solar_siliconvalley_biz2.html?.v=1.

22. Incentive programs by state may be found at the Database of State Incentives for Renewable Energy (DSIRE), http://www.dsireusa.org/.

23. "California Approves Legislation for Million Solar Roofs," EERE Network News, U.S. Department of Energy, August 23, 2006, http://www.eere.energy.gov/news/news_detail.cfm?news_id=10210.

24. Kammen, "The Rise of Renewable Energy."

25. "Google, Microsoft, and Yahoo faced spiking energy demands from running the hundreds of thousands of servers they need to power an economy increasingly conducted over the Internet," http://biz.yahoo.com/hbusn/061030/102606_solar_siliconvalley_biz2.html?.v=1.

26. "Amtech Systems Reaches $16.5 Million in Solar Orders; Announces New Solar Customers," *Business Wire*, June 12, 2007, http://home.businesswire.com/portal/site/google/index.jsp?ndm ViewId=news_view&newsId=20070612005379&newsLang=en.

27. "MEMC Electronic Materials Inc WFR (NYSE)," Reuters, http://stocks.us.reuters.com/stocks/fullDescription.asp?rpc=66&symbol=WFR.

Chapter 10 Pressure Cooker: Tapping the Earth's Heat

1. U.S. Department of Energy, Energy Efficiency and Renewable Energy, "Geothermal FAQs," www1.eere.energy.gov/geothermal/faqs.html.

2. Geothermal Education Office, Copyright 2000, http://geothermal.marin.org/GEOpresentation/sld051.htm.

3. Jeff Siegel, "The Big Bang," *Green Chip Stocks*, www.angelnexus.com/o/web/1625.

4. Kevin Bullis, "Abundant Power from Universal Geothermal Energy," *MIT Technology Review*, August 1, 2006, www.technologyreview.com/read_article.aspx?id=17236&ch=biztech&sc= &pg=1.

5. "Energy from Hot Rocks," *Economist,* September 14, 2006, www.economist.com/science/displaystory.cfm?story_id=E1_SJDVPDT.

6. Siegel, "Big Bang."

7. U.S. Department of Energy, Energy Efficiency and Renewable Energy, "A History of Geothermal Energy in the United States," www1.eere.energy.gov/geothermal/history.html.

8. Energy Information Administration, "Geothermal Energy," July 2007, www.eia.doe.gov/cneaf/solar.renewables/page/geothermal/geothermal.html.

9. U.S. Department of Energy, "A History of Geothermal Energy."

10. Ibid.

11. Jeff Siegel, "Powering Up for Geothermal Plants," *Green Chip Stocks,* December 7, 2005, http://wealthdaily.net/article.php?id=22&pub=gcr.

12. Geothermal Energy Association, "Update on US Geothermal Power Production and Development," May 10, 2007, http://geo-energy.org//publications/reports/May2007GEAUpdateon-USGeothermalPowerProductionandDevelopment.pdf.

13. Ibid.

14. David Rosenberg and Alisa Odenheimer, "Ormat Aims to Increase Alternative-Power Capacity," *Jerusalem Post from Bloomberg,* October 11, 2006, www.jpost.com/servlet/Satellite?apage =1&cid=1159193415338&pagename=JPost%2FJPArticle%2FShowFull.

15. Ormat Technologies Inc. ORA 11/16/04 $15.50 11/8/06 $37.61 142.65%.

16. Rosenberg and Odenheimer, "Ormat Aims to Increase."

17. Ormat press release, "Ormat Technologies, Inc. Reports Fourth Quarter 2006 and Year-End Results," February 27, 2007, http://phx.corporate-ir.net/phoenix.zhtml?c=181999&p=irol-news Article_print&ID=968169&highlight=.

18. Rosenberg and Odenheimer, "Ormat Aims to Increase."

19. Ormat press release, "Ormat Technologies, Inc. Reports Third Quarter 2007 Results," November 6, 2007, www.ormat.com/news-and-events/new-releases/07::11::06—ormat-technologies,-inc.-reports-third-quarter-2007-results-.html.

20. Rosenberg and Odenheimer, "Ormat Aims to Increase."

21. Ibid.

22. U.S. Geothermal, "Consolidated Financial Statements," March 31, 2007, www.usgeothermal
.com/FinancialReports/YE03312007.pdf.

Chapter 11 Nuclear's Second Act

1. Australia Uranium Association, "What is Uranium?" http://www.uic.com.au/uran.htm.

2. World Nuclear Association, "Advanced Nuclear Power Reactors," February 2008, http://www
.world-nuclear.org/info/inf08.html.

3. Thomas B. Cochran, Christopher E. Paine, Geoffrey Fettus, Robert S. Norris, and Matthew G.
McKinzie, "Position Paper: Commercial Nuclear Power," *Natural Resources Defense Council,*
www.nrdc.org/nuclear/power/power.pdf.

4. Australian Uranium Association, "Nuclear Power Reactors," May 2007, www.uic.com.au/nip64
.htm.

5. Australian Uranium Association, "Nuclear Power in the World Today," www.uic.com.au/nip07
.htm.

6. Ibid.

7. Energy Information Administration, "U.S. Nuclear Generation of Electricity," www.eia.doe.gov/
cneaf/nuclear/page/nuc_generation/gensum.html.

8. Data source: EIA, 2006, www.eia.doe.gov/oiaf/aeo/excel/aeotab_1.xls.

9. Greg Walker, "Peak Oil Requires New Thinking for a New Age," *PR-inside,* May 28, 2007,
www.pr-inside.com/peak-oil-requires-new-thinking-for-r136542.htm.

10. Energy Information Administration, "International Energy Outlook 2007," 2007, www.eia.doe
.gov/oiaf/ieo/pdf/electricity.pdf.

11. Ariana Eunjung Cha, "China Embraces Nuclear Future," *Washington Post,* May 29, 2007, www
.washingtonpost.com/wp-dyn/content/article/2007/05/28/AR2007052801051_pf.html.

12. Council on Foreign Relations, "Prepared Statement before the Select Committee on Energy Independence and Global Warming U.S. House of Representatives," April 18, 2007, www.cfr.org/
publication/13128/.

13. Ibid.

14. John Vidal, "Nuclear Expansion Is a Pipe Dream, Says Report," *Guardian Unlimited,* July 4,
2007, http://business.guardian.co.uk/story/0,,2117711,00.html.

15. *Star Phoenix,* "Nuclear Demand Will Outstrip Supply: CEO," June 30, 2007, www.canada.com/
saskatoonstarphoenix/news/business/story.html?id=a96783d2-7976-43f4-9879-c3ae3262677c.

16. Jan Willem Storm van Leeuwen and Philip Smith, "Can Nuclear Power Provide Energy for the
Future; Would It Solve the CO_2-Emission Problem?" *Great Change,* June 16, 2002, http://
greatchange.org/bb-thermochemical-nuclear_sustainability_rev.html.

17. Jan Willem Storm van Leeuwen, "Energy Security and Uranium Reserves," *Oxford Research
Group,* July 2006, www.oxfordresearchgroup.org.uk/publications/briefing_papers/energyfact
sheet4.php.

18. Ibid.

19. John Vidal, "Nuclear Expansion Is a Pipe Dream, Says Report," *Guardian Unlimited,* July 4,
2007, http://business.guardian.co.uk/story/0,,2117711,00.html.

20. Energy Watch Group, "Uranium Resources and Nuclear Energy," December 2006, www.lbst.de/
publications/studies_e/2006/EWG-paper_1-06_Uranium-Resources-Nuclear-Energy_
03DEC2006.pdf.

21. Ibid.

22. Ibid.
23. Ibid.
24. van Leeuwen, "Energy Security."
25. Vidal, "Nuclear Expansion."
26. Keith Kohl, "Uranium in 2008: $255/lb. Is Just the Beginning," *Energy and Capital,* June 19, 2007, www.energyandcapital.com/articles/uranium-investing-nuclear+power/453.
27. "USEC Inc USU (NYSE)," Reuters, http://stocks.us.reuters.com/stocks/fullDescription .asp?rpc=66&symbol=USU.

Chapter 12 What's Needed: A Manhattan Project for Energy

1. European Commission, "European Smart Grids Technology Platform," www.smartgrids.eu/ documents/vision.pdf.
2. Council on Foreign Relations, "Prepared Statement before the Select Committee on Energy Independence and Global Warming, U.S. House of Representatives," www.cfr.org/publication/ 13128/.
3. Robert Hirsch and Roger Bezdek, "Peaking of World Oil Production Impacts, Mitigation, & Risk Management," February 2005, www.netl.doe.gov/publications/others/pdf/Oil_Peaking_NETL .pdf.
4. The Oil Drum, "Updated World Oil Forecasts, Including Saudi Arabia," August 5, 2007, www .theoildrum.com/node/2716#more.
5. Apollo Alliance, "The Apollo Alliance for Good Jobs and Clean Energy," Copyright 2003, www .apolloalliance.org/about_the_alliance/.
6. Apollo Alliance, "The Ten-Point Plan for Good Jobs and Energy Independence," Copyright 2003, www.apolloalliance.org/strategy_center/ten_point_plan.cfm.
7. Western Climate Initiative Scope Subcommittee, "Summary of Major Design Options Under Consideration," March 3, 2008, http://www.westernclimateinitiative.org/ewebeditpro/items/ O104F15977.PDF. A. Denny Ellerman and Barbara K. Buchner, "The European Union Emissions Trading Scheme: Origins, Allocation, and Early Results," Oxford Journals, Oxford University Press, Review of Environmental Economics and Policy 2007 1(1):66–87; doi:10.1093/reep/ rem003, http://reep.oxfordjournals.org/cgi/content/abstract/1/1/66. "Australia to launch carbon trading scheme by 2012," Reuters, June 3, 2007, http://www.reuters.com/article/environmentNews/ idUSSYD 26700820070603.
8. Carbon Tax Center, "Tax vs. Cap-and-Trade," September 20, 2007, www.carbontax.org/issues/ carbon-taxes-vs-cap-and-trade/.
9. "Hubbard Argues for a Carbon Tax," *Wall Street Journal,* June 28, 2007, http://blogs.wsj.com/ energy/2007/06/28/hubbard-argues-for-a-carbon-tax/.
10. Peerless Mfr. Co. corporate profile, http://phx.corporate-ir.net/phoenix.zhtml?c=117637&p=irol-homeProfile.
11. James Kanter, "In London's Financial World, Carbon Trading Is the New Big Thing," *New York Times*, July 6, 2007, http://select.nytimes.com/gst/abstract.html?res=F20E1EF6395A0C758CDD AE0894DF404482.
12. Bill Prindle, Maggie Eldridge, Mike Eckhardt, and Alyssa Frederick, "The Twin Pillars of Sustainable Energy: Synergies Between Energy Efficiency and Renewable Energy Technology and Policy," American Council for an Energy-Efficient Economy, May 2007, http://aceee.org/pubs/ e074.htm.

13. EnerNOC, Inc., "Customer Solutions," www.enernoc.com/solutions.html.

14. Lester R. Brown, "Ban the Bulb: Worldwide Shift from Incandescents to Compact Fluorescents Could Close 270 Coal-Fired Plants," Earth Policy Institute, May 9, 2007, www.earth-policy.org/Updates/2007/Update66.htm.

15. Richard Heinberg, *The Oil Depletion Protocol* (n.p.: New Society Publishers, 2006), 78.

16. Richard Heinberg, *Powerdown,* (n.p.: New Society Publishers, 2004), jacket copy.

17. *Transportation Energy Data Book: Edition 26—2007,* http://cta.ornl.gov/data/tedb26/Edition26_Chapter02.pdf.

18. Copulos, "Averting Disaster of Our Own Design."

19. Consortium for Electric Reliability Technology Solutions, "Integration of Distributed Energy Resources: The CERTS MicroGrid Concept," April 2002, www.localenergy.org/pdfs/Document%20Library/Microgrids.pdf.

20. International Energy Agency District Heating and Cooling, "A Comparison of distributed CHP/DH with large-scale CHP/DH," www.iea-dhc.org/010601.html.

21. Ibid.

22. U.S.-Canada Power System Outage Task Force, "Final Report on the August 14, 2003 Blackout in the United States and Canada: Causes and Recommendations," April 2004, https://reports.energy.gov/B-F-Web-Part1.pdf. Parks, Bill, 2003, "Transforming the Grid to Revolutionize Electric Power in North America," U.S. Department of Energy, Edison Electric Institute's Fall 2003 Transmission, Distribution and Metering Conference, October 13, 2003.

23. U.S. Climate Change Technology Program—Technology Options for the Near and Long Term, "1.3.2 Transmission and Distribution Technologies," November 2003, http://climatetechnology.gov/library/2003/tech-options/tech-options-1-3-2.pdf.

24. North American Windpower, "A Study of Wind Power Storage in Ireland," June 2007.

25. GE 2006 Ecomagination Report, "Delivering on ecomagination," http://ge.ecomagination.com/site/downloads/news/2006ecoreport.pdf.

26. Dave Rutledge, "Hubbert's Peak, the Coal Question, and Climate Change," www.its.caltech.edu/~rutledge/Hubbert's%20Peak,%20The%20Question%20of%20Coal,%20and%20Climate%20Change.ppt.

27. Ibid.

28. *AWEA Third Quarter Market Report,* November 2007, American Wind Energy Association, http://www.awea.org/Projects/PDF/3Q_Market_Report_Nov2007.pdf.

29. U.S. Department of Energy, "U.S. Continues to Lead the World in Wind Power Growth," May 31, 2007, www.energy.gov/news/5091.htm.

30. *AWEA 2007 Market Report,* January 2008, American Wind Energy Association. http://www.awea.org/projects/pdf/Market_Report_Jan08.pdf

31. "Wind Power Beat Nuclear, Says AD," *Dutch News,* July 12, 2007, www.dutchnews.nl/news/archives/2007/07/wind_power_beats_nuclear_says.php.

32. GE Energy press release, "U.S. Wind Industry Milestone: GE Ships 1,000th-Megawatt Wind Turbine for FPL Energy," June 4, 2007, www.gepower.com/about/press/en/2007_press/060407.htm.

33. Keith Johnson, "Turbine Shortage Knocks Wind out of Projects," *Post and Courier Charleston,* from the *Wall Street Journal,* July 15, 2007, www.charleston.net/news/2007/jul/15/turbine_shortage_knocks_wind_out_projects/.

34. Ibid.

35. Zoltek 2007 Annual Report, http://ir.zoltek.com/common/download/download.cfm?companyid=
ZOLT&fileid=154939&filekey=2874687A-D883-448A-BE9C-8778C35CEEA9&filename=Zolt
ek-AR-2007_Final.pdf.

36. Reuters, "Zoltek reports new expanded carbon fiber supply agreement with Vestas Wind Systems," May 22, 2007, http://www.reuters.com/article/inPlayBriefing/idUSIN20070522163346
ZOLT20070522.

37. Vestas Annual Report 2007, http://www.vestas.com/Admin/Public/DWSDownload.aspx?File=
Files%2fFiler%2fEN%2fInvestor%2fFinancial_reports%2f2007%2f2007-AR-UK.pdf.

38. Acciona press release, www.acciona-energia.com/cambioIdioma.asp.

39. *Mitsubishi Heavy Industries, Ltd. News,*"MHI Receives Massive Wind Turbine Orders from U.S., Almost Equal to Japan's Domestic Wind Power Generation Capacity," May 30, 2007, www
.mhi-ir.jp/english/new/sec1/200705301176.html.

40. Suzlon press release, "Suzlon Secures Single-Largest Order," May 2, 2007, www.suzlon.com/
images/you/Suzlon%20PPM%20400MW%20Order%20Release%20R2.pdf.

41. U.S. Department of Energy press release, "DOE Releases First Annual Report on U.S. Wind Power Market," May 31, 2007, http://www1.eere.energy.gov/femp/newsevents/release.cfm?
news_id=11003.

42. Eric Scigliano, "Wave Energy," *Discover*, December 2, 2005, www.discover.com/issues/dec-05/
features/ocean-energy/.

43. Scigliano, "Wave Energy."

44. Wayt W. Gibbs, "Plan B for Energy." *Scientific American* 295, no. 3 (2006), 112.

45. U.S. Department of Energy, EERE Network News, "FERC Aims to Simplify Licensing for Wave and Tidal Pilot Projects," July 25, 2007, http://www.eere.energy.gov/news/news_detail.cfm/
news_id=11125.

46. Adam Hochberg, "Power Turbines Will Rely on Tidal Forces," *NPR,* October 19, 2006, www
.npr.org/templates/story/story.php?storyId=6344642. Heather Timmons, "Energy from the Restless Sea," *New York Times,* August 3, 2006, www.nytimes.com/2006/08/03/business/
worldbusiness/03tides.html?ex=1312257600&en=a0172afbc7c00d14&ei=5088&partner=rssnyt
&emc=rss.

47. Phillip Matier and Andrew Ross, "Mayor's Current Idea: Catch a Wave to Make Power," *San Francisco Chronicle,* June 25, 2006, www.sfgate.com/cgi-bin/article.cgi?f=/c/a/2006/06/25/
BAGATJK5D51.DTL.

48. U.S. Department of Energy, EERE Network News, "FERC Aims to Simplify Licensing for Wave and Tidal Pilot Projects," July 25, 2007, http://www.eere.energy.gov/news/news_detail.cfm/
news_id=11125.

49. Peak Energy blog, "Tapping The Source: The Power Of The Oceans," February 25, 2008, http://
peakenergy.blogspot.com/2008/02/tapping-source-power-of-oceans.html.

50. "The new wave: Energy from the ocean," *International Herald Tribune,* August 2, 2006. http://
www.iht.com/articles/2006/08/02/business/tides.php.

51. "Energy from the Restless Sea," *New York Times,* August 3, 2006, http://www.nytimes.
com/2006/08/03/business/worldbusiness/03tides.html?ei=5088&en=a0172afbc7c00d14&ex=
1312257600.

52. Gibbs, "Plan B," 112.

53. Ibid.

54. Power Projects Limited, "Wave Energy Technology the WET-NZ Programme," June 2006, www
.wavenergy.co.nz/wetnz-2006-06.pdf.

55. Scottish Government, "Progress on Wave Power Development," August 30, 2006, www.scotland .gov.uk/News/Releases/2006/08/30103302.

56. E.ON UK press release, "E.ON UK and Ocean Prospect Look to Plug in to One of the World's First Large-Scale Wave Energy Farms," September 13, 2006, www.oceanpd.com/docs/ Eon%20PR.pdf.

57. "Scotland Vows Support for Wave Power," Environmental Data Interactive Exchange (EDIE), August 30, 2006, www.edie.net/news/news_story.asp?id=11937&channel=0.

58. WELL's Guidance Documents are available here: www.willitseconomiclocalization.org/ GuidanceDocs.

59. This data is a typical calculation, taken from this essay: *PR-inside,* "Peak Oil Requires New Thinking for a New Age," May 28, 2007, www.pr-inside.com/peak-oil-requires-new-thinking-for-r136542.htm. Other calculations based on other assumptions have produced losses as low as 10% and as high as 90%.

60. Ibid.

61. Matt Savinar interview in the documentary film, *A Crude Awakening.*

Chapter 13 A Future Electric

1. Robert Rapier, "The Future Is Solar," The Oil Drum, July 27, 2007, www.theoildrum.com/ node/2812.

2. Angela Greiling Keane, "Union Pacific, Icahn Win as Soaring Oil Lifts Rails," *Bloomberg,* June 21, 2007, http://www.bloomberg.com/apps/news?pid=newsarchive&sid=af4K2vSsWVNk.

3. Lupe C. Valdez, "SCAG's Goods Movement Task Force," March 15, 2006, www.scag.ca.gov/ goodsmove/pdf/gmtf031506_UnionPacificPresentation.pdf.

4. Alan S. Drake, "Electrification of Transportation as a Response to Peaking of World Oil Production," *Light Rail Now,* December 2005, www.lightrailnow.org/features/f_lrt_2005-02.htm.

5. Robert Malone, "Railroads Can Move Forward," *Forbes,* May 5, 2006, www.forbes .com/2006/05/04/railroads-intermodal-shipping-cx_rm_0505rail.html.

6. "The World's Billionaires, #2 Warren Buffett," *Forbes,* March 8, 2007, www.forbes.com/lists/ 2007/10/07billionaires_Warren-Buffett_C0R3.html.

7. "Warren Buffett Bought Two Other Rail Companies," *Guru Focus,* April 9, 2007, www.gurufocus .com/news.php?id=5263.

8. "The World's Richest People," *Forbes,* www.forbes.com/lists/2006/10/Name_13.html.

9. Angela Greiling Keane, "Union Pacific, Icahn Win as Soaring Oil Lifts Rails," *Bloomberg,* June 21, 2007, http://www.bloomberg.com/apps/news?pid=newsarchive&sid=af4K2vSsWVNk.

10. "The Two Other Rail Companies Warren Buffett Bought: Norfolk Southern Corp (NSC) and Union Pacific Corp (UNP)," *Guru Focus,* March 15, 2007, www.gurufocus.com/news .php?id=5851.

11. Alan S. Drake, "Electrification of Transportation as a Response to Peaking of World Oil Production," *Light Rail Now,* December 2005, www.lightrailnow.org/features/f_lrt_2005-02.htm.

12. *PR-inside,* "Peak Oil Requires New Thinking for a New Age," May 28, 2007, www.pr-inside .com/peak-oil-requires-new-thinking-for-r136542.htm.

13. Comment from Alan Drake on The Oil Drum, www.theoildrum.com/node/3152#comment-255805.

14. CityData.com, "Top 100 Biggest Cities," www.city-data.com/top1.html.

15. Dylan Rivera, "Adams Sees Web of Streetcars," *The Oregonian,* July 21, 2007, www.oregonlive .com/business/oregonian/index.ssf?/base/business/118498652393360.xml&coll=7   www.pr-inside .com/peak-oil-requires-new-thinking-for-r136542.htm.

16. *PR-inside,* "Peak Oil."

17. A123 Systems, "Plug-In PHEV Benefits," Copyright 2007, www.a123systems.com/newsite/ index.php#/applications/phev/pchart6/.

18. David Roberts, "New Study Finds That Plug-In Hybrids Rule All Possible Futures," *Gristmill,* July 20, 2007, http://gristmill.grist.org/story/2007/7/20/111715/427.

19. Technically, it should be possible to use electricity to derive hydrogen from water, and reform it into syngas and then into a liquid hydrocarbon fuel. But the EROI would be atrocious.

Epilogue Why We're Energy Optimists

1. Carl Mortished, "Energy Crisis Cannot be Solved by Renewables, Oil Chiefs Say," *Times Online,* June 25, 2007, http://business.timesonline.co.uk/tol/business/industry_sectors/natural_resources/ article1980407.ece.

2. Council on Foreign Relations, "National Security Consequences of U.S. Oil Dependency," www .cfr.org/publication/11683/.

3. "Jevons Paradox," Encyclopedia of Earth, Horace Herring, ed. by Cutler Cleveland, October 8, 2006. www.eoearth.org/article/Jevons_paradox.

INDEX